Prior to reading the Words of Solomon, it is strongly recommended that the reader read Chapters 1 thru 9 of the Proverbs

All verses quoted are from the Old King James Bible, except where noted.

THE
WORDS

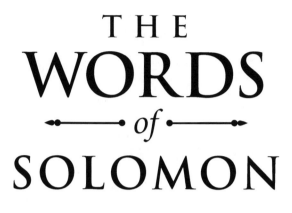

of

SOLOMON

Ancient Wisdom for Today's World

WAYNE GRAHAM

WESTBOW
PRESS®
A DIVISION OF THOMAS NELSON
& ZONDERVAN

Scripture taken from the New King James Version®. Copyright © 1982 by Thomas Nelson. Used by permission. All rights reserved.

Scripture taken from the King James Version of the Bible.

THE HOLY BIBLE, NEW INTERNATIONAL VERSION®, NIV® Copyright © 1973, 1978, 1984, 2011 by Biblica, Inc.® Used by permission. All rights reserved worldwide.

Scripture quotations marked HCSB are taken from the Holman Christian Standard Bible®, Copyright © 1999, 2000, 2002, 2003, 2009 by Holman Bible Publishers. Used by permission. Holman Christian Standard Bible®, Holman CSB®, and HCSB® are federally registered trademarks of Holman Bible Publishers.

WestBow Press books may be ordered through booksellers or by contacting:

WestBow Press
A Division of Thomas Nelson & Zondervan
1663 Liberty Drive
Bloomington, IN 47403
www.westbowpress.com
1 (866) 928-1240

ISBN: 978-1-5127-8008-6 (sc)
ISBN: 978-1-5127-8010-9 (hc)
ISBN: 978-1-5127-8009-3 (e)

Library of Congress Control Number: 2017904246

Print information available on the last page.

WestBow Press rev. date: 7/14/2017

INTRODUCTION TO PROVERBS

The book of Proverbs is best described as a Hebrew wisdom book. It was written during the tenth century BC. Some biblical scholars believe Solomon began writing his proverbs just prior to his anointing to be the next king of Israel (approximately 973 BC). Solomon is said to have written three thousand proverbs and 1,005 songs (1 Kings 4:32). The partial collection of Solomon's writings, preserved for us in the Bible and commonly known as the book of Proverbs, consist of 915 verses which are organized into thirty-one chapters. The first nine chapters of Solomon's Proverbs are written as short stories or sermons of instruction. Beginning with chapter ten, the writing style changes from a continuous narrative to that of single verses, or small groups of verses which can stand alone as an illustration of wisdom. The last two chapters of Proverbs identify different writers, Agur and Lemuel, as their authors. It is generally accepted that Solomon wrote the previous twenty-nine chapters of the Old Testament Proverbs, but some scholars do not share this opinion. They theorize there was an additional writer or writers because of the change in format beginning with chapter ten.

The change in writing style can also be explained by Solomon himself changing due to age and circumstances. As a young man, Solomon was very obedient to God's will, whereas later in life he began to stray from God's prescribed path of wisdom. This eventually led to the worship of foreign idols into Israel. It should be noted that during his later years, Solomon was probably without the accompaniment of his mother, Bathsheba, and Nathan, the prophet. Despite his being the wisest king of Israel, these two trusted allies had to have been an important source of support and guidance for a young king. Solomon had a throne set for Bathsheba so she could sit at his right side, as we are told in 1 Kings 2:19. Note this verse also states Solomon bowed down to his mother. There is no recorded evidence suggesting Solomon had such a relationship with his father, King David.

Solomon and his father, David, by all accounts seem to have been outstanding kings in their early years. They both were effective leaders, excellent writers, and men who loved God. After establishing their fame and prominence, they both fell out of God's will by failing to restain their sexual lust. These are the only traits these two Old Testament saints seem to have had in common. David's accomplishments can be rivaled by few in scripture, but being a good father was not among his achievements. David, the shepherd boy, became Israel's mightiest warrior; whereas Solomon grew up in a palace surrounded by beauty and comfort. Solomon never had to go to war because his father had subdued all of Israel's enemies. Solomon and Israel were given peace and prosperity during the forty years of his reign.

The inheritance Solomon received is almost beyond comprehension. He truly was a fortunate son. This strikes an interesting parallel with our own heavenly Father—God too will place His sons and daughters in a paradise—one that is beyond comprehension. Christianity is not the only religion teaching that its followers have a fantastic reward awaiting them, after physical life on earth is complete. What separates Christianity from other religions is it teaches Jesus Christ paid the entire price for our future heavenly rewards.

Despite his eventual shortcomings, God allowed Solomon to accumulate much wealth and knowledge. He was humble enough, and wise enough as a young man to request that God give him a wise and discerning heart for the purpose of ruling God's people. This request pleased God so much He responded with the following: *Wisdom and Knowledge is granted unto thee; and I will give thee riches, and wealth, and honour, such as none of the kings have had that have been before thee, neither shall there any after thee have the like"* (2 Chronicles 1:12). It is worthy to note that God never promised Solomon children. Scripture only records the name of one son, Rehoboam, who was born to Solomon. This is very interesting; given the fact Solomon had one thousand wives and concubines with whom he could have fathered children.

It has been said, "Solomon was the wisest man who ever lived." This verse (2 Chronicles 1:12) does not claim that—it states Solomon was the wisest king who ever lived. First Kings 3:12 does make a stronger argument for Solomon's wisdom by saying: *"I have given thee a wise and an understanding heart; so that there was none like thee before thee, neither after thee shall any arise like unto thee."* This would be the strongest claim made in the Bible for Solomon's being the wisest man who ever lived. The Bible does not exclude Solomon from being the wisest man to have ever lived, but the books of Kings and Chronicles were written a long time before men such as the apostle Paul, Galileo, or Abraham Lincoln could be considered. Solomon's writings, have withstood the test of time because his ability to explain matters of everyday life by using metaphors and comparisons are a fascinating means of instruction.

The Bible teaches that God's opinion is the only one that really matters. Real Christians should have a thirst for the knowledge of His Holy Bible so our thoughts will be pleasing to Him. The Bible instructs its readers to live peacefully and honorably within their communities. This type of lifestyle positions us to maximize our witness for Him. Studying Proverbs will help us know the Lord better, so that we can serve Him better. A functional knowledge and understanding of Solomon's Proverbs can be as beneficial in the twenty-first century as it was three thousand years ago when they were written.

In addition to wisdom, Solomon also discusses anger, dishonesty, drinking, family, fear, fools, friendship, goodness, jealousy, knowledge, laziness, love, prayer, pride, riches, sexuality and work. A study of the book of Proverbs can be profitable for everyone: the young, the old, the rich, the poor, the wise, and especially the not so wise.

WISDOM SPEECH ONE

Proverbs 1:1–9

**"The proverbs of Solomon the son of David,
King of Israel" (Proverbs 1:1).**

A proverb is usually thought of as a poem or riddle which contains valuable information that is useful in everyday life. The word *proverb* is translated from the Hebrew word *mashal*, which can mean to use figurative or comparative language. It can also imply a sense of superior mental action or hidden wisdom. *Unger's Bible Dictionary* describes a proverb as a "dark saying" that requires interpretation. Numbers 12:6–8 records our Lord telling Israel's first high priest, Aaron, and his wife Miriam, that He (God) communicated directly with Moses. They had questioned the authority of Moses which caused God to proclaim in verse eight, *"I speak with him [Moses] face to face, even plainly, and not in dark sayings."*

Earlier verses indicate God spoke directly to Moses because he had learned to be totally faithful in all things pertaining to the Lord. God had chosen only Moses to be His spokesman. Those who were not chosen, as Moses was, did not have the privilege of direct communication with God. They were required to interpret God's "dark sayings" as recorded in scripture. How many times have you heard someone say, "I read the Bible, and it makes no sense to me"? These are the ones who recognize that God does not always speak plainly. Some of them will mistakenly put their faith into other sources of authority besides the living God of Israel. They want a God who talks directly to them, such as science or the written laws of humanity.

God put Aaron and Miriam in their place that day for claiming they had position and authority equal to that of Moses. This event records that pride, as displayed by Aaron, can blind us from having a true understanding of God's ways. It also tells us that God's wisdom is not given to just anybody. He expects us to work for it. Why should anyone expect God to share His magnificence with someone who is unwilling to honor and obey what He has already plainly revealed, such as the Ten Commandments? God expects us to seek Him out. This is why, one thousand years later, Paul told Timothy, *"Study to show thyself approved unto God"* (2 Timothy 2:15). The Bible is God's treasure map—He expects us to dig for its wealth.

Knowledge found within the Holy Scriptures will enhance one's life not only spiritually but in other dimensions as well. The book of Proverbs is concentrated with practical advice, which is as applicable in today's complex culture as it was in ancient Israel's agricultural society. Some will feel it is a shame we do not have access to Solomon's other 2,971 proverbs mentioned in 1 Kings 4:32. A strong argument can be made that the best of Solomon's writings have been divinely preserved for us. These ancient writings provide us with everything to which God wanted us to have access. Without God's editing, Proverbs would be a lengthy piece of literature that few would take the time to read in its entirety.

In Proverbs 1:1, Solomon introduces himself as "the son of David, King of Israel." Solomon wasted no time introducing the perspective from which his early proverbs are written—that of a father instructing his son. The phrase "my son" is used fifteen times throughout the first seven chapters of Proverbs. It is used as a term of endearment and as a call to attention. It could be compared to a coach saying "listen up!" This opening statement also lets us know that David is still king when Solomon began writing his proverbs. The Bible does not tell us how old Solomon was when he became king, but 1 Chronicles 29:1 gives us a clue: *"Furthermore David the King said unto to all the congregation, Solomon my son, whom alone God hath chosen, is yet young and tender."*

This verse also tells us Solomon was chosen by God, not by David, to be Israel's next leader. It reveals to us Solomon was woefully unprepared for his new duties. What kind of father would put his son in this position?

David was a father who had many children with multiple wives (at least eight) and an unknown number of concubines. David also had an assortment of family problems, which by all accounts were never fully resolved. Among these problems were adultery, murder, rape, and the death of at least three children. David also had an army to command and a growing kingdom to rule. Despite all these activities, David found time to write the Psalms, design a temple, and assemble most of the materials needed for the construction of that temple. But he found little to no time for his children. Perhaps being excluded from his father's attention inspired Solomon to want to be a better father. This desire could have inspired him to write his early proverbs for a son he had not yet had.

When Solomon began his written works, he had little to no actual experiences to draw upon. What he did have going for him was a loving and wise mother, every available resource for his education, and God's blessing. Despite David's alienation of affection, his well-known conquests and failures undoubtedly provided all the ideas and inspiration a young Solomon needed to write about in his early proverbs. To his credit, Solomon never implied any disrespect or resentment toward his father in his writings. It does seem, though, that the phrase "my son" might represent the sentiment of a lonely young teenager who would have given just about anything to have had a complete and loving relationship with his father, "King David the giant slayer."

Shortly after Solomon's birth, the prophet Nathan was dispatched to reveal God's love for the child Solomon. Nathan revealed God's favor for the baby Solomon, by naming him Jedidiah, which means "beloved of God." This name served as notice to David that he had been forgiven for his sin of adultery with Solomon's mother, Bathsheba, and for the consequential murder of her husband, Uriah the Hittite. David had arranged for Uriah to be killed in battle, making Uriah's already pregnant wife, Bathsheba, available to David for marriage. This was a marriage intended by David to cover up his secret sin. Had Uriah lived, he would have been within his legal rights (according to mosaic law) to have had Bathsheba (while pregnant) stoned to death for being a partner in adultery with his king.

Nathan's message from God had to be a great relief to David because Nathan's previous message to David had informed him that Bathsheba and David's first child would not live. It is worthy to note that God was no longer communicating directly with David, as in the past. David, because of his sin, had lost his privilege of direct communication with God. Reading 2 Samuel chapters 11 and 12, we learn about the events leading to Solomon's birth and of God's judgment, as revealed through

3

the prophet Nathan. Knowledge of these two chapters is necessary to understand Proverbs and the man who wrote them. Reading Psalm 51 is also highly recommended at this time so you can gain insight of David, the man whose writings seem to have been so inspirational for Solomon. This psalm can help us understand why God later refers to David as a man after His own heart, despite his being an adulterer and a murderer.

Just as Moses was not allowed to enter the Promised Land, David was prohibited from building the temple that would house God's holy ark of the covenant (1 Chronicles 17:1–15). God eventually revealed to David, through Nathan, it would be Solomon who would build His temple. This revelation provided a strong incentive for Nathan and Bathsheba to encourage a young Solomon to work and study hard for his upcoming role as Israel's king. God's spiritual influence placed a hunger in Solomon for knowledge. He was probably in the palace studying most days while his older half brothers were out causing problems, as we are told in 2 Samuel 13. Solomon's childhood was definitely one of privilege, but it was also one of confusion, disappointment, and controversy. Like Joseph with his coat of many colors, Solomon was probably despised by his older brothers. But unlike Joseph, he was not his father's favorite son.

Given the extensive consequences of David's sin, Nathan, Bathsheba and David himself all had to be in agreement that Solomon's life should not be patterned after David's. Perhaps this contributed to David's distancing himself from the son he knew was chosen to be Israel's next king. It appears that God's choice of Solomon was a closely guarded secret. Given the history of David's dysfunctional family, this was necessary to secure the safety of Israel's next king from his older throne-seeking brothers.

Solomon's early proverbs were written by a young man who had expressed a sincere desire for purity and for obedience to God's will. His later writings began to reflect the thoughts of a young adult destined for greatness. Despite his God-given wisdom, it seems Solomon's priorities did change, and this once-dedicated child of God wound up with seven hundred wives and three hundred concubines!

Sorrow and regret are what fueled the thoughts of a disgraced Solomon, who later wrote the book of Ecclesiastes. I think God's purpose for this book is to show us why the world's wisest king ended up with such a sorrowful soul. When reading Solomon's Ecclesiastes, we find the thoughts of a broken man who had repented of his sin, received forgiveness, and then could once again discern right from wrong (Ecclesiastes 1:12–15; 2:10–17; 4:13; 11:8–10).

These verses reveal a repentant king who wished he had never allowed the worship of false gods into Israel. The passing pleasures of his youthful lust were now just a distant memory, but the consequences of his past folly remained very real and quite vivid. Solomon now had firsthand knowledge of how and why his father, David, had been lured away from wisdom's cry for obedience and had succumbed to his own personal foolishness. There is a repetitive pattern in the Bible of men being crushed before God was finished with them. Sin always has its consequences. They are sometimes delayed and often misunderstood, but always fulfilled!

Following Solomon's introduction in verse one, the next five verses provide us the purpose of the Proverbs, which lead us to verse seven7, the key verse for the entire book of Proverbs. **"The fear of the Lord is the beginning of knowledge: but fools despise wisdom and instruction"** (Proverbs 1:7 KJV). It is a very common opinion among those who study the scriptures that verse seven is the mission statement of Solomon's Proverbs. An understanding of this verse should result in a continuous awareness of God's presence, and His complete control of both the physical and the spiritual worlds of His creation. What sane person would want to defy the will of anyone with this kind of power?

"To know wisdom and instruction; to perceive the words of understanding" (Proverbs 1:2).

The first stated purpose for the study of Proverbs is to know wisdom. Wisdom is the ability to use knowledge properly. Knowledge is the awareness of existing facts. Awareness is acquired through life experiences, which collectively becomes our databases to draw upon. We need positive experiences in our databases, so we have productive information to guide us through the decision-making process. This is why a young child's brain is like a sponge, absorbing everything the central nervous system presents to it. We need knowledge to grow and function.

Verse two also reveals the necessity for instruction, in addition to accumulated wisdom, if we expect to increase our understanding.

5

Instruction is a major component of the parent/child relationship. It is a sad situation when a young child does not receive the mental and emotional nourishment that our Lord wants every child to have. Some parents are unable to pass on what they themselves did not receive as children; **they can't give away what they don't have**. Other parents are too busy to pass on adequate instruction, but those who do are sometimes met with opposition from their children/students. If children do not respect their parents as instructors, the transfer of knowledge is greatly hindered. Twenty-first century Christian parents have the additional challenge of competing with today's politically correct public school system, making it difficult for parents to maintain a position of authority.

Good instruction requires good reception for it to be effective. A disturbed child or an angry child will be hindered from learning. Some children tend to feel bombarded by instruction, or lack the necessary discipline to give it the thought and concentration it requires to be effective. Children will sometimes need extra encouragement or maybe even an occasional rebuke to serve as motivation to conquer life's many challenges. Proverbs 1:2 in the New International Version (NIV) uses the word *discipline*, instead of the word *understanding*, for this verse. Discipline is the training that corrects or molds for the purpose of achieving a desired effect. Discipline is the control gained by an enforced, deliberate action. Some students will require discipline to help them "perceive the words of understanding."

"To receive the instruction of wisdom, justice, and judgment and equity" (Proverbs 1:3).

Verse three adds justice, judgment, and equity to the list of virtues given by Solomon as reasons to study his proverbs. Justice refers to the fair treatment of those around us, according to the law of the land and the expectations of its culture. In addition to these standards, Christians must also consider the expectations of God's law. America is getting further and further away from God's law, thus creating a greater need than ever to study God's Word. God's instruction of justice not only teaches us how to treat others; it also urges us to lead by example.

The instruction of judgment refers to the judgment of our own thoughts, words and actions, not the conduct of others. Good judgment allows for the accurate evaluation of information. It can also alert us to the types of information we should ignore. Good judgment will cause us to avoid the people, places, and situations to which God's Holy Spirit does not want us exposed.

The last word of verse three in the King James translation is *equity;* which is taken from the Hebrew word, *meyshar*, which usually means evenness, straightness, in agreement, things that are equal, right, or upright. Figuratively, it can refer to being prosperous. Webster's dictionary assigns three definitions which include: "justice according to natural law," "a system of laws," or "the money value of a property." The first definition fits nicely with the Hebrew definition of upright, straight, and definitely prosperous, and who else but God can be credited with establishing natural laws?

"To give subtilty to the simple, to the young man knowledge and discretion" (Proverbs 1:4).

Subtilty is a form of the word subtle, which can mean to be: delicate, mentally alert, highly skilled, cunning, or crafty. Translated from the Hebrew word, *ormah*, this word can take on the meaning of trickery but only in a good sense. This was a skill that saved David's life, as recorded in 1 Samuel 21:10-15. *Subtil* is also the word used by the Old King James Version of the Bible to describe the serpent, who misled Eve in the Garden of Eden. The word subtil in Genesis 3:1 is translated from the Hebrew word, *aruwm*. This word serves as an example of trickery in a bad sense.

Verse four adds the word *discretion* to Solomon's list of valuable virtues. Discretion is the ability to make reasonable and responsible decisions. Discretion is the result of good judgment, as mentioned in the previous verse. Discretion is a God-given gift that He expects both children and their parents to cultivate. Smashed fingers and bloodied knees will be replaced with much more serious problems; which is why everyone needs discretion. **One of the main purposes of Solomon's Proverbs is to help young people avoid costly mistakes by assessing the wisdom and discretion their elders have already acquired.** Solomon knew the importance of willingness to learn. This was one of the traits that set him apart from his older brothers, and it contributed immensely to his success.

"A wise man will hear, and will increase learning; and a man of understanding shall attain unto wise counsels" (Proverbs 1:5).

Verse five tells us those who benefit from listening will continue to do so. The Holman Christian Standard Bible (HCSB) translates verse five as *"a wise man will listen and increase his learning, and a discerning man will obtain guidance."* Discernment is one of the spiritual gifts mentioned by the apostle Paul (1 Corinthians 12:10). It refers to the ability to know and recognize with accuracy what our senses are telling us. A discerning mind, by definition, is one that possesses understanding. Seven different Hebrew words are translated into three forms of this word—discerned, discerner, and discerneth—are all found in the Old Testament. Perhaps the best over-all definition to collectively represent these Hebrew words, is to know with certainty.

"To understand a proverb and the interpretation; the words of the wise, and their dark sayings" (Proverbs 1:6).

We already have defined what a proverb is. The New King James translation uses the word *enigma*, which is defined as an obscure speech or writing that is hard to understand or explain. It can also mean a mystery. The Holman Christian Standard Bible uses the word *parable* here. Psalm 78:2 states, *"I will open my mouth in a parable; I will utter dark sayings of old."* Christians interpret this verse as prophecy concerning the coming Messiah, Jesus Christ; who frequently spoke in parables. He is the one who provides the spiritual insight (referred to frequently as "the light" in the New Testament) required for understanding Old Testament dark sayings.

There is nothing dark about the next verse. It not only is the key verse of chapter one, but it also is the theme of the entire book of Proverbs. I have heard this verse criticized as much as any other verse in the Bible. I have heard atheists, agnostics, and those who mistakenly think they are real Christians say something such as: "I don't think a loving God wants us to fear him." It is so easy to spot the wannabe Christians. They want to play it safe, just in case the Bible really is God's Word, but they haven't quite wrapped their heads around the fact that God is all powerful and all knowing. They haven't read the Bible enough to know that almost every time God—or even one of His angels—made an appearance, those whom He appeared to were usually very scared.

Genesis 3:7–10 tells us how Adam and Eve hid from the presence of God once they had eaten of the forbidden tree, and their eyes had been opened. Verse ten quotes Adam as saying, *"I heard thy voice in the garden, and I was afraid because I was naked; and I hid myself."* We are all an "open book" in the eyes of God; therefore, we are naked, and if we have any sense at all, we, like Adam, will be afraid—we may not be physically naked, but we are naked in every other sense! Exodus 3:6, Deuteronomy 10:12, 2 Samuel 6:7–9, Daniel 5:5–6, Luke 2:8–9, Matthew 17:5–6, and Romans 14:11 all tell us it is a fearful thing to come into the presence of the living God.

"The fear of the Lord is the beginning of knowledge: but fools despise wisdom and instruction" (Proverbs 1:7).

Yirah is the Hebrew word for fear. It is the word used by Solomon in verse seven to describe man's natural relationship with God. In addition to fear, it also can mean reverence, dread, or awe. Yirah is a reverent respect for God, as evidenced by continual obedience and motivated by love, faith, and free-will. If this concept is not deeply ingrained into our souls, then any other knowledge we manage to acquire is just data in our brains—whereas a proper and sincere fear of the Lord will free us from the distractions of sin. We first must confess our sin; then acknowledge that the sacrificial blood of our Savior, the Lord Jesus Christ, is the only means of removing this sin from our souls. Once this happens, then—and only then—our heavenly Father's Holy Spirit can come in to unite with our own spirits. The indwelling of God's Holy Spirit is what gives us the ability to serve Him as our Lord, Master, and Savior.

Verse seven is the first verse of Proverbs to utilize antithetic parallelism. This refers to the second phrase of this (or any other) verse, stating the opposite viewpoint or result of the first phrase. This is a type of Hebrew poetry that usually emphasizes making wise decisions. Playing the fool is the opposite of worshiping the Lord. If we continue doing foolish things, we will eventually become fools, we will suffer the consequences of our foolishness, and we will be alienated from God's Holy Spirit. This will leave us vulnerable to Satan's suggestions. Fearing the Lord includes a hatred for foolishness and evil.

A fool is one who lacks the ability to make good judgments. He is often thought of as being stupid or easily deceived. Some will consider a fool to be harmless or possibly even entertaining, but the Bible does not support this position. Solomon's Proverbs will tell us to avoid not only the fool but also his folly. A man is often judged by the company he keeps. We will find more information about the fool in later chapters.

"My son; hear the instruction of thy father, and forsake not the law of thy mother" (Proverbs 1:8).

After issuing the advice to "fear the Lord," Solomon redirects our attention towards parental authority. Never in the history of mankind have we had a greater need for the command of this verse than we do today in twenty-first century America. Our once Christian country has been led away from God's law by the doctrine of political correctness. America's children are continually bombarded by it in our public schools and the growing influence of public media. We may be surprised, as we read through the Bible, by all the false gods that ancient civilizations would worship. Does not the current American culture worship materialism, political correctness, and the gods of the electronic age? Would season tickets behind home plate constitute a tithe to your local Major League Baseball team?

Solomon is telling his students it takes a caring father and a loving mother to raise a child, not the teacher, not the television, not the neighbors, and certainly not the older kids in the neighborhood! This is one of the most important concepts in the Bible—it expands upon the fifth commandment, **"Honor thy father and thy mother: that thy days may be long upon the land which the Lord thy God giveth thee"** (Exodus 20:12). Solomon valued this information enough to issue for the first time his intimate call to attention, "My son." This verse begins the direct instruction of the young student to whom these first nine chapters of the Proverbs are written.

The words "my son" signal the beginning of what author, David Hubbard, refers to as a wisdom speech in his excellent commentary on Solomon's proverbs. For the purpose of this book, the first nine chapters of Solomon's proverbs are broken down into sixteen wisdom speeches. Twelve of these sixteen speeches begin with these some-what affectionate words: "my son."

The Hebrew word for instruction is *muwcar*. Its meanings can include chastening, correction, discipline, or rebuke, in addition to its use here for instruction. Verse eight tells our student to hear the father's *muwcar*. Verse eight also tells our young student, "Do not forsake the law of your mother." Solomon seems to be setting a bit of a double standard here—it's almost like he is saying, "Listen to what I tell you because it is important, and remember, what your mother says is important too." This is an effective means of Solomon's prioritizing any conflicting instructions.

There are two reasons for this: first, Israel and all the other societies of that era were male-dominated. Second, Solomon, and David both had many wives and concubines with whom they legitimately could have children with. Please read 1 Kings 11:1–13 to better understand the magnitude of this situation. When Solomon was young, there is evidence he greatly respected his mother, as signified by setting up a throne for her next to his. This gives reasonable cause to believe the bulk of his foreign wives were probably acquired after the death of his mother, Bathsheba. Solomon had to have realized his older half-brothers were receiving different instruction from their mothers than he was from Bathsheba. Some of these other wives of David had grown up with other gods from other lands, thus they had no respect for the written laws given to Israel by God through Moses. This was the catalyst for the eventual demise of Israel. Had Solomon written this proverb later in life, Mom's law may not have received such honorable mention.

"For they shall be a graceful ornament of grace onto thy head, and chains about thy neck" (Proverbs 1:9).

Since verse nine refers to the plural by saying, "they," it is referring to Mom's law as well as Dad's instruction. The Holman Christian Standard Bible (HCSB) uses the word *garland* instead of ornament. A garland was a wreath made of material from plants or trees. It was a common practice for pagan societies to place garlands on the heads of victims selected for human sacrifice. They would also place garlands on the heads of the idols to whom the sacrifices were being offered. This practice is referenced in Acts 14:13, when the priests of Zeus thought the apostle Paul and Barnabas were gods.

The word *ornament,* as used in both the Old and New King James Versions is defined by *Webster's* as a useful accessory or something that lends beauty or grace. With this definition in mind, verse nine could be telling us that by respecting our parents' teachings we will acquire God's blessing, which could include, among other things, beauty and grace. If a person uses these blessings to promote God's kingdom, more blessings will follow. It's been said we can't out-give God.

The second line, or part B, of verse nine refers to "chains about thy neck." Anything worn around the neck is usually seen by others. Some chains around the neck, such as those worn by military personnel, are worn for identification purposes. Just like a dog-tag, our words and actions can serve as identification for who we really are. When we obey our heavenly Father's instructions, our words and actions identify us as one of His. We should take the time to ask ourselves, **"If Christianity were a crime, is there enough evidence to convict me?"** If not, then I suggest reading God's Word to not only know Him better, but to know how to serve Him better as well. Christians have a lot going for them. The Apostle Paul confirms this in 2 Timothy 1:7 when he says, *"For God hath not given us the spirit of fear; but of power, and of love, and of a sound mind."*

Who in his or her right mind wouldn't want what God has to offer? All it takes is faith that God is all He says He is and a commitment to be obedient to His will, all of which is revealed to His followers in His Word, the Holy Bible. Anyone who sincerely seeks Him will want to know Him a little better every day. Perhaps one of the most effective means of acquiring this knowledge is by reading what was written by the man proclaimed by God Himself to be the wisest king of Israel. These early chapters of Proverbs are what that same king wanted his own son to know. If you take the time and make the effort to understand them, you too can be blessed by God—if not in this world, then in the next.

Wisdom Speech Two

Proverbs 1:10–14

"My son if sinners entice thee, consent thou not" (Proverbs 1:10).

This is Solomon's second call to attention initiated by the words "my son," a loving yet stern verbal alert. The words "my son" serve the same purpose as when Jesus would say, "Verily verily I say unto you." An accurate interpretation for "verily verily" could be surely surely. The call to attention given by Jesus meant He was going to say something very important, just as Solomon has here in verse ten. Solomon uses the phrase "my son" eleven more times in the first seven chapters of Proverbs.

Solomon's instruction, given after his first call to attention in verse eight, *"hear the instruction of thy father and forsake not the law of thy mother,"* is the foundation for all the following instructions issued in Proverbs. Both parents and children need to recognize this first piece of proverbial wisdom as the beginning of God's path. Pleasing Mom and Dad needs to be every child's first objective. Even a toddler should know what **"NO"** means, and then stop doing whatever it is that caught Mom's or Dad's attention.

Wisdom's path begins with obedience to a known authority, usually our earthly mothers and fathers. Then, as we grow and develop; knowledge accumulates and we begin to recognize God as an additional authority figure. Through faith and obedience we eventually gain access to God's road to wisdom, but we will also have a force inside urging us toward sin's downhill path. The other road, also known as the "high road" is an uphill journey, but this is necessary because God always raises us up. He never pushes us down. Mom and Dad's training at an early age is crucial for the mental and spiritual toughness required for pre-adolescents to continue their up-hill climb.

While still at home and under the close supervision of at least one loving parent, it's not too difficult for children to remain on track for success. As children mature and become more independent, new challenges and temptations will come into play. Detours from wisdom's path can mislead children from the spiritual and emotional prosperity God intends for them to have. Sin has the capability to blind us all of its certain consequences. Solomon later wrote in Proverbs 4:19, **"The way of the wicked is as darkness; they know not at what they stumble"** This verse is the most valuable piece of information found in Solomon's Proverbs, second only to verse seven of this first chapter.

You may not want to think of any young child, especially a toddler, as being wicked. What should be recognized and accepted here is; **early disrespect for parental authority will eventually lead to wickedness if not promptly corrected**. The longer one strays from wisdom's way, the harder it will be to get back onto its path. An established pattern of rebellion toward authority, if left unchecked, will eventually lead to wickedness.

Verse ten begins its instruction for when our young student of Solomon's Proverbs begins to encounter the influence of outsiders who, unlike his parents, do not have his best interest at heart. Verse ten describes these outsiders as sinners who are going to entice the innocent to try something new, to join them in their wickedness. The sinners of verse ten can represent older siblings, neighborhood friends, or schoolyard acquaintances. Growing up includes the gradual independence from parental guidance. Children eventually must journey away from the safety and security of the home to experience the outside world—a world that will include people who did not have the benefit of growing up in a Christian environment. As young students mature, they will eventually visit the homes of new friends, where they will encounter parents who are different from their own. Some homes may have just one parent, parents who have fallen out of love with each other, or parents who have to work multiple jobs just to keep the bills paid. Among the saddest of homes are the ones that include an alcoholic or drug-addicted parent. There is little to no hope for a child to emerge emotionally stable from a home that includes drinking, fighting, or disorganization. A disorganized home could be thought of as one with emotional as well as physical clutter.

Parents from previous generations in America did not have as much legal and social accountability as they do today. I can recall spending much of one summer in the late sixties with a friend who had an alcoholic father. Alcoholism had reduced this once-talented man to an unemployable drunk who was in the final stages of alcoholism. He would lie around the house all day in a stupor, while his wife worked to support the family. Being teen-aged boys, we naturally chose to hang out at my friend's house rather than my house where there were rules and parental expectations. We soon took advantage of the situation and began sneaking drinks when his father was passed out. Drinking alcohol made us feel grown up because we were doing what other boys our age were not yet doing. The feeling of whiskey burning our throats soon got old, so we began sneaking out his father's pickup truck to drive it around the neighborhood. This would further our feelings of superiority to our peers. Little did we know that his father would soon die in an alcoholic coma, and that we were rapidly losing sight of wisdom's path.

Rather than learning from the example God had put before me of the dangers of alcoholism, I instead continued to use it as a means to quiet my conscience. Alcohol would stifle the guilt and shame caused by my disobedience to the godly instruction of my parents. As my guilt grew, so did my drinking. This led to my eventual use of marijuana. I secretly did not want to try it the first time it was offered to me, but I could not stand the thought of my peers perceiving me as scared to try it. My pride had cornered me into a need for fitting in with the "cool crowd."

Looking back on that time, I now find it no coincidence that this was when I stopped participating in sports. Wrestling and baseball were now expendable, as was following God's instruction. I did not know why there were tears in my eyes when I told that high school coach, "I quit." That was because I was still unfamiliar with Proverbs 4:19 (*"The way of the wicked is as darkness, they know not at what they stumble"*). I now only wanted to pursue what I thought was "cool" in the eyes of my peers: sex, drugs, and rock 'n' roll. I did not yet realize these were merely the devil's tool for diverting me very far from wisdom's path by purging all discipline from life.

The home God had provided for me to grow up in was a clean home. One free from clutter and dirt, and it was clean in more than just a sanitary respect. It was spiritually clean as well. Free from drinking, cursing, and smoking. Clean Christian homes were quickly dwindling in a society where more and more parents became fixated on acquiring more stuff. Americans in the sixties were no longer content with one car in the driveway—they now had to have two cars in the garage. America's big businessmen, also known as the "captains of industry," took full advantage of America's greed for more stuff. They knew the more hours people worked, the more money they would be able to make. The result was more Americans working longer hours, leaving less time for the parental instruction of America's children.

Today's high-paced urban society makes verse ten an even more important warning than it was long ago in ancient Israel. The competition within a highly technical job market requires a lot more preparation for a career than what was required when Solomon wrote this verse three thousand years ago. This means children of today must stay in school well into their twenties to qualify for the best-paying jobs. America's youth must begin competing early if they are going to get into the right schools, meet the right people, and make the right connections. It also means sexually mature young adults have to constantly struggle with their biological urges, if they are going to remain sexually pure until marriage. This issue was never a concern for the politically correct crowd or America's captains of industry.

The verses following verse ten describe a situation where the young Hebrew teenager of chapter one, is obviously away from home and being enticed to join with a gang of outlaws. This is an example of what could happen to young restless males of ancient Israel who were uninterested in pursuing the family's business and lifestyle. They would venture out on their own where they would probably meet up with an outsider, who might ask, "Do you really want to take care of those stinking sheep for the rest of your life? Why don't you come with me, and I will show you an easier way to make more money than you could ever have by herding livestock. I can introduce you to people your own age, people who will love you like a brother, people on whom you will always be able to depend. You will never again be poor, bored, or lonely if you join us."

This is a perfect example of how Satan lies by telling a half truth. It is probably true that the young man will have more money if he joins the gang, but Satan leaves out the little fact that the money will have to be stolen, not earned or produced. He did not tell the young recruit, "Oh yeah, by the way, you are going to greatly reduce your life expectancy and probably have to be looking over your shoulder for the rest of your life."

Gangs are still a major problem—they are nothing more than an organized group of criminals who would rather hurt innocent people, than pursue honest work. The head of all the gangs is Satan himself. His methods of recruitment have been refined and enhanced to be effective in today's society. The most common gang threatening children today does not promote violence; it promotes secular humanism in our public schools. This gang is different from most gangs of the past. It does not want to remove its members from the home in a physical sense. It simply wants to introduce an element of doubt into the minds of any child who still believes God created the earth and all of its life-forms.

The management of Satan's organized gangs consists of a wide range of people, from evil dictators and corrupt politicians to well-meaning science teachers who impress on young, vulnerable minds that evolution, not God, is their creator. This seemingly nominal event causes a young Christian mind to ponder, "Do I continue to think like Mom and Dad, or do I join in with my friends and believe what the teacher is telling us?" Little does that child know that some of his or her classmates are struggling with the same questions, "Who should I believe? Why am I being told two different stories?" It can be tough to break away from the "programmed herd mentality," especially when there's a strong sociological urge to fit in.

In a situation like this, what a child thinks has happened will be the most influential, rather than what actually has transpired. Children will look around at their fellow classmates to determine if they appear to be agreeing with what they are being taught. If the teacher presents an interesting argument for the validity of evolution, which might include stories of ancient volcanoes and dinosaurs, a child's imagination will be very stimulated and thus open to suggestion. Well-trained, politically correct professionals will make the study of evolution a fun and exciting experience for their students. They will probably even have toy dinosaurs for the class to play with, while the Christian child wonders, "How can this be? The Bible doesn't say anything about dinosaurs being in the Garden of Eden."

Any young students who have not been grounded in a Christian belief will have no reason not to believe what they're taught. Christianity was—and still is—the only institution threatening the success of the "God created nothing" gang. **This is why Satan has fought so hard to have God, prayer, and the Bible removed from America's public school systems.**

The teaching of evolution was once illegal in America. This was when nearly every American student not only knew but also believed the first sentence from the Bible—*"In the beginning God created the heavens and the earth."* The devil is smart enough to know that if he can discredit the very first sentence of the Bible, then there always will be a degree of doubt about all the following verses. The Bible is then reduced in the minds of the deceived children to a book of fairy tales, along with Santa Claus and the Easter Bunny. When a young mind is persuaded to believe a non-believing educator instead of a Christian parent, that child has unknowingly joined the gang.

Adolescence is a period of declining parental influence, while peer pressure grows. Often the greatest danger is what adolescents think their peers are doing, rather than what is actually happening. If a teenage boy begins to brag about a made-up sexual conquest of a girl, even though it never happened, you can be sure this will have a bad influence on any other teenage boys who hear that false story. Today's music, television, and other electronic communications are all capable of causing America's youth to believe their peers might be participating in sinful and even illegal behaviors, even if they really aren't. All it takes is one or two popular teens to say they have participated in an immoral act to tempt another teen to think, *"I want to try that."*

If young Christians are brave enough to question an older, well-trained professional teacher, they often run the risk of appearing unsophisticated before their classmates. If, because of their beliefs, they stand their ground and say, "No, I refuse to believe I evolved from a monkey," this will cause them to be thought of as different by any non-believing peers. It can be psychologically traumatizing for an innocent child to be placed in the position of deciding whether to believe a teacher or their parents. It is unlikely that a child will be happy if there are no other children in whom the child can confide or with whom the child can compare his or her inner thoughts.

Sooner or later, parental authority and control will be reduced in all children's lives; it's a necessary part of growing up. America's government prefers that it be sooner rather than later. America's political machine is convinced it can do a better job of raising America's children than America's parents can. Just turn on any network news program, and you will hear, over and over again, the values they think should be taught to your child. For example, you will hear how important it is to make free condoms available for teens, rather than how important it is to remain sexually pure, as the Bible teaches. Political correctness is the government's current preferred authority. Satan, his generals, and their captains of industry do not want any resistance to liberal America's current idol, political correctness. Christian parents need to plant their seed in fertile ground. This requires convincing children to believe in God and to be involved with other Christian children in a Bible-believing church.

The teaching of evolution and political correctness presents all parents with the need to recite Proverbs 1:10 to their children on a regular, if not daily basis: *"My son, if sinners entice thee, consent thou not."*

Now Solomon will use the next four verses to describe a more likely reason to teach this verse to the children of his era.

"If they say, Come with us, let us lay wait for blood, let us lurk privily for the innocent without cause" (Proverbs 1:11 KJV).

The verbs of this verse describe an ambush, but against whom? It is a trap set for the innocent, or as the Holman Bible reads, *"Let's attack some innocent person just for fun!"* Satan does not want a fair fight. The young, the innocent, and the harmless are his favorite targets. This would explain why pedophiles are so compelled to do their disgusting deeds—they are encouraged by the devil. The expression, "to shed blood" may sound extreme, but every time one steals, whether it's a child's innocence, a person's property, or even an idea, is that not a part of the victim's life being stolen?

"Let us swallow them up alive as the grave; and whole, as those that go down into the Pit" (Proverbs 1:12).

The power from this verse is derived from Solomon's graphic example of a predator swallowing its prey—not only alive but whole, with no chewing required. Verse 12 illustrates how the power of a gang's influence can appeal to the ego of a potential young recruit. An experienced gang recruiter will be on the lookout for young people who both are vulnerable and have the capability to carry out similarly violent behavior. Children who are not grounded in Christian faith are the easier targets. Those who do not have the benefit of living with both of their biological parents also are more likely to succumb to the allure of the gang. Satan's recruiters will attempt to convince younger recruits that the gang will give them a feeling of strength and satisfaction. He will project the feeling of invincibility as he describes how a victim will struggle to free himself or herself from the gang's jaws of death.

This verse also can be applied to a spiritual battle as well. The grave, or *sheol*, is the Old Testament Hebrew term that refers to the domain of the dead. It is the equivalent of the New Testament Greek word, Hades. The King James Version and New International Version Bibles both use the word grave. A grave is commonly thought of as where only the corpse will remain once its spirit has departed. The first use of the word grave is in Genesis 37:35, when Jacob said, *"In mourning I will go down to the grave."* Jacob, who was a righteous man, used this word to describe where his body would go after his death.

The story of Lazarus and the rich man, found in Luke chapter 16, quotes Jesus, making reference to "Abraham's Bosom" or "Abraham's Side" (NIV) as the resting place for Lazarus's departed spirit, while the rich man's spirit was imprisoned in Hades. The Holman Christian Standard Bible states that Jesus, while on the cross, told the thief next to him, *"I assure you: Today you will be with Me in paradise"* (Luke 23:43). Most Christian scholars believe the paradise Jesus spoke of is the same place spoken of in the Old Testament as Abraham's bosom. Hades is the New Testament name for the pit.

King David makes reference to the grave and seems to distinguish it as a different destination than the pit. *"O Lord, Thou hast brought up my soul from the grave: thou hast kept me alive, that I should not go down to the pit"* (Psalm 30:3). The grave, as stated here by David, is a different place than the pit. David seems to use the word grave to refer to death, not to a tomb or grave. Only the body is buried; the spirit will continue being a spirit after physical death, but without the body it once indwelt. There are two possible destinations for the spirit. These would be the pit, where David obviously did not want to go, or Abraham's bosom, also known as paradise, which was where Jesus told the thief they would soon be. There are nine references to the bottomless pit in the book of Revelation, with all of them describing it as a prison for demons and the eventual eternal residence for Satan as well.

Proverbs 1:12 describes those going down to the pit as being swallowed whole, which refers to the whole man, including his spirit, whereas the grave will house the dead's physical bodies only. The righteous man's spirit eventually will be reunited with a body, but it will be a new and improved body, like the one the resurrected Jesus possessed after His ascension from the tomb. This is what Christians have to look forward to—eternal life without the demands and limitations of a physical body.

Satan's gang gives no thought to a heavenly body. What they seek are the material possessions of their victims, but the members will lose something much more important when they arrive at the pit to join the founder and CEO of all the gangs for all of eternity. They will miss out on the wonderful opportunity to spend eternity with their true Creator. Please carefully consider Psalm 28:1–5, taken from the Holman Christian Standard Bible (HCSB):

> Lord, I call to you; my rock, do not be deaf to me. If you remain silent to me I will be like those going down to the Pit. Listen to the sound of my pleading when I cry to you for help, when I lift up my hands toward Your holy sanctuary. Do not drag me away with the wicked, with the evildoers, who speak in friendly ways with their neighbors while malice is in their hearts. Repay them according to what they have done—according to the evil of their deeds. Repay them according to the work of their hands; give them back what they deserve. Because they do not

consider what the Lord has done or the work of His hands,
He will tear them down and not rebuild them.

**"We shall find all precious substance, we shall fill
our houses with spoil; Cast in thy lot among us; let
us all have one purse" (Proverbs 1:13–14).**

This is the reward the young man is promised if he joins one of Satan's many gangs. The sought-after possessions of the gang's fallen victims are the rewards acquired for a deal with the devil. Satan is still using the same bait he has always used—he appeals to that part of human nature that wants something for nothing. This was essentially the deal Adam had in the Garden of Eden, with one exception—God required obedience. Satan, on the other hand, just wanted to deprive Adam of his fellowship with God. When Adam failed to remain obedient, God punished him and his descendants by cursing the earth, which is described in Genesis 3:17–19. This was when God essentially told Adam that if he wanted to eat, he would have to work hard; hard enough to sweat.

God cursed the ground, cursed the serpent, and cursed Adam's first son, Cain, all within the first four chapters of Genesis. As you read through the Bible, you will find a whole lot of blessing and almost as much cursing being pronounced upon mankind. Some sin carried a curse that could be passed on for four generations, as described in Exodus 20:5–6. Pride has encouraged many, down through the centuries, to design their own God to fit with their personal beliefs and needs. When people insist upon fashioning a personalized god who will not condemn a sinner to punishment, it's a safe bet that they have not studied, nor understand the Bible. God is patient and forgiving, not forgetful—more importantly **He is the Creator, not the created!**

WISDOM SPEECH THREE

Proverbs 1:15–33

"My son, walk not thou in the way with them; refrain thy foot from their path" (Proverbs 1:15).

How can a plan for staying out of trouble be made any simpler than this? God created His animal kingdom with protective instincts, one of which is to stay away from predators. Humans however, frequently ignore or misuse their God-given instincts because they also have been endowed with free will. The ability to choose is why children need to learn early to obey their parents. They need encouragement to make wise decisions and to be guided away from the frivolous path of foolishness. Our Creator, understands the hazards and the limitations of our human condition; more so than any other intelligence. The psalmist knew the importance of avoiding evil, as he wrote in Psalm 119:101, *"I have refrained my feet from every evil way, that I might keep thy word."* The apostle Paul puts this same concept in very plain language: *"Do not be deceived: Bad company corrupts good morals"* (1 Corinthians 15:33 HCSB). An even plainer way of stating it is, "If you play in the pigpen, you're going to smell like a pig!"

"For their feet run to evil, and make haste to shed blood" (Proverbs 1:16).

This verse begins the description of the type of people Solomon is urging his young student to avoid. Reading through the Proverbs will provide us with a comprehensive list of characteristics that define the foolish and the wicked. Solomon is advising his student to be on the

23

lookout for these personality traits so he can avoid the demonic influence of Satan's recruiters. Verse 16 describes the enthusiasm of Satan's followers in carrying out their master's work, which is to steal, kill, and destroy (John 10:10).

Eve sinned because of her curiosity, Adam sinned because of peer pressure, and Cain sinned because of anger and jealousy. These are just a few examples of what can motivate a person to sin. The sinners described in verse 16 do not need any motivation to sin because they enjoy it. Sin became the identity of their souls. They no longer sensed any guilt or remorse from their spirits despite their continuing sin. The apostle Paul describes this broken spiritual condition in Romans 1:21–32. Romans 1:28, in the NIV translation, specifically tells us God gave these habitual sinners over to depraved minds. The word *depraved* means they were corrupt or marked by evil. The New King James Version uses a more general term, debased, which can mean a lower quality or status, perverted, moral deterioration by evil, or a loss of soundness. The Old King James Version states, "God gave them over to a reprobate mind to do those things that are not convenient." Reprobate, when used as an adjective, can mean condemned, foreordained to damnation, or morally abandoned.

The King James Version tells us that God's Holy Spirit no longer places these people under conviction when they sin; even if it's obvious sin. This verse is not saying they can or cannot be saved— it's saying they have been doing wrong for so long that they no longer realize what they are doing is wrong. In a sense, they are no longer slaves to sin; they're volunteers! Their feet run swiftly toward evil. If this is not bad enough, the King James Version tells us they were doing those things which were not convenient (verse 28). This describes an addiction—if the sin is causing inconvenience, then why is the sinner still doing it? Why does the alcoholic continue to drink? Why do some of those with emphysema continue to smoke? **Sin, if allowed to continue, can become the ultimate addiction!**

> **"Surely in vain the net is spread in the sight of any bird. And they lay wait for their own blood; they lurk privily for their own lives" (Proverbs 1:17–18).**

These verses refer us back to the gangsters, of verse 11 who were attempting to lure the young student from wisdom's path. Solomon compares their words to a trap being set. He states that these gangsters have less understanding than any free flying bird, because they unknowingly have become trapped. Their gang membership will close many future doors of opportunity. This is especially true for the younger gangsters who do not have enough sense to conceal their gang affiliations. What they do not yet realize is the gang lifestyle has a lasting stigma that will later cause them substantial inconvenience. Sin, just like a disease, produces progressive symptoms in the bodies and souls of its victims. In some cases, the effect is permanent. If they survive to reach middle age and eventually manage to get out of the gang, they still will have the reputation and the mannerisms of a hoodlum. Informed people still will remember them as gangsters, and employers will avoid hiring them. The life of crime can pay well in the beginning, but the gang has no use for the old or the weak.

The eternal destination for an unrepentant gangster is the pit, where Satan is waiting to claim his own spoils; which are the spirits of those who rejected wisdom's ways. Lurking secretly for their own lives means the gangsters are their own worst enemies. Older friends and relatives, who have witnessed the long-term effect of the gang lifestyle, can plainly see its effect on the lives and the personalities of the gang's membership. They can foresee the coming demise of the young gangster, whom they can still remember as a young child with a future—a future the gang has destroyed.

"So are the ways of everyone that is greedy of gain; which taketh away the life of the owners thereof" (Proverbs 1:19).

Solomon is now expanding the list of people the young student needs to beware of. Our human condition causes us to want more than our share of nearly everything except work and responsibilities. Our God-given instincts are what drive us to survive and to provide for the continuation of our species. Verse 19 describes those whose instincts go beyond God's intended purpose as being "greedy for gain." *Batsa* is the word translated to greedy—it usually means to plunder. Solomon is suggesting that those who are greedy enough to plunder will lose their lives rather than preserve them.

Greed is basically an extension of self-centeredness, which means we are more concerned about our own desires than the will of God. Greed also can be described as a lack of faith because a true faith in God will give us the assurance our needs will be provided for. Once we have a saving faith, God's Holy Spirit will lift us from the limitations of our self-imposed burdens. When endowed by the Holy Ghost we no longer are concerned about our survival, because we are given the faith to know that God will provide for our safety, as well as our needs. Faith of this magnitude produces within us a peaceful spirit that has been calmed by God's love, mercy, and grace. We can be sure of this because the Bible states, *"There is no fear in love; instead, perfect love drives out fear, because fear involves punishment. So the one who fears has not yet reached perfection in love. We love because He first loved us"* (1 John 4:18–19 HCSB).

Verse 19 tells us the greedy person will eventually suffer the same consequences as those described in the earlier verses of chapter one, the ones who lie in wait for innocent blood. The greedy have the same general motivation as the gangsters, so they also will share the same fate. They have not been perfected by love—they are only capable of loving themselves. Proverbs 1:19 tells us that sin (specifically greed) takes away, or controls, the life of its owners.

Greed is often associated with money, but it can become woven into other areas of one's life. For example, the use of steroids for the enhancement of athletic performance is a growing problem. The greed for recognition of athletic accomplishment is usually what compels an athlete to cheat his or her competitors. Steroids may give the greedy a competitive advantage on a given day, but at what long-term costs? Students who put off studying to socialize excessively will later have to cram for exams. This may result in the use of excessive caffeine or maybe even amphetamines to stay awake. Some celebrities cannot accept they are getting older, and have thus ruined their appearances by having too many cosmetic surgical procedures. These are all examples of people wanting to satisfy their mislead instincts for more fame, more money, or more recognition of their success. These are the goals of people who lack in spirituality because they are greedy for gain. Moderation in the pursuit of instinctual satisfaction is necessary if we expect to hear wisdom's cry.

The apostle Paul masterfully covers the topic of greed in his first letter to Timothy. *"For the love of money is a root of all kinds of evil, and by craving it, some have wandered from the faith, and pierced themselves with many pains"* (Timothy 6:10 HCSB). Paul is claiming these people sabotage their own success when overreacting to their instinctual self-serving desires. If you don't believe what Paul and Solomon are saying, try doing an Internet search on the winners of the larger state lotteries. You will find many of these big-time "winners" wound up being big losers. Solomon will now point out another voice that is crying out to us besides our pride and self-centeredness.

"Wisdom crieth without; she uttereth her voice in the streets: She crieth in the chief place of concourse, in the openings of the gates: in the city she uttereth her words, *saying*" (Proverbs 1:20–21 KJV).

These two verses formally introduce us to the solution for out-of-control greed—God's wisdom. We earlier discussed how faith in God can relieve us of our instinctual sin nature. If God were to appear before us and perform an undeniable miracle to demonstrate His ability, it's a pretty good bet we would experience an increase of faith in Him. However, it usually doesn't happen that way. Jesus is quoted when speaking to (doubting) Thomas, *"Because you have seen Me, you have believed. Those who believe without seeing are blessed"* (John 20:29 HCSB). God's primary method of communication is the voice of His Holy Spirit. If a sinner is exposed to enough wisdom, he or she should become aware of God's existence, which is why wisdom cries out. God wants all of mankind to recognize His greatness through the magnificence of His living creations and the immensity of His star-filled heavens. He wants sinners to hear His cry and to believe in His wisdom, so they can learn how to be blessed through obedience, rather than cursed by ignorance. Solomon had a great appreciation for wisdom—he was blessed more than any other man because of his earthly father's obedience to God. Obedience to God should be the core concept of every family's creed.

Wisdom cried out to Solomon in the open streets of Jerusalem because of their beauty and magnificence. Does wisdom still cry out in the streets of twenty-first century America? What would Solomon think about young men wearing their pants below their buttocks or young women mutilating themselves with facial piercings? First Kings, chapter three records how Solomon shrewdly dealt with two harlots who each claimed the same baby was her child. What would Solomon think about a nation killing its unborn children? How much longer can we expect even a loving God to keep crying out to America?

We're also told wisdom cries out at the gates of the city. The gates of the city could be compared to the ports of America's coastal cities. They are currently filled with rail containers full of foreign merchandise that represents the betrayal of the American worker. Solomon would find no wisdom with America exporting her jobs. What he would find is poorly manufactured junk instead of the quality products America was once known for manufacturing. Today's political policies allow for and even encourage importing poorly crafted products that will soon break and then have to be replaced. This is how the economy is kept rolling. The politically correct do not seem to have a concern for the American consumer, who has the financial burden of replacing or fixing broken goods, but they regularly advertise their concern about America's landfills flowing over with broken, plastic, foreign products.

America's current god, political correctness, dictates it is America's responsibility to promote the economy of a new world order. America's elected officials really are not as concerned about the foreigners as they pretend to be, but they are consumed with the interests of international corporations who donate to their reelection funds. America, like ancient Israel, has sought to please foreign gods and, just like Israel, will suffer the consequences. Psalm 73:27 warns us of this by declaring, *"For, lo, they that are far from thee shall perish; thou has destroyed all them that go a whoring from thee."* These seemingly harsh words merely corroborate earlier warnings from the book of Exodus, where we are told Israel's God is a jealous God (Exodus 20:5 & 34:14). Those who rule countries, as well as those who populate them, need to listen to wisdom's cry.

"How long, ye simple ones, will ye love simplicity?
and the scorners delight in their scorning, and
fools hate knowledge?" (Proverbs 1:22)

The Hebrew word for simple is *pthiy*, which refers to the foolish. The Hebrew for scorner can also mean mocker, which is the word used by the NIV translation. To scorn means to reject with vigorous or angry contempt. Mockery can be done through speech or actions; its purpose is to insult whoever is being mocked. Imitation can be a method of learning. Body language is very obvious to children, which is why adults need to be alert to both the verbal and the visual messages they send. Solomon is addressing two types of people, the foolish and the scorners, who choose to amuse themselves with the unfortunate state of the disadvantaged. If an authority figure does not step in to change the ways of a young scorner, he or she will graduate the school of mockery to become a student of the University of Foolishness.

Verse 22 concludes with telling us why it is so difficult for fools to change their ways; it's because "Fools hate knowledge." Short of God's help, there is very little hope for a fool to avoid his or her self-imposed destiny with the pit. The first mention of the fool in Proverbs was verse seven, which declared, "But fools despise wisdom and instruction." *Becoming a fool is a process, not an event—it usually begins with parents' reluctance to discipline the beautiful, young children they love so much.*

"Turn you at my reproof: behold, I will pour out my Spirit onto you, I will make known my words unto you" (Proverbs 1:23).

This verse provides the believer with the assurance that God will pick us up, clean us up, and continue to love us, even if we have fallen into sin's pigpen. How blessed we are to have a God who is willing to "pour out" His Spirit on us, even if we have strayed from His will. It's important to note the effect God's Spirit has on the believer. It makes His words known to us. As an informed Christian, it should be our desire to know God's words, so we can minimize the need for His rebukes. No one, including our Lord, enjoys issuing rebukes.

When my dog, Max, was just a puppy, I did not enjoy issuing the many rebukes inflicted by my pulling on her leash, but the corrective action of that choke chain is what taught her to walk by my side in a straight path. It was this training—or, it could be said, the continual rebukes—that eventually enabled Max to walk freely, without a leash, by my side wherever I led her. As Max's master, it was my responsibility to teach her where she could walk safely and where she had better not walk at all. I am sure she eventually understood that the discomfort I inflicted upon her was for her own good. My yanking on that leash meant I loved her and that I was always looking ahead to ensure her safety. I was able to do this because God put me in charge. He made humans a higher form of intelligence than He did dogs. In a sense, I was Max's god, in that I determined everything in her life, which included making that final decision for her, which was to have her put asleep.

If I could be as obedient to God as Max was to me, I would be a better Christian than I presently am. Perhaps I will be allowed to walk beside our Lord on the sidewalks of heaven, and then I will be able to please Him as much as Max did me. I still thank God for giving me the special relationship I had with Max. As smart as she was for a dog, her intelligence still could not be compared to a human's, just as my human intelligence cannot be compared to God's. Isn't it ironic that dog spelled backwards is God?

It is an awesome feeling to have the Spirit of God upon you, as verse 23 suggests. Those who have experienced it are forever changed. The same Spirit that provided Solomon with wisdom manifested itself in a totally different manner within Samson's body, as described by Judges 15:14–15. *"The Spirit of the Lord took control of him; and the ropes that were on his arms became like burnt flax and his bonds fell off his wrists. He found a fresh jawbone of a donkey, reached out his hand, took it, and killed 1000 men with it"* (HCSB). God's Holy Spirit produced the super-human strength necessary to transform Samson into an invincible warrior. Joel 2:28–31 (HCSB) describes for us yet another form in which the Holy Spirit can manifest itself upon mankind:

> After this I will pour out MY Spirit on all humanity; then your sons and your daughters will prophesy, your old men will have dreams, and your young men will see visions. I will even pour out My Spirit on the male and female slaves in those days. I will display wonders in the heavens and on the earth: blood, fire, and columns of smoke. The sun will be turned to darkness and the moon to blood before the great and awe-inspiring Day of the Lord comes.

These verses tell us how to recognize the outpouring of the Spirit just prior to the return of God's Son, Jesus Christ. The Holy Ghost will be crying loudly before that great day of the Lord, but many will be unable to hear or recognize His call to attention. The knowledge of God's Word will give us the necessary insight to recognize God's plan, so these events will be understood for what they are. Isaiah 55:8–9 tells us, *"For My thoughts are not your thoughts, neither are your ways My ways, saith the Lord. For as the heavens are higher than the earth, So are My ways higher than your ways, and My thoughts than your thoughts."* When we begin to know God, only then do we realize how much God loves us, which should, in return, cause us to love Him. When we truly love God, we will want to work toward His great commission, which is to feed His sheep (John 21:17). It all begins with studying His instructions for us, as found in His Holy Bible.

"Because I have called and ye refused; I have stretched out my hand, and no man regarded; But ye have set at nought all my counsel, and would (accept) none of My reproof" (Proverbs 1:24–25).

These two verses continue the description of the simple ones, the scorners and the fools, which began in verses 22 and 23. We are told these unfortunate people rejected God's advice. This means they now are in worse shape than when they started out, because having moved further away from God, they are closer to Satan and his pit. It could also mean that God, without their knowing it, might remove any existing protection these fools once had from satanic attack. The first chapter of Job, beginning with verse six, describes God's removing His hedge of protection from a righteous man as a means of testing. This scripture plainly tells us it was Satan—not God—who was responsible for Job's problems. Despite his wife's advice to "curse God and die," Job remained faithful to God and was eventually blessed with twice the possessions he had had before his trials (Job 42:10).

This author knows of only two reasons why people ignore God's counsel—they either doubt God's unlimited power and knowledge, or they are addicted to sin, which means they are so close to Satan's influence they can no longer sense God's Holy Spirit. The apostle Paul describes the fallen spiritual state of addiction in a passage referred to by many as the "Double-Minded Man":

For I do not understand what I am doing, because I do not practice what I want to do, but I do what I hate. And if I do what I do not want to do, I agree with the law that it is good. So now I am no longer the one doing it, but it is sin living in me. For I know that nothing good lives in me, that is in my flesh. For the desire to do what is good is with me, but there is no ability to do it. For I do not do the good that I want to do, but I practice the evil that I do not want to do. Now if I do what I do not want, I am no longer the one doing it, but it is the sin that lives in me. (Romans 7:15–20 HCSB)

"I also will laugh at your calamity; I will mock when your fear cometh; When your fear cometh as desolation, and your destruction cometh as a whirlwind; when distress and anguish cometh upon you" (Proverbs 1:26–27).

This passage reveals an aspect of God's personality with which some Christians are not familiar: God has a sense of humor. King David writes about God's laughter in Psalms 2:4—"He that sitteth in the heavens shall laugh." Judges 6:11–12 give us a firsthand account of God's humor by sarcastically referring to Gideon as a "mighty man of valor" while he was hiding from Israel's enemy, the Midianites.

The book of Judges gives an account of Gideon and his greatly outnumbered three-hundred–man army defeating the Midianites. God was using sarcasm to motivate Gideon to eventually do something that he would have never dreamed of being able to do. God wants us to be all we can be. Can you recall any situations where God's Holy Spirit injected a little humor into a situation that everybody except you thought was funny?

Solomon then goes on to compare the fool's coming terror to that of a whirlwind—or its modern-day equivalent, a tornado. Nature's powerful forces are just one of the many means God can use to bless us or to curse us. A display of power is often what it takes to get a proud man to become aware of his own powerlessness. Verse 28 says when a fool becomes overwhelmed, then and only then will he be willing to ask for advice or help.

> **"Then shall they call upon me, but I will not answer; they shall seek me early, but they will not find me" (Proverbs 1:28).**

This verse is telling us there are situations where God does not answer prayer. It's describing for us those who previously ignored God but have now begun to seek Him diligently—which means a lot of effort is put into their search, but there is still no mention of confession or repentance for sin by these troubled seekers. Verse 28 confirms that works alone do not gain us favor or even an audience with God. God does not listen to the prayers of an unrepentant sinner. To verify this claim, please read Isaiah 1:1–20. This was written by the prophet Isaiah approximately two hundred years after Solomon's reign. God is telling His chosen people that it seems useless to punish them because they had failed to recognize their own powerlessness. In the third verse, God tells Israel they have less sense than an ox or a donkey. God was telling Israel, "I can't hear you."

Because the people of Judah had been sinning for so long on a regular basis, God tells them their offerings are no longer wanted. Their attempts for formal worship had become meaningless because God knew their hearts. Despite their fallen state, God tells Judah their sins can be removed if they become willing and obedient (Isaiah 1:19). Solomon addresses those who continually refuse to submit to God's authority, despite their fallen state. The next two verses reveal the specific action that constitutes rebellion against God.

> **"For that they hated knowledge and did not choose the fear of the Lord: They would (have) none of My council: they despised all my reproof" (Proverbs 1:29–30).**

Verse 29 takes us right back to the previously designated key verse of the Proverbs: *"The fear of the Lord is the beginning of knowledge, But fools despise wisdom and instruction"* (Proverbs 1:7). Solomon has set the stage to inform us of the consequences for men who fail to lay down a solid foundation of knowledge built on biblical principles. The human brain's physiology is still not completely understood by men of science. Like a house, our brains can be thought of as a storehouse for our worldly possessions, and it is built piece by piece. As time passes, both the house and the mind become closer to completion. No matter how well built or how beautifully designed a house is constructed, it will not stand up to a storm without a solid foundation placed on solid ground. God's wisdom is the only foundation Christians should rely upon. Knowledge of Jesus Christ and a healthy, reverential fear of His unlimited power and glory is what we, as His children, can rely upon to last for an eternity. Without a solid foundation, a prideful man will reject God's counsel and, just like Judah, will fail to recognize God's rebuke. Do you think twenty-first–century America is still capable of recognizing God's rebuke?

"Therefore they shall eat of fruit of their own way, and be filled with their own devices. For the turning away of the simple shall slay them, and the prosperity of fools will destroy them" (Proverbs 1:31–32 KJV).

"They shall eat the fruit of their own way"—this tells us that as we sow, so shall we reap. God does not have to punish us here on earth for our foolishness. Like a boomerang, the consequences of sin will come back to manifest itself into our lives. The Holman Christian Standard Bible reads the "complacency of fools," instead of the "prosperity of fools" will destroy them. The word complacency fits well for this application because prosperity should not be associated with fools. Any prosperity a fool enjoys is usually at someone else's expense. If you want fools for children, just provide for all their wants, shield them from all responsibility, and never say anything that could hurt their feelings. This simple formula will provide you with fools for children.

"But whoso hearkeneth unto me shall dwell safely, and will be quiet from fear of evil" (Proverbs 1:33).

This verse echoes the twenty-third Psalm, which reads:

> The Lord is my shepherd; There is nothing I lack. He lets me lie down in green pastures; He leads me beside

quite waters. He renews my life; He leads me along the right paths for His name's sake. Even when I go through the darkest valley, I fear no danger; for you are with me; Your rod and Your staff—they comfort me. You prepare a table before me in the presence of my enemies; You anoint my head with oil; my cup overflows. Only goodness and faithful love will pursue me all the days of my life, and I will dwell in the house of the Lord as long as I live (HCSB).

Solomon's final verse of Proverbs chapter one promises those who walk in wisdom's way will experience peace, safety and security. These promises serve as powerful incentives, but Solomon knew from experience that wisdom's path is narrow and often challenging. He knew Satan's recruiters would continually put up their detours of deception and temptation, so he wanted to impress upon his students just how valuable wisdom's words are in the next chapter of his proverbs.

WISDOM SPEECH FOUR

Proverbs 2:1–22

My son, if thou wilt receive my words, and hide my commandments with thee; So that thou incline thine ear unto wisdom, and apply thine heart to understanding (Proverbs 2:1–2).

Chapter one concluded with Solomon's informing his student about the power of God's words and how they are capable of providing a refuge from evil. In chapter two, he informs his student and future readers how to access this valuable resource. He attempts to teach his student how to listen to God because listening requires an effort beyond simply hearing or reading what is being communicated—it requires continued concentration on what's being said. When Solomon was writing this second chapter of Proverbs, he may have been meditating upon the words of his father's first psalm.

> Blessed is the man that walketh not in the counsel of the ungodly, nor standeth in the way of sinners, nor sitteth in the seat of the scornful, But his delight is in the law of the Lord; and in his law doth he meditate day and night. And he shall be like a tree planted by the rivers of water, that bringeth forth his fruit in his season; his leaf also shall not wither; and whatsoever he doeth shall prosper. The ungodly are not so: but are like the chaff which the wind driveth away. Therefore the ungodly shall not stand in the judgment, nor sinners in the congregation of the righteous. For the Lord knoweth the way of the righteous: but the way of the ungodly shall perish. (Psalm 1:1–6)

You can be sure, that if God knows the way of the ungodly, He certainly will know if we, His children, are really listening to Him with an undivided attention. We may be able to deceive our earthly fathers, but our heavenly Father knows our innermost thoughts before they are ever conceived. The human condition necessitates continual meditation upon God's words if we are striving to think pure thoughts. David alerts the readers of this psalm and of the required preparations for being able to listen closely to God's words—he begins by telling us to first get away from the influence of active sinners.

God knows when we are truly sincere in our decision to serve Him as Lord and Master. A commitment of this magnitude requires total acceptance, which is the message of the HCSB translation of Proverbs 2:1, which reads, *"If you accept my words and store up my commands within you."* The word *accept*, compared to the word *receive*, as used in the King James translation for verse one, implies God not only wants obedience from His children in respect to His laws and commands, but He wants us to realize they are good for us. He wants us to understand His laws are given to us from the love He has for us; they are not to be perceived as simply a means of control. **It is our responsibility to know and to pass on His statutes to the next generation. This is the purpose for Solomon's wisdom speeches. They seek to facilitate the successful transfer of God's wisdom from generation to generation.** God wants and expects our obedience so He can bless us, but what God also expects and really wants is for His children to accept His perfect will in their lives, because only He can see the "big picture." When we're not happy with our circumstances, we must remember this world's cruelty was not by God's intended design. The world we live in has been cursed by God (Genesis 3:17). It and its inhabitants are heavily influenced by satanic powers wherever God's hedge of protection is not in place.

The King James Version translates verse one as *"hide my commands with thee,"* whereas some other translations state "treasure my commands within you." The original Hebrew text uses the word *tsaphan*, which, in addition to hide, can mean to hoard or to store in a secret place. When the two commands of verse one are honored, verse two says we will incline our ear to wisdom. Godly wisdom comes from above, so Solomon's words can cause readers to visualize the student of Proverbs listening to God with the fingers of one hand cupped around his ear, which is then pointed up toward the heavens, straining to hear every word God has to say. Once we have received God's message, He wants us to continually listen so we can store, or hoard up as much of His wisdom as possible.

Hoarding is normally thought of as a compulsive disorder that eventually becomes obvious to all the hoarder's neighbors. Once the hoarder's house is full, he or she will begin stacking the plunder on the porch. When the porch is filled, the plunder will then begin to accumulate in the yard for everyone to see. Like the hoarder, a true student of wisdom will hoard up God's words until the evidence of His Holy Spirit is obvious for everyone to see in his or her life. God's Holy Spirit will then be able to flow out (like the hoarder's plunder) into the lives of those around him or her, so they too can hear God's wisdom.

Successful students of the Proverbs will continually keep their ear inclined; otherwise, the reservoir of wisdom's treasure will no longer be able to overflow. If you are fortunate enough to be surrounded by any who are overflowing with God's wisdom, you know that His Holy Spirit is still very much alive and still in complete control. We can be sure God communicates to us from above and that He always raises us up, never down, as indicated in Isaiah 55:9, which says, *"As the heavens are higher than the earth, so are my ways higher than your ways, and my thoughts than your thoughts."* When we listen to God and accept His Word, then we too can apply our hearts to the understanding of His Word, as revealed to us by His Holy Spirit.

> **"Yea, if thou criest after knowledge, and liftest up thy voice for understanding; If thou seekest her as silver, and searchest for her as for hid treasures; Then shalt thou understand the fear of the Lord, and find the knowledge of God" (Proverbs 2:3–5).**

God's biblical concepts determine how His kingdom operates. Solomon repeats them over and over again. He takes us right back to the basic universal law: "As you sow, so shall you reap." If you sow with the efforts of seeking godly wisdom and understanding, you will reap the understanding of the one and only true God. The understanding of His unlimited power, unlimited knowledge, and unlimited presence will result in the normal human response of reverential respect—unless one's judgment has been hijacked by satanic devices.

It is a tremendous blessing to be living in this currrent age of convenience, made possible for us by technology, but on the other hand, (because of technology) many Americans no longer feel dependent upon God's provision. They instead tend to put their faith in the world's many layers of sophistication and convenience. Those who are blinded by worldly wisdom should be a very real concern for every mature Christian because they, along with all the world's systems, are doomed to fail. If you profess to be a Christian but are not praying for the lost people around you, it should be a red-light indicator of your own spiritual condition. No informed, rational human being should want to hide God's good news. This is why we are instructed by verse three to cry out for knowledge of how He wants His universe to function and, more specifically, what role He wants us to assume in it on a daily basis. We, as committed Christians, have an important job to do, and it needs to be done right, so we need all the instruction we can get from the sole source of true knowledge.

"For the Lord giveth wisdom: out of His mouth cometh knowledge and understanding. He layeth up sound wisdom for the righteous: He is a buckler to them that walk uprightly" (Proverbs 2:6–7).

Solomon personified wisdom in the female gender throughout chapter one. It is obvious for any believer that wisdom comes from God, yet Solomon does not plainly state this until now. What he earlier said was, "The fear of the Lord is the beginning of knowledge" (Proverbs 1:7). A Christian reading Proverbs will readily agree with verse six, but for unbelievers, these promises are frequently doubted. Verse seven tells us God favors the upright by storing sound wisdom for them. It is stored, or hoarded, to be there when needed. This is His method of shielding us from evil. Just like an earthly father, our heavenly Father protects His own. The spoken word of God is what the book of Genesis declares brought this world into existence. Most of us will not directly hear His spoken word while on planet earth. We instead will sense His presence and then almost feel his words being soaked up by our souls. This is just one of the ways we can know God's Spirit has been received into our hearts.

Verse seven stated, *"He layeth up sound wisdom for the righteous; He is a buckler to them that walk uprightly."* The word, *Righteous* is translated from the Hebrew word *yashar,* which can mean straight or prosperous in addition to righteous or upright. The word *buckler* is from the Hebrew *mginnah,* which means a shield or protector. It can also refer to the scaly hide of a crocodile. God defends His children against Satan's dark forces in the spiritual plane of God's creation. We who are presently living in His physical plane of existence usually remain unaware of what He and His angels are doing for us in the spiritual realm. If God were to remove His *mginnah,* or hedge of protection, we would be in the same position Job was in when Satan made his life a living hell on earth. Without God, we are no match for the powers of Satan. Psalms 84:11 reads, *"No good thing will He withhold from them that walk uprightly."*

"He keepeth the paths of Judgment, and preserveth the way of His saints" (Proverbs 2:8).

The Hebrew word *mishpat,* which refers to a verdict or a decree, is what the King James Version translates as *judgment.* The Hebrew for preserveth is *shamar,* which means to put a hedge, with thorns about, as a means of protection. The shamar, or hedge of protection, used by God to protect Job is a part of His spiritual domain because it is used as a means for protection against spiritual enemies. Verse eight is telling us God has provided a means of protection for the righteous within the physical domain. God seems to be saying He will protect us from a corrupt system of justice. In a perfect world, there would be only one path to justice, but a corrupt justice system will breed alternate paths. We are assured in verse eight, that God is able to overcome a crooked legal system when it persecutes a righteous man.

Notice that despite the multiple paths to justice, verse eight goes on to say there's only one way of the saints. That sole way of the saints is the way in which God's Holy Spirit directs them. Volumes could be written on all of the ways God can, has and will continue to preserve His way, His laws, and His words found in the Holy Bible. Isaiah 55:8–9 tells us God has no need of any other means or methods for His glory to be manifested. God only preserves the superior aspects of His creation because He is a perfect

God. Sin is why the world, as we presently know it, is still under a curse. God's heaven will not have sin or sinners to corrupt His perfect creation. This is His long-term plan for preserving the way of the saints. God began preserving the way of the saints all the way back in the third chapter of Genesis, when He said, *"I will put enmity between thee and the woman, and between thy seed and her seed; it shall bruise thy head, and thou shall bruise His heel"* (Genesis 3:15).

The Hebrew word for enmity is *eybah*, which implies hostility or hatred. The first phrase of this verse—*"I will put enmity between you and the woman"*—refers specifically to Eve and the serpent. It's commonly accepted from that moment forward, Eve and all existing species of snakes avoided contact with each other. The second phrase— *"between your offspring and hers"*—tells us this instinctual repulsion would pass on from generation to generation. Have you ever been to a circus side show where a snake crawls around on a nearly naked woman? I have, and despite its having been over forty years ago, I still remember feeling the presence of evil.

Any child of God with whom the Holy Spirit abides will be gifted with the ability to sense evil wherever God's decrees are being rejected. It has been a violation of natural law every time a woman showed affection for a snake, since this prophecy was spoken in the garden of Eden. My mother and her five sisters grew up working in the fields of a backwoods farm, and they all dreaded snakes. We have all probably seen men and women affectionally handling their pet snakes, but it's a good bet if those same folks ran into a den of copperheads when out in the woods, they would not pick them up and play with them.

The third phrase of this verse—*"It will bruise your head"*—refers to a very specific individual of Eve's offspring. "It," in the King James Version of Genesis 3:15, refers to the one who eventually would put a permanent end to Satan's influence on humankind. Most modern Bible translations will say "He" instead of "It," and "He" will be capitalized because "He" refers to the deity of Jesus Christ. The sin transaction that took place between Eve and the serpent was both a physical and spiritual event. When Adam and Eve sinned, they both incurred a spiritual separation, or death, from God and were no longer a part of His perfect creation. This is why the curse, as described in the remainder of Genesis chapter three, and which we still live under, was put into place. However, there is coming a day when Jesus will crush Satan's head. This event will complete the preservation of the saints because it will eliminate Satan's influence on God's creation.

John the revelator describes this event: *"The Devil who deceived them, was thrown into the lake of fire and sulphur where the Beast and the False Prophet are, and they will be tormented day and night forever and ever"* (Revelation 20:10 HCSB). The Bible records countless other measures God has taken to preserve the way of His saints. Following the fall in the garden of Eden, God declared in Genesis 6:7, *"I will destroy man whom I have created from the face of the Earth."* God accomplished this with a great flood that killed all humankind except Noah and his family. We are told God did this because man had become exceedingly wicked, and God had come to regret that He had created man—but one man found grace in God's eye. Noah and his family were saved through God's grace, and it was only by His grace that these eight people were allowed to repopulate the earth and thus preserve the way of His saints.

After Noah and his family came out of the ark, Genesis 9:11 records God promising He would never again wipe out all flesh by water. Noah, like Adam, was instructed to be fruitful and to multiply. Unfortunately, Satan managed to ruin another covenant through Noah's drunkenness, and another curse was put into place. Chapter 11 of Genesis goes on to record ten generations, over a period of 367 years, before God told Abraham to leave Haran because of widespread idolatry. The men of Genesis 10 and 11 worshipped lifeless manmade idols, rather than the living God—of whom Noah and his sons could still give a firsthand account. They were able to say, **"We heard God say He would destroy this earth because of wickedness, and then we saw Him do it!"**

But by Genesis 12, man's world had become full of idolaters, so God started over again. Rather than again destroying all life as He had with the flood, He started over with just one man by telling him to get away from all of the sin and all of the sinners.

> Now the Lord said to Abram, Get thee out of thy country, and from thy kindred, and from thy father's house, unto a land that I will shew thee: And I will make of thee a great nation, and I will bless thee, and make thy name great; and thou shalt be a blessing: And I will bless them that

bless thee, and curse him that curseth thee; and in thee
shall all families of the earth be blessed. (Genesis 12:1–3).

Abram, whose name was later changed to Abraham, was the earth
father of the Jewish nation. His grandson Jacob also was also renamed by
God. His name was changed to Israel, and it was though Israel's twelve
sons that God's promise would be carried out. All nations will have the
opportunity to be blessed because of what one descendant of Abraham
(Jesus) did about two thousand years ago, which was forty-two generations
after Abraham.

Abraham's descendents were repeatedly warned to stay away from idols
and idolaters, which was the eventual means of Israel's (as a nation) repeated
failures. Despite Israel's disobedience, God was tolerant enough to preserve
the way of His saints through men like Moses, Joshua, Samuel, David, and,
finally, Jesus, whose sacrificial blood made possible the covenant of grace
under which we presently live.

Following the Crucifixion, forty-six Roman emperors, over a span of
three hundred years, tried to eradicate the Christian movement. Finally
the emperor Constantine was smart enough to know Christianity was
not going away, so he decided to change it. He did this by doing what the
Constitution of the United States forbids—he united church and state. He
then invited Christians to come out from hiding and to worship openly
in the existing pagan temples of Rome. These temples had been acquired
from all the previously fallen empires that had worshiped the likes of
Zeus, Diana, Molleck, Bahl, and other false gods. Some of these temples
had housed temple prostitution and even child sacrifice. The only earthly
temple God had fully recognized was the one built by the Jews in Jerusalem
during Solomon's reign. Rome's temples contained pagan art, furniture
with symbolic pagan carvings, pagan books, and priests with their pagan
rituals, who were all eager to Romanize Christianity.

This was the birth of Roman Catholicism. Constantine ordered the
entire Roman army to be baptized, believing this would make them
Christians. Those who were already Christians knew baptism was a
public confession of faith and an act of obedience, nothing more. It was
obvious to them that Jesus Christ was not resurrected because He was

baptized by John the Baptist. They knew it was only God and not any ritual performed by the church, who could raise the dead.

It must have been a great embarrassment for both the Romans and the Jews that the Son of God was mistakenly put to death, so the new state church would put emphasis on Peter, Mary and an array of sacraments, including baptism, which all served as a distracting substitution for the one and only true means of salvation: **the shed blood of Christ**. Those who remained loyal to the teachings of Jesus were soon being hunted, persecuted and even put to death for their faith-based defiance toward the new *politically correct state religion.* Real religious freedom was never officially established until the Constitution of the United States was recognized as the law of the land in the colonies of America—the same Constitution that now is under attack by many of our elected officials.

God not only preserved the way of the saints; He also preserved His Word, the Holy Bible—the book we are so privileged to read, despite its having under gone centuries of satanic attack. Many men lost their lives to make this book available for the common people in a language they could read and understand. It is estimated as many as fifty million Christians were martyred during the thirteen-hundred year period of time known as the Dark Ages. Books such as *Foxe's Book of Martyrs* and *The Trail of Blood* describe the sacrifices that were made for the preservation of God's Word. Mark 13:31 tells us, *"Heaven and Earth shall pass away, but My words will never pass away"* (HCSB).

"Then shalt thou understand righteousness, and judgment, and equity; yeah, every good path" (Proverbs 2:9).

When the Lord gives wisdom, as verse six 6 assures us He will do, then—and only then—will we understand real righteousness, know perfect justice, experience true equity, and recognize every good path, as we're told here in verse nine. Righteousness is the defining characteristic of the upright for whom God reserves wisdom, as verse seven tells us. When we are obedient to God, we begin to know and understand His way. This is what enables us to understand righteousness and justice. Justice refers to the law of the land or what is acceptable by the existing culture. Justice in the United States was once patterned after biblical righteousness, but just as in past civilizations, America has wandered off the biblical course. America's leaders no longer recognize the good path. Our leaders and educators fear global warming more than they do God.

"When wisdom entereth into thine heart, and knowledge is pleasant unto thy soul; discretion shall preserve thee, understanding shall keep thee" (Proverbs 2:10–11).

Verse 10 tells us how God protects us from sin. Chapter one warned the young student about gang involvement; now Solomon is preparing to warn the young man of other dangers that are capable of separating him from God's blessing. Proverbs 1:8 told our young man to **"Hear the instruction of your father, and do not forsake the law of your mother."** In chapter two, the young man is a little older, so now Satan uses a more age appropriate lure of attraction to interrupt the young student's relationship with godly wisdom.

Chapter one declared the initial means of acquiring wisdom and understanding was to respect and obey God. Chapter one then instructed its readers to respect their parents and to obey their instruction, especially when being tempted. Chapter two followed up by describing a higher level of obedience by telling us to seek and treasure God's commands. If we follow God's directions, the result will be what verse 11 promises; knowledge will be pleasant to our souls. This is telling us God's words have become the guiding force of our lives, which includes our personalities. People should not have to be around us very long before they recognize the love and respect we have for both God and His commands.

When we reach this level of commitment and understanding, verse 11 says, *"Discretion will preserve you."* Discretion is the ability to adapt our conduct and speech appropriately for given situations and circumstances. Discretion is one of the gifts from God that can help preserve the way of His saints. Discretion will help us to make wise decisions that will keep us within God's hedge of protection. Obedient Christians who are in continual communion with God's Holy Spirit will find themselves instinctually making good decisions. The Holy Spirit will work in ways that is not always consciously understood; real Christians instinctively know they are doing God's will. This is why verse 11 declares, *"Understanding will keep you."* It is an indescribably great feeling to know, without any doubt, that God considers you a "keeper." Solomon goes on to describe four different types of satanic attack from which God's hedge of protection can protect us.

"To deliver thee from the way of the evil man, from the man that speaketh froward things; Who leave the paths of uprightness, to walk in the ways of darkness" (Proverbs 2:12–13)

The "way of evil" is the first category of satanic attack that can be avoided through discretion and understanding. The first step for avoiding evil is to be able to recognize it for what it is. This may sound simple, but Satan is a master of disguise and deception. Genesis 3:1 states, *"The serpent was the most cunning of all the wild animals that the Lord God had made"* (HCSB). The New International Version uses the word *crafty*, while the King James Version uses the word *subtil*, which is translated from the Hebrew word *aruwm*. Aruwm, pronounced *au-room*, can have all these meanings, but when used it always implies in a bad sense. It is no coincidence that Satan's chosen vessel through which he spoke to Eve was the serpent, just as it is no coincidence he will use the physically beautiful people of this world to attract the innocent towards the passing pleasures of sin. The "way of evil" can be dressed up with many layers of sophistication, making it possible to deceive anyone whose mind strays, even momentarily, from the way of God.

"The man who speaketh froward things" refers to those whom Satan uses to communicate through, as he did the serpent. They are the chosen means of communication for the advancement of Satan's agenda. The Holman Christian Standard Bible uses the word perverse, instead of the King James Version's word, *froward*. Both words are translated from the Hebrew word *tahpukah,* which means perversity or fraud. *Webster's* dictionary defines froward as "habitually disposed to disobedience and opposition." The froward person could include anyone from a gang recruiter to a college professor who proclaims there is no God. Satan is happy to use anyone who is not protected by God's hedge of protection to spread his false doctrine.

"Who leave the paths of uprightness to walk in the ways of darkness" describes those who have temporarily lost their fellowship with God.

Despite having once had a relationship with God, Satan has managed to creep into their souls, which deprives them of their relationship with God and destroys their conscious contact. This is why it's so important to flee the very appearance of evil. We can never know the full extent or all the consequences of sin, despite how trivial some sin may seem. It delights Satan to use one Christian to trip up another Christian. The guilt and remorse a child of God can feel for any harm done to a Christian brother is a weakness Satan will continually exploit for future attacks. When God forgives our sin, He does it perfectly and completely. If we fail to acknowledge this tremendous truth by wallowing in self-pity, we provide an opening in God's hedge of protection that will enable Satan to slither through.

"Who rejoice to do evil, and delight in the frowardness of the wicked; whose ways are crooked, and they froward in their paths" (Proverbs 2:14–15).

Solomon seems to be addressing the fourth category of sinners in verse 14, but he really isn't. He is describing the insanity that a habitual sinner will experience before giving in again to an addictive temptation. Insanity is defined as repeating the same actions and expecting different results. Those who delight in repeating the same evil over and over again expect some type of pleasure from their actions. When the pleasure is great enough, it will remove all other conscious thought from the habitual sinner's mind. Unfortunately for the sinner, the brief mental and emotional escape achieved through the means of sin is only a temporary relief from whatever is really haunting his or her soul. Each time a false means of escape is used, it becomes harder and harder for even a brief return to the blissful state the now-addicted sinner has come to crave.

These are the sinners who take delight in their perversity, but it comes at a tremendous cost. They will eventually ignore every other aspect of their lives to recapture the initial "high" they first achieved. The escape they so desperately need becomes harder and harder to achieve, and so begins the process known by some as "chasing the dragon." The sin of addiction makes returning to reality a little more difficult each time the means of escape is utilized. Satan will use any addiction to twist the addict's mind into believing there is no escape from the deadly cycle, but there's good news. First John 4:4 states, *"Greater is He that is in you, than he that is in the world"*. This verse should assure all Christians, including those who have relapsed into an addictive lifestyle, that a functioning faith in the living God will provide us safe refuge from whatever is oppressing our fellowship with His Holy Spirit. The price of repeated sin will only continue to go up until it owns not only our souls but our spirits as well.

What's really being described here is the outer manifestation of an inner spiritual condition. A sinner may appear happy on the outside for a while; but that is only because his outward self, the physical man, has not yet caught up to the inner spiritual turmoil caused by sin. To further illustrate this, I will refer to the sin of habitual drunkenness (alcoholism) as an example.

When I experienced intoxication for the first time, I was visiting my older cousin who lived in a farming community. He had been obsessed with fast cars for as long as I could remember and having just passed his driving test, he was ready for some action. That evening we went to town in his '56 Chevy and soon met up with two of his friends. It didn't take long for the three of them to find an older acquaintance who gladly bought us a case of beer for a nominal fee.

We continued riding around as each one of us began drinking his six-pack. It wasn't long before my cousin was driving faster and spinning the Chevy's tires much more frequently. I wondered why the others, who were in the backseat, had began laughing so much. The conversation soon went from silly to sexual. The way these guys were talking, it sure seemed the local girls they knew were much friendlier than those I went to school with in the city. I didn't even know I was affected by the beer until we all got out of the car to relieve ourselves on the side of the road. That was when I realized my coordination and sensory perception had become blurred, but I still did not understand why the others were acting so unusual. I thought to myself, *I'm sure glad alcohol doesn't affect me like that.* It was only a few months later before I was acting just as those older boys were on that particular night—which fulfilled the warning of Proverbs 1:31 *"Therefore they shall eat the fruit of their own way, and be filled with their own devices"*.

My first date with alcohol was identical to the story of Proverbs chapter one. What I experienced that night was essentially the older boys saying,

"Come with us; we can show you how to have some real fun" (verses 10–11). I then forsook the instruction of my father and the law of my mother (verse 8). I suffered no immediate consequences for my disobedience—I didn't even have a hangover the next morning—but I now know for certain that something big changed inside of me that night. I had been introduced to my new best friend and eventual lover, Queen Alcohol, and I was very loyal to her every command. I would never be the same. By age fifteen I was willing to go to nearly any lengths, just to get a drink. It was only a matter of time before my outer flesh was a true reflection of my inner turmoil. What shames me the most was that I would go back home to where I lived to play the "Big Shot" by showing my friends what I had learned in the country. **I had unknowingly become one of Satan's recruiters!**

"To deliver thee from the strange woman, even from the stranger which flattereth with her words"(Proverbs 2:16).

The strange women is the fourth category of sinners of which Solomon warns us in chapter two. The Holman Christian Standard Bible translates this verse as, *"It will rescue you from a forbidden woman, from a stranger with her flattering talk."* The Hebrew word *zuwr* is what the King James Version translates to "strange." Both biblical translations are accurate for this word. An additional interpretation could be "foreign women." The Old Testament tells us idols were continually smuggled into Israel, usually by those described as strange or foreign women. It appears that Solomon, as a young writer, prophesied his own future downfall, which involved foreign women (whom he married) and their idols. God has given us some insight, through Solomon, about human nature—this is an obvious example of how much easier it is to give advice than it is to follow it. Each stage of human development seems to have its own age-specific vulnerability. Satan, who is very aware of these chronological and biological tendencies, is eager to exploit them.

To fully appreciate verse 16, it should be pointed out that adultery is considered by God to be the physical version of idolatry, which would mean idolatry is the spiritual form of physical adultery. The Old Testament book of Hosea is centered on this concept. Hosea was instructed by God to marry a prostitute. *"Go, take onto thee a wife of whoredoms and children of whoredoms: for the land hath committed great whoredom, departing from the Lord"* (Hosea 1:2). God instructed this man, Hosea, to marry a harlot so he could use this harlot's future adultery as a parallel example of Israel's worshiping idols. Hosea was then shown, through his wife's unfaithfulness, how God felt when Israel was also unfaithful by loving other gods.

Hosea's wife, Gomer, then went on to give birth to three children, who probably were not fathered by Hosea, and then left him to pursue other lovers. God then instructed Hosea to get his wife back and to love her again so that he could understand how God felt concerning Israel's committing spiritual adultery with her false gods. The five verses of Hosea chapter three tell this story.

Proverbs chapter two is written from the perspective of a teacher who is encouraging his student to fully surrender his will to the voice of wisdom, but for him to do so will require a greater effort than what he has thus far exhibited. This is why the young student was earlier told, *"If you call out to insight and lift your voice to understanding, if you seek it like silver and search for it like hidden treasure,* **then you will understand the fear of the Lord and discover the knowledge of God"** (Proverbs 2:3–5 HCSB). These verses are describing a young man who has been taught to grab onto God's wisdom as a drowning man would a life preserver. This is the type of young man Satan really wants to distract and then entrap. Verse 16 is warning the young man about one of Satan's most effective tools in his arsenal—seduction. Like many young men in the prime of their youth, Solomon's young student will be tempted with more than just the visual stimulation of a beautiful woman; he will be verbally seduced as well. Solomon will later devote an entire chapter (chapter seven) to acquaint his student with the methods and tactics of the seductress.

Proverbs 12:26 reads, *"The righteous man is more excellent than his neighbor: but the way of the wicked seduceth them."* This verse reveals that righteous men are not commonly found, so it would be logical to assume the odds are against two righteous men living next door to one another. We are also told that righteousness does not make one immune to temptation. The Hebrew word *taah*, which is translated to "seduceth," can mean to make one go astray or to cause to wander. Solomon is telling us Satan will go the extra mile for the bigger prize. He takes greater pleasure in the corruption of a righteous man than he would for the fool or the spiritual underachiever. Flattery from the lips of a sexy woman is a one-two punch, in that a mental seduction is added to the more obvious visual seduction. The late Dr. J. Vernon McGee wrote, "Flattery is like perfume—it's okay to wear, but you ought not to drink it."

"Which forsaketh the guide of her youth, and forgetteth the covenant of her God" (Proverbs 2:17).

The Hebrew word *alluwph,* which is translated to "guide" by the King James Version, normally refers to the leading or the guiding of an ox or a cow. This verse could be encouraging its reader to visualize God's Holy Spirit acting as a bit and a bridle, helping Christians to work together as a team for the accomplishment of God's will. The woman of verse 17 seems to have willingly broken communion with the God of her youth and is now encouraging others to do likewise. What she may or not know is that disobedience toward the one true and living God amounts to carrying out the will of Satan. Whether she knows it or not, she too has become a recruiter for Satan.

You may ask, "How can this be? How can anyone unknowingly worship the devil?" It is very important to remember that Satan runs a covert operation. He is not particular about with whom he will spend eternity. God, on the other hand, is very particular. God wants only those who truly want to be with Him and are willing to serve Him as the only ones to accompany Him in His heaven. If God were not so protective of who did and who did not get into His heaven, it would be no different from our present earth—sin-infested. The human spirit becomes a part of Satan's domain automatically with its failure to know and accept Jesus Christ as God and Savior.

Imagine for a minute that Satan and Jesus were two businessmen who were competing for the same customers in a given market. Does it not make sense that the salesman with the inferior product would have to spend more time, effort, and money on advertising? Science and its modern technology have provided the almost-perfect environment for the earth's occupants to ignore God. With the exception of aging and natural disasters, modern technology can usually overcome almost any problem. When a drought or some other natural disaster does occur, rather than considering the possibility that it's a judgment from God, the news media will repeatedly tell us it is global warming or some other man-made problem that middle-class America should feel guilty about and become willing to pay for.

Verses 16 and 17 can be interpreted as Solomon prophesying his own future. Throughout his life, he probably experienced hundreds of attempts by beautiful women to seduce him into granting them favor. This was how strange gods eventually came into Israel. Satan has many forms of seduction from which he can choose to target his victims. He will pick the right time, the right place, and the right circumstances to use his weapon of choice against you—without Christ and His hedge of protection, men are seriously disadvantaged against the power and devices of Satan.

For her house inclineth unto death, and her paths unto the dead" (Proverbs 2:18).

The Hebrew word *bayith* is translated to *house* for verse 18. An additional application for this word, besides house or palace, is family. It was a strong Hebrew tradition for heads of families to prearrange marriages, so this could very well have been a consideration Solomon had in mind when he wrote this verse. If it was, it would seem that Solomon was continuing to prophesy his own future downfall. The foreign women Solomon married managed to bring their families' idols into Israel, which eventually seduced Israel's wisest king, Solomon, into participating with his wives in their pagan rituals (1 Kings11:1–11). Despite his own continual written warnings to his students about wisdom, Israel's wisest king was successfully seduced.

Had Solomon not repented of his sin, the successful seduction of Solomon would have led him down to the pit. The whole Jewish nation suffered because their king's weakness was successfully exploited by Satan, making Solomon one of the biggest disappointments in biblical history. If Satan can succeed in distracting a man like Solomon from the "way of understanding," then all Christians should recognize him as a dangerous adversary. One whom we should go to any length to avoid—which is why the apostle Paul writes in 1 Thessalonians 5:22, *"Abstain from all appearance of evil."* Evil acts as a spiritual magnet attracting the presence of Satan, while at the same time repelling the presence of God's Holy Spirit.

"None that go unto her return again, neither take they hold of the paths of life" (Proverbs 2:19).

This is a verse that should get everybody's attention; it foretells us the end result of un-confessed sin. Wisdom's student of chapter two is now at an age when sexuality has become an influential force in his life. Our God-given instincts all have a purpose, and the sex drive is no exception to this biological principle. While in the early stages of human development, moderation in all things can be a wise approach. Too much reading might hinder a young man's physical development. Muscles and tendons need to be used to be strengthened, and bones need to be stressed to develop density. Too much physical activity will result in a strong body but not an informed mind. Every young person can benefit from a balanced menu of activity.

The practice of moderation, when applied to our human cravings, is a challenging discipline to practice. Too much sex, too much food, too much sleep, and yes, even too much work will all lead to an imbalanced spirituality. A cold drink of water on a hot day can be a lifesaver, but too much water is known as drowning. A dehydrated man crossing the desert is going to drink water wherever possible, but if that water contains hazardous bacteria he will likely die. Solomon is warning his adolescent student about the end result of consumption from the wrong sources in verse 19.

David's sexual sin with another man's wife caused enough turmoil to be considered the probable inspiration for Solomon's writing this verse. Considering that Solomon's mother was the very same woman with whom David had committed this adultery, he probably had an array of thoughts concerning sexual immorality. The King David that Solomon knew as a young man was only a shadow of the mighty warrior who had previously defeated Israel's enemies. It was often a very remorseful David who wrote the psalms, some of the most beautiful and insightful literature ever given to man. God used the misery of a sorrowful sinner to write the very words that would go on to lift and strengthen those who would later be under similar satanic attack. This is just one of many examples found in the Bible where God remanufactured Satan's evil into a beautiful and very significant outcome. David's psalms have helped and inspired countless people over thousands of years. Much like raising the dead, only God can reshape something as ugly as sin, and fashion it into something beautiful.

We can read about another important example of God's taking evil and making it good in Genesis 45, where Joseph forgives his brothers for having sold him into slavery. He then goes on to explain how it was God's plan all along for him to be in Egypt for the purpose of preserving life. Joseph's being in Egypt was necessary to fulfill God's promise to an old and childless Abraham, as recorded in Genesis 15:12–16. God has a specific plan for each one of his children. Most of us will not play as important a role as did Abraham, Isaac, or Jacob, but we can remain on the path of righteousness if we continually honor God's will for our lives.

"That thou mayest walk in the way of good men, and keep the paths of the righteous" (Proverbs 2:20).

Verse 20 gives us a warning, in that it tells us association with sin and sinners prevents Christians from achieving what God wants them to have. Righteousness is an absolute requirement for any type of relational experience with God's Holy Spirit. Before an offering was presented to the Lord in Old Testament times, the priest had to be clean. This meant he had to be righteous, as defined by Mosaic law. If a priest went in to the Holy of Holies to approach the ark of the covenant where God dwelt, and he was not ceremonial clean, God would strike him dead. What do you think would happen to today's church if twenty-first-century Christians were struck dead while attending church on Sunday morning if they had fresh sin in their hearts from Saturday night? This next verse encourages us to keep our hearts and minds clean so God can lift us up with the reward of His blessing.

"For the upright shall dwell in the land, and the perfect shall remain in it" (Proverbs 2:21).

Dwelling in the land was one of the promised blessings for Israel. It was promised to Abraham by God Himself in Genesis 12. This blessing is passed down from generation to generation forever, but this blessing is just one part of God's covenant with the chosen children of Abraham and Sarah. The blessing was contingent upon obedience to God's laws, which were gradually revealed to the nation of Israel in God's time and in God's way. Verse 21 reminds Solomon's young student what is at risk if he gives in to his youthful biological desires. An informed young Israelite could not consider himself righteous without resisting the call of the seductress.

The normal human tendency is to follow biological and psychological urges, unless he or she is wise enough to know the temporary pleasure of sin is not worth the price of disobedience to God's law. Obedience can sometimes seem impossible unless God has stored up sound wisdom, as He has told us He will do for the upright (Proverbs 2:7). The upright are those who continually incline their ears (Proverbs 2:9) to receive divine communications from a God whose ways are higher than our ways and whose thoughts are higher than our thoughts (Isaiah 55:9). To "dwell in the land" was the evidence of having been blessed by God. Leviticus 25:18–19 tells us, *"You are to keep My statutes and ordinances and carefully observe them, so that you may live securely in the land. Then the land will yield its fruit, so that you can eat, be satisfied, and live securely in the land"* (HCSB). When Christ comes back to rule and reign on this earth, it will begin in the very same land referred to in these verses.

"The blameless will remain in it." This statement was true when it was written and will remain true throughout all of eternity. Those who dwelled in the land were required to remain in fellowship with the Lord; otherwise, those following their own will were on their way out of the land. Those who stayed in communion were considered by God to be blameless, as verse 21 alludes to here. The word *perfect*, used here in the King James Version, is translated from the Hebrew word *tamyim,* which can mean blameless, without spot, whole, complete, upright, or undefiled. These are the adjectives that were repeatedly used to describe the Old Testament sacrifices, which all symbolically pointed to the only acceptable sacrifice, which was the one our God made by allowing His Son to die a substitute death on our behalf.

Only by the sinless blood, shed by Jesus for our sins, can we be perfect, in a positional sense. This means our sin is covered by the blood of our Savior, thus God no longer sees it—what He does see is how much His Son, Jesus, loves us. He loves us enough to have endured extreme pain and suffering so we could be perfected through His perfect sacrifice, as stated in Hebrews 10:14, *"For by one offering He has perfected forever those who are sanctified"* (HCSB). The writers of the New King James Version of the Bible very alertly wrote this verse as "those who are *being* sanctified" (my emphasis), instead of "those who are sanctified." "Being sanctified" puts emphasis on sanctification being an ongoing process, which continues with our continual obedience. God never kicked Israel out of the land immediately because of sin—He removed them from the land only after continual disobedience.

When reading through the Bible, it is very easy for us to wonder, "How could the children of Israel continually make the same mistakes, generation after generation?" The only logical explanation is that each generation of Israel lost some of the faith in God that the previous generation possessed. Some may have even begun to doubt God's existence. Is this not the prevailing condition of twenty-first–century America? Do not America's prominent educational institutions train our young people to believe that science, not God, holds the key to their destiny? If this continues, we, like Israel, will eventually be removed from this great land that was created by and given to our forefathers by the God of Abraham, Isaac, and Jacob. Some of us will go to the land spoken of in verse 21— while all others will be subject to the promise of verse 22.

"But the wicked shall be cut off from the Earth, and the transgressors shall be rooted out of it" (Proverbs 2:22).

You do not want to be in this group of people. It is my prayer that you are among those who enter the land. If you refuse to incorporate the before-mentioned disciplines into your life, then you will not be among those who enter the land. Those who fail to submit their will to God are exercising their freedom of choice, but few, if any of them, are considering the long-term consequences of deliberate disobedience. They will continue living in ignorance until God's wisdom is allowed to shed His light on their situations. God is capable of doing this upon whoever He chooses, but He expects His chosen to not only be committed but also eager to spread His gospel to those still lacking salvation. This is how we express our love and obedience to Him—we work to expand His kingdom. **We can choose to be blessed, or we can choose to be cursed—the decision is ours.** Deuteronomy 28:58–59 tells us what's at stake: *"If you are not careful to obey all the words of this law, which are written in this scroll, by fearing this glorious and awesome name—Yahweh Your God—He will bring extraordinary plagues upon you and your descendants, severe and lasting plagues and terrible and chronic sicknesses"* (HCSB).

The word *transgressor* from verse 22 is taken from the Hebrew word *bagad,* which can mean to act deceitfully, unfaithfully, covertly, or treacherously, as translated in the Holman Christian Standard Bible. The word *wicked* comes from the Hebrew word *rasha,* which means morally wrong, to be an actively bad person, condemned, or ungodly. Men who are *bagad* or unfaithful will go on to become *rasha* or wicked if they live long enough to do so unless they make a decision to turn their lives over to the living God.

Verse 22 does tell us what continual bad decisions or even seemingly innocent indiscretions can lead to. It states, "The wicked will be cut off." The expression "cut off" first appears in Genesis 9:11 to describe all those who were destroyed by the flood. The term "cut off" was also used by Saul in 1 Samuel 24:21, when he petitioned David to not cut off his seed. David later wrote in Psalm 37:28, *"For the Lord loveth judgment, and forsaketh not His saints; they are preserved for ever: but the seed of the wicked shall be cut off."* These verses are telling us that being "cut off" by God affects more than one specific sinner. It can affect his or her children and grandchildren as well. Psalms112 describes the preferred legacy of the faithful. We are told, *"Blessed is the man that feareth the Lord, that delighteth greatly in His commandments. His seed shall be mighty upon earth: the generation of the upright shall be blessed. Wealth and riches shall be in his house: and his righteousness endureth for ever."*

Deuteronomy 28, beginning with verse 15, informs the children of Israel of the curses they will endure if they choose disobedience. Verse 20 alone should be enough to repel us from the darkness of sin. It reads, *"The Lord will send against you curses, confusion, and rebuke in everything you do until you are destroyed and quickly perish, because of the wickedness of your actions in abandoning Me*" (HCSB). Despite the warnings in chapter 28, sin caused the children of Israel to eventually suffer all the curses listed in this chapter, including cannibalism, which is listed in verse 53. Can anything be more disgusting than starving mothers and fathers eating the corpses of their own dead children? How could God have issued a stronger warning than this one, found in Deuteronomy? Yet God's chosen people eventually experienced the "generational drift," rendering the warnings of Deuteronomy, along with all the other scriptures, powerless to fulfill their intended purpose.

Have you ever known someone who appears to be afflicted with some of these curses? If so, do you think sin played a role in this person's demise? The life of sin does have its eventual consequences. Just like a physical disease, the spiritual effect of sin will manifest itself into an obviously ugly condition if left untreated. All sin in the eyes of God is just as disgusting as the act of cannibalism would be to a modern-day person who is accustomed to eating well-prepared meals in a sanitary environment. If you hate sin the way God wants us to, then what are you prepared to do to halt its advancement in your own life and the lives of those around you?

WISDOM SPEECH FIVE

Proverbs 3:1–10

"My son, forget not my law; but let thine heart keep my commandments: For length of days, and long life, and peace, shall they add to thee" (Proverbs 3:1–2).

Chapter three of Proverbs begins with some repeated advice, but there is good reason for Solomon's redundancy. Israel's wisest king had read all the existing scriptures, beginning with his father, David, and all the way back to the writings of Moses. This would have made him keenly aware of his ancestors' repeated failures caused by their repeated disobedience, so Solomon addresses the problem of repeated sin with repeated warnings. This is the second mention of both law and commands in the Proverbs. The first reference to law was in Proverbs 1:8, which referred the young student to the law of his mother, whereas these verses in chapter three direct the reader's attention to a higher law—the law of wisdom, which is the law of God.

Let's consider the law of Solomon's mother and the mothers of all his siblings. As previously mentioned, the family of David's house included several wives and concubines. Some of these wives came from outside the Hebrew culture, which meant they would have grown up with a different set of laws and values than did Solomon's mother, Bathsheba. Even as a youth, Solomon had enough insight to recognize the differing maternal influences in some of his siblings. If Amnon, Solomon's oldest half brother, had been taught the values dear to Bathsheba's heart instead of the values taught to him by his mother, Ahinoam the Jezreelitess, maybe he would not have raped and then rejected his innocent half sister, Tamar, as recorded in 2 Samuel 13.

Chapter one tells our young student to respect his mother's law because that is what young children are supposed to do. Solomon's student is now an older person in chapter three. He will now have a different set of problems and responsibilities than he did as the child written about in chapter one and the teenager of chapter two. When young men and young women reach an age of accountability, it is time for them to begin acquiring their own understanding of God, which would necessitate an understanding of God's law. Living within the laws of God should by definition, be every Christian's top priority.

Beginning with Abraham and continuing throughout the days of the Old Testament, every Jew was expected to know and obey what is known today as Old Testament law. It's also sometimes referred to as the Law of Moses. Since the Crucifixion of Christ, the Old Testament law has been replaced by the grace of God, which was made possible by the love and obedience of Jesus Christ. Jesus loved both His Father and us, enough to shed His innocent blood. This incomprehensible act of love and obedience is what God required to make possible His gift of salvation. This was made possible solely through His grace, which is why it's said we live in the age of grace; also known as the church age. We no longer are required to live under Old Testament law. We are instead commanded to live under a Christ consciousness, made possible through the leading of God's Holy Spirit and knowledge of God's words in the Holy Bible.

Most young adults are extremely busy acquiring the necessary skills required for a career in today's demanding job market. This, along with normal social activities, leaves little spare time for spiritual development. God is aware of all the challenges today's young adults face, which is probably why He inspired Solomon to write, "Do not forget my law." The law of God, as taught by committed, loving Christian parents, will adequately guide young adults during these challenging years, if their hearts remain loyal to God's Holy Spirit.

Young Christians who have the advantage of a Christian upbringing will know that 2 Corinthians chapter six instructs believers not to be "yoked" together with unbelievers. Being married to a Christian spouse should put both spouses in agreement with what God's laws are. This will prevent a lot of future stress and disagreements. When God's commands are passed down from generation to generation by unified parents, who are working (yoked) together, they are much more likely to be accepted and obeyed by their children. Can you imagine trying to reconcile the laws and beliefs to the children of multiple women from multiple countries, all while remaining loyal to the teachings of your own God? Now, take a moment to think about the problems Solomon must have experienced by having a thousand wives and concubines.

Learning and following God's words will greatly reduce our problems and the internal stresses they cause in our minds and bodies. This is why verse two tells us that peace and the length of days are the reward for (our) obedience. Solomon is reinforcing what he had learned from the writings of Moses: *"Honour thy father and thy mother, as the Lord your God hath commanded thee; that thy days may be prolonged, and that it may go well with thee, in the land which the Lord thy God giveth thee"* (Deuteronomy 5:16).

> ### "Let not mercy and truth forsake thee: bind them about thy neck; write them upon the table of thine heart; so shalt thou find favour and good understanding in the sight of God and man" (Proverbs 3:3–4).

This is the first mention of mercy and truth in the Proverbs. Like wisdom in chapter one and discernment in chapter two, mercy and truth are personified here in chapter three. When Solomon writes, "Let not mercy and truth forsake thee; bind them about thy neck," he is describing a personal relationship with these two disciplines. Proverbs 2:10–11 reads, *"When wisdom entereth into thine heart, and knowledge is pleasant unto thine soul; Discretion shall preserve thee, understanding shall keep thee."* This is instruction for a young person who is still learning why she or he should want wisdom and knowledge. In chapter three Solomon is addressing those who have already been introduced to knowledge and discretion. He now urges them to deepen their knowledge and wisdom by remaining in God's will. This is what mature, intelligent Christians who have had the benefit of proper instruction and discipline will want to do—unless they are distracted by temptation.

The Hebrew word from which *mercy* is translated is *checed*. Its possible meanings include kindness, favor, and good deeds. Modern dictionaries give definitions such as compassion shown to an offender, relief from distress, and divine favor or blessing. *Webster's Dictionary* cites charity as being a synonym for mercy; its meanings include benevolence, goodwill, generosity, tolerance of others, and a forgiving nature. Before a person can exercise mercy, it must first be within the person's power to do so; for example, one must first have some type of strength before he or she can attempt to lift up the weak.

Our Lord wants His people to be both merciful and truthful, which is the other characteristic mentioned in verse three. Everyone knows that truth is the absence of fiction, but some have difficulty distinguishing between the two. It's human nature to want to be right. This normal tendency often causes a skewed perception of reality. John 14:6 does a wonderful job of describing what truth really is: *"I am the way, the truth and the life, no man cometh unto the Father but by me."* Jesus is plainly telling us He is the truth. If men would acknowledge this one simple claim, there would be no need for a judicial system, prisons, or wars. Wouldn't that go a long way toward ending our nation's current budget crisis?

John 18:37 quotes Jesus telling Pontius Pilate, *"I was born for this, and I have come into the world for this: to testify to the truth. Everyone who is of the truth listens to My voice"* (HCSB). God wants us to know truth because He knows the truth can set us free from the entanglements of sin. When we diligently pursue mercy and truth, it not only benefits us, but it also benefits everyone we encounter along life's way. Who doesn't like being the recipient of mercy and truth? God wants us to be positive examples to those around us so our witness of Him will be effective. This is why verse four says we will find favor with God and our fellow man. This verse tells us how to get along with both God and man.

The Christian community, as a whole, has not done well in the public promotion for God's kingdom, while the devil has managed to use the liberal media very efficiently for his purposes. With a little help from the devil, a nominal or artificial Christian can be tricked into helping the media make the church appear full of greed and hypocrisy. A mature Christian, in comparison, who has acquired truth and mercy can promote the true Christ-given mission for the church body. Those who are unsaved seem almost eager to believe the Christian Church is more interested in money than it is in mercy and truth. Sadly, this is the norm for some churches, but the genuine Christian body still has a responsibility and a desire to help promote God's truth. If we are not including truth and mercy in our code of living, the chances are nil we will be successful Christians. **We cannot give away what we do not have!**

> **"Trust in the Lord with all thine heart, and lean not**
> **unto thine own understanding" (Proverbs 3:5).**

The word *trust* is translated from the Hebrew word *batach,* which means to be confident, to be bold, or to be sure. The real source of power contained in this verse comes from the descriptive phrase, *with all thine heart.* It requires total commitment to do something with all your heart. Solomon is not just describing a good or adequate effort here; he is talking about being **"ALL IN."**

These words bring to mind memories of the old black-and-white television western scenes of a poker game played in the town's saloon. There would always be dancing going on in the background to lively piano music, when suddenly one of the gamblers would say, "I'm all in." He then would push a pile of poker chips to the center of the table, which is being carefully watched by the other poker players and spectators standing closely around the table, with drinks in hand. It suddenly gets quiet around the table, and sometimes even the piano quits playing. All eyes are on that man who is positive he has the winning hand and conveys that thought to everyone when he bets all he owns, signaling his confidence.

We all know what usually happens next—the cards are shown, and the winner leans over the table to rake in his winnings, when suddenly a fight breaks out. This familiar drama is eerily similar to what happens when wisdom calls out to us. God's commands, like a potentially winning poker hand, are first assessed and then determined if it is the best hand for us to play. The devil will immediately cause a person to wonder if there is a more enjoyable or more profitable set of life procedures. The only way to win is to step out in confidence and announce we have a hand in which we are willing to invest our whole lives because we think it's the best hand at the table. When we understand that wisdom comes from God, we are expected to step out in confidence and trust in the Lord with all our hearts. This means, just like that fictional poker player, we have to signal the others around us that we are totally committed by trusting in God with all—not just part—of our hearts. This is the only way we can claim what God wants us to have. Unfortunately, just like in any poker game, there is going to be a loser who will want to start a fight. That would be Satan who is upset because he has just lost the title deed to a human spirit, one who will not be joining his gang for all of eternity.

Verse five also tells us, "lean not onto thine own understanding." Most ambitious young adults in today's society have at least a couple of years of college or technical school in addition to a high school education. Prior to World War II, it was not uncommon in the United States to have only an eighth grade education. Knowledge is currently growing at an exponential rate, making it easier than ever for the world's population to proclaim their independence from God. Today's college curriculums are producing a higher percentage of atheists than previous generations, and some of them are dedicated to dragging the rest of the world's population down their intellectual path of spiritual apathy. The world's "wise-guys" are leaning on their own understanding because they are full of the world's knowledge, yet devoid of godly humility. A person lacking humility fills that void with pride, and wants to be the master of his own destiny. This makes him an idolater because he has set himself up to be his own God.

"In all thy ways acknowledge Him, and he shall direct thy paths" (Proverbs 3:6).

This verse is no small order. It is telling us we not only have to be "all in," but we also have to remain all in, so God can direct our paths. Jesus did not give up on His mission while suffering on the cross. Being dedicated, or all in, to complete his job is the example He set for us. He knew Satan was (and remains) determined to conquer our souls and spirits. He knew there would be future temptations to which even His elect would give in, yet he continued to willingly suffer for those he knew would eventually let Him down.

Solomon probably had no direct knowledge about the coming Crucifixion of Jesus Christ. He did know however, of the leadership God provided for the children of Israel across the desert to the Promised Land. He knew God had directed their path with a cloud to follow during the day and a tower of fire above the tabernacle to make camp by at night. We do not have visual confirmation, as Israel had for those forty years across the desert, but we do have God's Word, the Holy Bible, and if you are a Christian, you have access to the fellowship of God's Holy Spirit.

"Be not wise in thine own eyes: fear the Lord, and depart from evil" (Proverbs 3:7).

Verse seven has a similar tone as verse five. This verse tells us, "Do not be wise in your own eyes." This is essentially the same message as "lean not on your own understanding." Solomon wisely chose to drive this point home because he knew human nature. Being as intelligent as he was and also being surrounded with beauty and splendor, he knew better than most how hard it is to remain humble. Chapters one and two provide the young student with basic instruction on what to do and not do. Now, in chapter three we find instruction on how to think. Early Christian instruction accompanied by loving corrections, is the formula to be used by the parents of young people who are willing to work themselves into proper thinking.

I still recall my grandma telling me idle hands are the devil's workshop. Grandma was born in 1900 and was probably the busiest woman I have ever known. Raising seven children on a backwoods farm without running water and cooking on a woodstove consumed a great deal of her time and energy, yet she found time to teach Sunday school. Two of her young students from the early fifties went on to pastor churches in that same small farming community. Being in church or riding to church was the only predictable time you could see her sit down. I recall Grandma saying people were never late to church when they were still driving horse-drawn wagons to church. One thing that had not yet changed when I sat in that same small country church, with Grandma during the early sixties, was the sincere gratitude expressed by prayer for things we today take for granted, such as a summer rain. I recall the sweat running down that preacher's face on those hot July Sundays, and people wearing their coats inside the church during freezing January services. These were people with callused hands and with skin that looked like leather, yet they were happy just to be in God's house, with God's people, on God's day.

Working people who seek to please God through their daily routines understand what pleases God. Because of their faith, they are content with their wages no-matter how minimal their positions. This was the example Jesus was setting for His disciples when He insisted upon washing Peter's feet. A well-thought-out job, humbly done to the best of our ability, can sometimes be our strongest testimony. A spirit of humility and a mind of pure thought is a place where the Holy Ghost is happy to dwell. Isaiah 26:3–4 tells us, *"Thou wilt keep him in perfect peace, whose mind is stayed on thee: because he trusteth in thee. Trust ye in the Lord forever: for in the Lord JEHOVAH is everlasting strength."* These two verses should be engraved upon the tablets of every Christian's heart, as Proverbs 3:3 suggests.

The next verse of Isaiah tells us the fate of those who are wise in their own eyes. *"For He bringeth down them that dwell on high: the lofty city, He layeth it low; He layeth it low, even to the ground; He bringeth it even to the dust"* (Isaiah 26:5). It doesn't matter if you're alone or if you're one of many, God will put you in your place. Twenty-first-century America is no exception to this rule.

The second phrase of verse seven: "fear the Lord and depart from evil" —repeats the core message of the Proverbs. To depart from evil, we would already have to be in its presence. Verse seven in its entirety is telling us, "If you're proud of how smart you think you are, then you are practicing evil, and if you are practicing evil, you had better get out of its presence because it will lead you straight to hell!" Now that we know what will happen if we don't follow the advice of verse seven, let's look at verse eight to read what happens when verse seven is followed.

"It shalt be health to thy navel, and marrow to thy bones" (Proverbs 3:8).

The "it" in this verse is referring to God's law, the same topic with which this chapter began. We were told in Proverbs 3:1–2, "Let your heart keep my commands; for they will bring you many days, a full life, and well-being" (HCSB). Verse eight is informing us of additional blessings in store for those whose hearts are loyal to God. An argument could be made that the "it" to which Solomon is referring at the beginning of verse eight, is fearing the Lord and departing from evil, as we are told to do in verse seven. Either interpretation tells us how to go about keeping God's commands. Our fear can help motivate us to ignore what our flesh wants us to do, which is to satisfy our human instincts. Our pleasing God is what secures His blessing, which includes the health, strength and sound sleep only He can provide.

The word *navel* is translated from the Hebrew word *sher*, which means umbilical cord. It also can figuratively refer to a center of strength. The umbilical cord is the lifeline for an unborn child. Like the umbilical cord of a child in the womb, our obedience to God's commands is what nourishes us. Our conscious contact with God's Holy Spirit is the nourishment we get through that lifeline, which every Christian needs to keep open, so God's nourishing instruction can flow freely.

Solomon tells us what medical science finally confirmed about three thousand years later: the mind, which is a large part of our souls, does indeed affect the body. It has only been within the last century that empirical studies have shown those who pray and those who are prayed for heal faster than those who, for whatever reason, refuse to pray. Studies confirm that when humans pray for wounded monkeys, they heal faster than other similarly wounded monkeys who receive no prayer. These are proven facts that the mainstream media chooses to bury behind other news they deem to be of greater importance. If prayer can bring health and strength to a monkey, there should be no doubt concerning its effectiveness in human beings. In theory, this should be especially true for the evolutionists, as they insist on believing they have evolved apes.

"Honour the Lord with thy substance, and with the firstfruits of all thine increase: So shall thy barns be filled with plenty, and thy presses shall burst out with new wine" (Proverbs 3:9–10).

How do we honor the Lord with our possessions? To fully appreciate this verse, we first must recognize exactly what we own. *We own nothing*, including our own bodies, because true ownership belongs to the Creator. The Hebrew word Solomon used for substance was *huwn*, which can mean wealth, riches, or possessions. Substance refers to the actual material of which an object is composed. God told Adam he came from the ground, and he would return to the ground. God knew the exact combinations of the substances that comprised Adam's body. He knew all the laws of magnetism and electrical charges that bond and repel each other to amass the human body and power its functions. Everything we think we possess is actually God's, but we do get to choose what to do with His possessions, which are temporarily put at our disposal.

If I get into an automobile that I legally own, and drive that car to church, being careful to obey all the traffic laws, then it's safe to say I am honoring the Lord with that particular possession. If I later place a bumper sticker on that same car, conveying my approval for public nudity, and drive it recklessly through the neighborhood while consuming a six-pack of beer, then that automobile has become a tool of the devil.

Imagine you have a business, and you have given your favorite employee a truck with which to deliver your product to paying customers. This would be a business strategy based on the belief that if your product is delivered, then you should be able to sell more of it. Now, suppose you happen to see that employee unloading some other product that you don't sell from the back of that truck and delivering it to your next-door neighbor. Let's say he even drove the truck through your front yard so he could unload the cargo into a side door of your neighbor's garage.

No businessman would remain in business very long if he allowed his employees to disrespect him in this manner. You would have no choice but to terminate that employee for the improper use of your company's resources. Well, in a sense, God is a businessman. His business is saving souls; we are His employees, and the devil is His competitor.

Proverbs 3:10 tells me if I use that previously mentioned car to take needy people to church, then God has cause to fill my barn with possessions. If I don't have a barn, then He is going to bless me in some other way. The terms *barns*, *presses*, and *firstfruits* from verse nine, are all agricultural terms that were applicable in Solomon's lifetime. In today's society he might have used terms such as income, investment, or business.

This fifth wisdom speech is a tall order. Being "all in" is a huge commitment. Many people say that marriage is the biggest decision of one's life; others may say their choice of career is the most important decision. If you ask a truly committed Christian, "What's the most important decision you have ever made?" he or she will say, "To serve Jesus Christ with all my heart, with all my strength, and all my soul."

If you have not made this commitment, please find someone who has, and learn all you can from him or her. Better yet, why not pray to God right now, and invite Him into your soul as Lord, Master, and Savior? A sincere prayer to God, petitioning for forgiveness from sin, will provide you the strength and the knowledge of His Holy Spirit. This, followed by a commitment to be "all in" will ensure your place in God's heaven.

Wisdom Speech Six

Proverbs 3:11–20

My son, despise not the chastening of the Lord; neither be weary of His correction: For whom the Lord loveth He correcteth: even as a father the son in whom he delighteth (Proverbs 3:11–12).

Some Christians want to believe they should be happy under all circumstances. It's true a heaven-bound saint has a lot to be happy about, but happiness needs to be genuine. There is no humility in a phony state of happiness. Some Bible teachers will interpret this verse to mean we should be happy all the time, but it's been said God does not want us so heavenly minded to where we're no earthly good. The Bible is full of examples where both good and bad men were unhappy. The shortest verse in the Bible, John 11:35, tells us "Jesus wept."

These verses are not telling us to be sad or happy; they are telling us to accept what is good for us, even if it seems unacceptable. An Olympic athlete endures years of training to force her or his body to do what a normal body cannot do. Should God expect any less dedication or hard work than this? We cannot all be as tough as the apostle Paul, but neither should we refuse to do whatever it is that God calls us to do. Let's clarify what *chastening* means before attempting to understand the command of these verses.

The modern definitions, given by *Webster's*, for this seldom-used word are, "To correct by punishment or suffering, or to prune off excess pretense or falsity." The original Hebrew word was *mowcerah*, which means correction or a place in the desert. The desert was often the chosen training site for some of God's most beloved people. The desert is where the children of Israel wandered for forty years while receiving the Mosaic law. Their instructor, Moses, had previously spent another forty years in that same desert. This is where God prepared him to be the "deliverer of Israel." The prophet Elijah was fed by the ravens in the desert, and if you were going to hear a sermon from John the Baptist, you probably would have had to go to the desert. Our Lord Himself was driven into the wilderness, where Satan tempted Him for forty days (Mark 1:11–13).

One purpose for going to the desert was to remove distractions so the Holy Spirit could be heard. God's Holy Spirit prefers quiet places free from satanic noise. The harsh desert environment is also representative for any "dry spells" of testing with which the Lord may choose to chasten his children. If God does chasten us, it means He is treating us just as He did His own Son. Testing and training by means of chastisement is how God molds us into the people He wants us to be.

We are told in Acts 5:41 that the apostles rejoiced after being beaten by order of the Sanhedrin. They were happy because they had been found worthy to suffer for the name of the Lord. These were the same apostles who were earlier scattered with fear when their shepherd was slain. Jesus had earlier told the disciples this would happen (Mark 14). This also was prophesied five hundred years earlier by the prophet Zechariah. *"Awake, O sword, against My Shepherd, and against the man that is my fellow, saith the Lord of hosts: smite the Shepherd, and the sheep shall be scattered"* (Zechariah 13:7).

If you are wondering why or how these frightened disciples managed to become so bold so quickly, take a look at Acts 2. For forty days after Christ had risen from the tomb, He was seen numerous times by different groups of people. His final appearance is known as the ascension. This happened on the Mount of Olives, where the disciples watched their risen Christ ascend up to heaven, where He presently resides with His heavenly Father. Ten days later, the Comforter was sent to them on what is known as the Day of Pentecost. This was when God's Holy Spirit filled the house where the disciples had assembled. They heard a rushing wind and saw tongues of fire and then began speaking in unknown languages.

These previously timid men were now filled with the Spirit of God! They recognized this as the fulfillment of what Jesus had told them prior to His physical death. John 13:15–18 and John 16 describe the Holy

Spirit being sent to dwell within God's chosen people while they are still physically alive on earth. It was the indwelling of this Spirit that enabled these early Christians to be faithful unto death for what they knew to be true. Otherwise, Christianity would have been quickly eradicated by the over-bearing cruelty of the Roman government.

God fully realizes some of us are not yet ready to welcome His chastening into our lives. This is why God through Solomon's Proverbs provides a set of instructions to prepare His saints for any future testing. These are the same written instructions found in the Proverbs. Trials and tribulation are how God trains us for the work He wants us to do while we're still living on the earth. Try to think of these sometimes inconvenient instructions as the steps of a training program designed to enable us to do what we otherwise would be unable to do. The nature of God's missions normally resembles a marathon more than a hundred-yard dash, so we must train to endure. Training is how we develop strength, endurance, and the necessary calluses, which will protect us from the frictions of our journeys.

The first (training) step, found in Proverbs 1:8, tells us to obey our parents. God wants our training to begin early because he knows the earliest lessons are those which have the most influence in our lives. Each call to attention issued by the phrase, "my son," is a reminder of this first step. Age does not excuse a Christian from honoring his or her parents.

The second step, found in Proverbs 1:10–15, tells us to avoid evil. It is difficult, if not impossible, to sense God's will when we are distracted by sin. This is why God sent so many Old Testament prophets to the desert.

Proverbs 2:1 tells us the third step—learn God's words and store them in our hearts. If we skip this step, we will not be able to draw upon the Holy Spirit's power when we really need it. A thorough third step will make step four, found in Proverbs 2:3–6, almost automatic; we're told to seek God for understanding. The following verses of chapter two tell us how valuable wisdom, knowledge, and understanding are. When we are granted these precious gifts of God, we have successfully worked step five, which provides discernment and discretion for us.

This brings us to chapter three where we are told to exercise mercy and truth in our lives. This sixth step is not always a convenient discipline to follow, but it strengthens us to be able to work the seventh step of Proverbs

3:5, which says, "Trust in the Lord with all thine heart, and lean not on thine own understanding." This step commands us to fully obey God and leave all the consequences to Him. You may remember this as the "ALL IN" step.

The next verse reveals step eight: "In all thy ways acknowledge Him" (Proverbs 3:6). Step nine, taken from Proverbs 3:9, tells us to honor God with our possessions (HCSB). Finally, we get to this all-important and difficult step ten: "Despise not the chastening of the Lord" (Proverbs 3:11). The writer of the book of Hebrews had this to say about chastening:

> My son, despise not thou the chastening of the Lord, Nor faint when thou art rebuked of Him: For whom the Lord loveth He chasteneth, and scourgeth every son whom He receiveth. If ye endure chastening, God dealeth with you as with sons; for what son is he whom the father chasteneth not? But if ye be without chastisement, whereof all are partakers, then are ye bastards and not sons. Furthermore we have had fathers of our flesh which corrected us, and we gave them reverence: shall we not much rather be in subjection unto the Father of spirits, and live? For they verily for a few days chasteneth us after their own pleasure; but He for our profit, that we might be partakers of His holiness. Now no chastening for the present seemeth to be joyous, but grievous: nevertheless afterward it yieldeth the peaceable fruit of righteousness unto them which are exercised thereby. (Hebrews 12:5–11)

"Happy is the man that findeth wisdom, and the man that getteth understanding. For the merchandise of it is better than the merchandise of silver, and the gain thereof than fine gold" (Proverbs 3:13–14).

It is good to note that Solomon immediately switches our attention to happiness after just two verses on the subject of chastisement. Neither God nor Solomon wanted us to dwell on the negativity of chastisement, but they knew we needed to be prepared for it. We need always to remember, especially when being chastened, that God wants to raise us up, not push us down. If He does choose to smack us down, it's only to prevent us from continuing down the wrong road. It is sometimes necessary to make a U-turn to get back to where God wants us.

When a man or woman possesses true godly wisdom, he or she will be happy. Godly wisdom leads to godly understanding, which produces a faith in us to know that God will provide for all of our needs. Faith in the living God, the Creator of all substance, the source of all life and positive energy, was what strengthened men like Peter, Paul and John to fight the good fight, regardless of their circumstances. They understood that Jesus never promised them a smooth trip, but He does promise a safe landing in eternal paradise. When times get tough, visualize the rewards of faith and obedience that are represented by the silver and gold mentioned in Proverbs 3:14. God's plan for His faithful followers will exceed any pleasure or riches available to us on planet earth while existing within our human limitations. His heaven has no pain, no death, no sorrow and no tears, as we are told in Revelation 21:1–4.

> **"She is more precious than rubies: and all the things**
> **thou canst desire are not to be compared unto her.**
> **Length of days is in her right hand; and in her left hand**
> **riches and honour. Her ways are ways of pleasantness,**
> **and all her paths are peace" (Proverbs 3:15–17).**

Proverbs 3:15 continues emphasizing the importance of wisdom and understanding for the development of human souls. Thus far in Proverbs, Solomon has spent more verses on the benefits of wisdom than he has any other specific topic. Why would a writer as knowledgeable and talented as Solomon continue to hammer away at the same point, which seems to have already been so thoroughly discussed? Perhaps Job 28:12–13 can give us some insight to Solomon's persistence. *"But where shall wisdom be found? And where is the place of understanding? Man knoweth not the price thereof; neither is it found in the land of the living."*

So Job is telling us that wisdom is an elusive commodity. In fact, he says it is nowhere to be found on the earth, yet Solomon tells us earlier in the Proverbs that wisdom cries out from everywhere (Proverbs 1:21–22). This seems to be a contradiction, but as Christians, we are supposed to believe the Bible is the inerrant word of God; so who are we supposed to believe—Job or Solomon? It does not matter if Job was right or if Solomon was right. What really matters here is that as ambassadors for Christ, we should never doubt the validity or the accuracy of the Holy Scriptures.

The short answer is that Job and Solomon were both right. There are different types of wisdom; which caused Job and Solomon to use different Hebrew words which were both translated into our modern English word, wisdom. The word used by Job was *chokmah,* which means wisdom in a good sense. The word used by Solomon was *chakmowth,* a collateral form of Job's word, which means just wisdom. The word used by Job has a more specific meaning than the word used by Solomon. To really understand what Job and Solomon said about wisdom, let's look into the circumstances and situations by which these Old Testament saints were inspired to make these statements.

Job was a happy, respected, and well-known man in the land of Uz. He feared God and shunned evil. Job 1:1 describes him as "blameless and upright." When God held Job up as an example of obedience, Satan's reply was, *"Haven't you placed a hedge around him, his household, and everything he owns? You have blessed the work of his hands, and his possessions have increased in the land. But stretch out your hand and strike everything he owns, and he will surely curse You to Your face"* (Job 1:9–11 HCSB). God then removed His hedge of protection from around Job and allowed Satan the opportunity to cause Job to curse God. The only limitation God placed on Satan's efforts was that he could not take Job's life.

When Job later made his claim that wisdom was nowhere to be found, all his worldly possessions had been taken away, including his ten children. His only surviving family member, his wife, chastised him with the words, "Curse God and die," and then Satan inflicted him with painful boils from the soles of his feet to the crown of his head (Job 2:7). Added to all these woes was Satan's sending three of Job's friends, who thought they were helping by pleading with him to confess whatever sin he was being punished for. These three proceeded to assume a position of moral superiority over Job and were critical of his character, instead of offering him any support or compassion. Satan threw everything he had at this man, but Job accepted his chastisement and remained loyal in his fellowship with God, who eventually restored Job to an even loftier position than he'd had prior to Satan's test of torment. Job accepted his chastening, and then God miraculously made him whole again.

God had allowed the presence of evil to not only enter Job's life but to surround and engulf him to the point where evil was lurking in every direction he looked. Then Satan sent his three pious ambassadors, who were supposed to be Job's friends, to inflict even more torment of a psychological nature. These were the conditions from which Job spoke when he proclaimed, *"But where can wisdom be found? And where is the place of understanding? Man does not know its value, nor is it found in the land of the living."* Job could find no *chokmah*, or good wisdom, because Satan's evil had surrounded him after God removed his hedge of protection.

We are eventually told in the last verse of Job 28, *"The fear of the Lord is this: wisdom. And to turn from evil is understanding" (HCSB).* The conclusion Job stated in this verse (Job 28:28) is identical to the conclusions found in the book of Proverbs, so a deeper investigation confirms there is no contradiction between Job 28:13 and Proverbs 1:21–22. Solomon, on the other hand, was indeed surrounded by beauty and wisdom because he had just inherited the most magnificent kingdom ever ruled by a mortal man—a kingdom so marvelous that God Himself had intended to rule it.

God informed Israel, through the writings of Moses that He personally was to be their king. The Old Testament judges and prophets were then commissioned to make God's will known for Israel to follow. God knew Israel would sin, and sin, being a progressive disease, would cause them to want a mortal man to act as their king. They wanted what all their surrounding pagan neighbors had—a man on a throne. God reluctantly told Samuel to ordain Saul as Israel's first king. This fulfilled what God had told Moses, 350 years earlier:

> When you enter the land the Lord your God is giving you, take possession of it, live in it and say, "I will set a king over me like all the nations around me," you are to appoint over you the king the Lord your God chooses. Appoint a king from your brothers. You are not to set a foreigner over you, or one who is not of your people. However he must

not acquire many horses for himself, or send the people back to Egypt to acquire many horses, for the Lord has told you, "You are never to go back that way again." He must not acquire many wives for himself so that his heart won't go astray. He must not acquire very large amounts of silver and gold for himself. When he is seated on his royal throne, he is to write a copy of this instruction for himself on a scroll in the presence of the Levitical priests. It is to remain with him, and he is to read from it all the days of his life, so that he may learn to fear the Lord his God, to observe all the words of this instruction, and to do these statutes. Then his heart will not be exalted above his countrymen, he will not turn from this command to the right or the left, and he and his sons will continue ruling many years over Israel. (Deuteronomy 17:14–20 HCSB)

God told Israel—and specifically, any sitting king of Israel—a few very simple rules that would ensure the prosperity of the kingdom. When these statutes were not observed and respected, God would then send His prophets to alert Israel, and especially the king, about the evil of their ways and the pending consequences of continued sin. Although there is no record of any prophet confronting Solomon, we know that Nathan and Bathsheba stood up for him when his older half brother, Adonijah, tried to seize the throne. Solomon and his father, David, probably knew these scriptures and the Mosaic law better than any other kings of Israel. This claim is made on the basis of David and Solomon being the only kings to have written books included in the Bible. These two Old Testament writers never lost their salvation, but they did lose the joy of their salvation because of disobedience. Solomon's later writings in Ecclesiastes reveal the thoughts and opinions of an older and wiser king who has lost his joy and whose views had began to sound similar to those of Job's.

Job, despite all of Satan's efforts, remained obedient to God's law and was exceedingly blessed as the result. He not only had his health and wealth restored, but he also had seven more sons and three more daughters. *"And in all the land were no women found so fare as the daughters of Job: and their father gave them inheritance among their brethren. After this lived*

Job an hundred and forty years, and saw his sons and his sons' sons even four generations" (Job 42:15–16 KJV).

This was the result of Job's obedience. The result of Solomon's disobedience is described in Ecclesiastes 7:23–26, which reads, *"I have tested all this by wisdom. I resolved, 'I will be wise'; but it was beyond me. What exists is beyond reach and very deep. Who can discover it?"* (HCSB). Despite his beautiful surroundings, Solomon now realizes that God's wisdom had departed from him. He also writes about why this happened to him in the two following verses: *"I turned my heart to know, explore, and seek wisdom and an explanation for things, and to know that wickedness is stupidity and folly is madness. And I find more bitter than death the woman who is a trap, her heart a net, and her hands chains. The one who pleases God will escape her, but the sinner will be captured by her"* (Ecclesiastes 7:25–26 HCSB).

More information about the life of Solomon would certainly increase our understanding of his writings. It does seem that a king as wise as he was should have been more dedicated to carrying out God's law, especially while being allowed to rule God's kingdom. He should have earnestly sought to secure God's blessing for the kingdom he was entrusted to rule. His description of entrapment originating from a woman's heart could be describing his own addiction to sex. Much like an alcoholic blaming his problems on everything but himself, Solomon claims to have been trapped. First Kings 11 says Solomon built "high places," which were places of worship, for *all* of his foreign wives (1 Kings 11:8). It is difficult to imagine any power, other than sex, that these women could have had over Solomon to have caused him to do what he knew was wrong. We do not know how many of Solomon's seven hundred wives and three hundred concubines were foreign; but it sounds like there was a substantial amount of idol worshipping going on in God's chosen land by God's chosen king. Satan might have failed with Job, but he sure succeeded with Solomon.

If Solomon was indeed a sex addict, it would certainly explain a lot about one of the most baffling periods of biblical history. If you looked at it from the perspective that Satan only used one woman to help bring down Adam, then a lot could be said about Solomon's having a thousand women to distract him from the will of God. As king, however, he could have started beheading every member of his harem who dared utter a word of disobedience toward the holy God of Israel. One night in the dungeon would have probably been sufficient incentive for most of these pampered women to stop worshipping their false gods.

The untamed passions of David and Solomon not only split their fellowship with God, but it split apart their kingdom as well. Solomon disobeyed God's commands to not multiply wives, to not multiply horses, and to not multiply silver and gold (Deuteronomy 17:16–17). Let's return to Solomon's earlier years, when he was still content with wisdom's way. He was still talking about his delight with wisdom and had every reason to believe he would remain a happy man in the will of God because of wisdom and understanding. It's too bad he left out obedience!

"She is a tree of life to them that lay hold upon her: and happy is every one that retaineth her" (Proverbs 3:18).

The tree of life referred to in verse 18 is a descriptive term used by Solomon to help expand the young student's understanding of knowledge. It is debatable whether or not Solomon is referring to the tree of life mentioned in the second and third chapter of Genesis. Most Americans, including the unbelievers, are aware of the tree from which Adam and Eve ate—which was the tree of knowledge of good and evil (Genesis 3:22). The other tree specifically mentioned in Genesis 2:9 was the tree of life. God drove Adam and Eve out of the garden of Eden, and placed cherubims around this tree to prevent man from eating of it and living forever (Genesis 3:23–24). It is probable that these cherubims continued to guard the tree of life until it and the entire garden of Eden were consumed about seventeen hundred years later in the flood. What Solomon did not know was the book of Revelation would later state the tree of life will be in God's Jerusalem (Revelation 22:1–2).

Solomon did know God held trees in high regard. Trees, especially fruit trees, were considered necessary for sustaining life—so much so that God commanded Israel, in Deuteronomy 20:19, to not cut down the trees when besieging a city. The King James Version states, "for the tree of the field is man's life." When Moses recorded Deuteronomy, and Solomon read it, I imagine they were primarily thinking in terms of trees supplying them food. Today, we know, as God has always known, that trees also produce the oxygen, which is necessary for all biological functions. God's wisdom, like trees, provides us the essentials of life.

The next two verses tell us of another form of wisdom, which is the creative wisdom of God. These verses remind us that God's wisdom is infinite. We should know this because He created everything we are aware of, as well as plenty more that we don't know about yet.

"The Lord by wisdom hath founded the earth; by understanding hath he established the heavens. By His knowledge the depths are broken up, and the clouds drop down the dew" (Proverbs 3:19–20).

Proverbs 3:19 refers us all the way back to Genesis 1:1, probably the most commonly known verse in the Bible. Even nonbelievers can quote this one. It is also the verse that Satan has worked the hardest to discredit. A father and mother in Solomon's day could teach their children that God created the heavens and the earth without being challenged. In fact, it has only been within the last century that the United States government has revoked absolute parental authority in our once-Christian country. Thanks to a string of consecutive Supreme Court decisions, the children of Christian parents are taught in public schools that God did not create our world. What this does is to make it the official policy of the United States of America to teach our children the Bible is nothing more than a storybook. **This is an action for which America will be judged!**

Matthew 18:1–6 issues a severe warning to those who harm a child. The teaching of evolution points children towards a belief in science, rather than to faith in an all-powerful Creator. Whenever you encounter a fellow human who tries to convince you the Bible is flawed, observe his actions and mannerisms closely so you can learn to identify those who belong to the propaganda division of Satan's gang. Those who worship science are usually very educated and often skilled in the art of debate. These are the ones who write many of the textbooks from which our children are taught from in America's politically correct school system. They, like Satan, have no interest in having a fair debate, so they discredit and then shut down any new evidence supporting the biblical account of creation. Science, politics, and America's judicial system now determine what our children will be taught in public school. What seems to be forgotten is that God created science, making Him the first scientist. It was God who established the laws of motion and electromagnetism. It was God who created the proton, the building block of His creation. God established all of this for humans to learn about it, and use it to benefit by. It was satanic suggestion that caused men of science to discredit Gods work, and then take credit for their own false theories—some of which are now taught to our children as fact!

Both the Bible and secular history books provide us example after example of human stupidity. We wonder how a pharaoh could again challenge the God of Israel by sending his army into the Red Sea in pursuit of Israel, after seeing Egypt devastated by the plagues. We wonder how a man such as Leonardo da Vinci could have been condemned and then imprisoned for believing the world is round. It was only about five hundred years ago when men were needlessly dying after surgery because doctors had not washed their hands! The book of Leviticus instructs Israel to wash and to be clean and to burn the bedding of a leper. This is because God, the Creator of the still-uncounted solar systems, also created the unseen world of microorganisms. He understood how disease and infections are transmitted long before man did. It was the middle of the twentieth century before the majority of American men were being circumcised, yet God had His chosen people doing it four thousand years ago. As Christians, we must wonder, "Why is America turning her back on God?"

Proverbs 3:20 is Solomon's comment on Genesis 7:11, which tells us *"all the fountains of the great deep were broken up, and the windows of heaven were opened."* The Bible says it rained forty days and forty nights, but evolutionists avoid commenting on Genesis 7:11, which describes a collapse of the inner earth. Could this be describing the rearrangement of inner layers of stratus within a cooling planet and the water being formed from all the condensation rising to the top of that planet's surface, increasing the size of its oceans? The evolutionists want you to think that it was sheer luck that the ancient writer of Genesis provides us an accurate account of what happened to form this planet. How many thousands of years was it after Moses wrote these words before science came up with some similar ideas? How many times have scientists rewritten or reversed their beliefs? God has never revised the Bible. Only He can produce and preserve a literary work, written over a period of fifteen hundred years by at least two dozen different writers that successfully stands the test of time.

The evidence is overwhelming that an intelligence other than that of mortal men was responsible for the knowledge and wisdom contained in the Bible. In depth biblical study will reveal countless predictions of historic events that were later fulfilled. The mere fact that Israel still exists as a sovereign nation, despite being surrounded by Arab nations who all hate Judaism, should be enough to convince any unbiased mind that the Bible is indeed the inspired Word of God.

WISDOM SPEECH SEVEN

Proverbs 3:21–35

My son, let not them depart from thine eyes: keep sound wisdom and discretion: So shall they be life unto thy soul and grace to thy neck (Proverbs 3:21–22).

These two verses echo the encouragement of Proverbs 1:8–9, which reads, "My son, hear the instruction of thy father, and forsake not the law of thy mother; for they shall be an ornament of grace unto thy head, and chains about thy neck" (KJV). The young student was also told in Proverbs chapter two, and now again in Proverbs chapter three: wisdom will save you, understanding will guard you, and discretion will preserve you.

Solomon presented parental guidance as entry-level instruction for the new students of wisdom in chapter one. If the instruction is adequate and administered by righteous parents who are seeking God's approval, the young child should go on to instinctively avoid Satan's people, and the danger of wickedness. He or she will then be strengthened because of a God-given ability to discern what is right and what is wrong. The graceful ornament referred to in Proverbs chapter one is the Christian character that the parents and their child have continually practiced in all their affairs. The reward is a teenager who is mature enough to know that inner character is more important than outward appearances.

Obedient children who go on to be discerning teenagers will evolve into wise adults, if they keep wisdom's precepts in their hearts. The challenging instructions of Proverbs chapters two and three are accompanied with promises of both physical and spiritual prosperity to serve as incentive to do right. This is made possible by thinking wisely and acting with discretion.

"Then shalt thou walk in thy way safely, and thy foot shall not stumble" (Proverbs 3:23).

Verse 23 continues the list of wisdom's promised blessings, the purpose of which is to encourage us to choose discretion over frivolous amusement. Solomon last wrote about discretion in Proverbs 2:11, where we were told how to receive discretion. Discretion is the result of having wisdom in our hearts. Discretion provides us the ability to make godly choices, which will enable us to live gracefully so our feet will not stumble. God-given discretion breeds pure motivation in our hearts, based on God's greater good, rather than our own self-centered desires. It will guide us to make the best possible decisions. God wants only the best for His chosen children.

"When thou liest down, thou shall not be afraid: yea, thou shall lie down and thy sleep shall be sweet" (Proverbs 3:24).

Verse 24 gives us two more reasons to include wisdom and discretion into our lives. The Hebrew word for sweet is *arab,* which means secure. In today's high-paced stressful world, this comforting verse assures us we will not be afraid. One of the benefits of having God's grace is we also will have peace, even under stressful circumstances. Internal peace is provided by God's Holy Spirit, who is also known as the Comforter (John 14:26). Faith assures us God is in complete control, so it is needless to worry because problems on this earth are only temporary. Having faith in God will make your sleep sweet. If you are having problems sleeping, try including Proverbs 3:24 in your bedtime prayer. If you're not praying before you go to bed, maybe that is why you are not being blessed with a soul-nourishing peaceful night's sleep.

Three thousand years ago—long before medical science discovered how harmful stress is to the human body—the Bible declared the benefits of a clean conscience, as we have been told in verse eight of this chapter. "This will be healing for your body and strengthening for your bones" (HCSB). We also were told, "Trust in the Lord with all your heart, and do not rely on your own understanding" (Proverbs 3:5 HCSB). Proverbs 12:18 tells us, *"The tongue of the wise is health."* and Proverbs 16:24 says, *"Pleasant words are as an honeycomb, sweet to the soul, and health to the bones."*

"Be not afraid of sudden fear, neither of the desolation of the wicked, when it cometh, For the Lord shall be thy confidence, and shall keep thy foot from being taken" (Proverbs 3:25–26).

These verses continue the list of benefits that godly living can make possible. Solomon had already warned his young student in chapter one of terror coming as suddenly as a whirlwind. Here, Solomon uses the Hebrew word *shoah,* which is translated by the KJV into *desolation*, and refers to the type of destruction caused by a storm. This is a perfect description of what the wicked can bring into a godly life. It is the opposite of the peaceful state of mind, body, and soul described in the previous verses. This is what the wicked do: inspired by Satan, they destroy Christian lives with their immorality. Verse 26 assures us that Satan cannot blindside us with his devices because, like Job, God's children have a hedge of protection around them.

"Withhold not good from them to whom it is due, when it is in the power of thine hand to do it" (Proverbs 3:27).

The Hebrew word *towb,* which Solomon uses in verse 27 for our English word good, has meanings that include cheerfulness, fairness, graciousness, kindness, and favor, in addition to promptness, but this verse requires more than goodness. It also instructs us to discern who is deserving of our good works and to know what we are capable of giving. This is no small order because accurate self-assessment is difficult, even for a discerning Christian.

Jesus is quoted in Matthew 7:6 (KJV), saying, "Give not that which is holy unto the dogs, neither caste ye your pearls before swine, lest they trample them under their feet, and turn again and rend you." Solomon and Jesus are both advising their students of wisdom to exercise discretion, in an effort to avoid the misuse of our God-given resources. If Solomon had had access to this quote from Jesus, he might have felt led to write a fourth Old Testament book dedicated to the development of discernment for character assessment.

Solomon tells us in Proverbs 3:27 to do good when we are able. It does not mean we always have to give until it hurts, as many wealthy fundraisers (some of whom are behind pulpits) would have us do. It is important to note that Jesus said to withhold what is holy, not what is good, from the dogs and the swine. The Hebrew people in Solomon's day did not go into foreign pagan communities, trying to convert Gentiles into Jews. Jesus did later give the Great Commission to his disciples, instructing them to *"GO ye into all the world, and preach the gospel to every creature"* (Mark 16:15). This final command obviously includes both Jews and Gentiles. What Jesus wants us to learn from this verse is that some people are not yet ready to receive the Holy Spirit. This is the same spiritual principle Solomon is teaching in verse 27 by specifying "do not withhold good from those to *whom it is due"* (emphasis added). Some are not ready to be saved, and some are not ready to be helped, period.

Without the Holy Spirit, there can be no salvation, regardless of how great our efforts are. This does not mean we are commanded to do no good works, but it does mean we should not witness to a person if we know it will anger him or her. For example, it is probably not a good idea to go into a tavern or a casino and invite a bunch of drunks to church. This could reinforce existing prejudiced views about how impractical Christians and Christianity can be. It would provide an opportunity for the mocker to mock and the scorner to scorn. Perhaps the greatest harm would be the potential negative influence such interaction could have on any spectators who are not yet intoxicated. There could be some younger bystanders whose minds have not yet been hardened by Satan's human agents—who would then think, *I don't want anything to do with Christianity if it means being the object of public scorn and laughter.*

This does not exclude us from striving to be the best living example of a Christian that we can be. Our words and actions can speak volumes to those around us. We may unknowingly be the closest example of God's Word to which some folks will ever be exposed. Solomon tells us in part B of verse 27 to do good when it is within our ability to do so. This is when we need to be wise enough to know what we are and are not capable of doing. For example, we are not supposed to give away anything that our family legitimately needs. To support this claim, please consider 1 Timothy 5:8, which reads, *"But if any provide not for his own, and specially for those of his own house, he hath denied the faith and is worse than an infidel,"* This means charity begins in the home!

Proverbs 3:27 encourages us to recognize good people and to reward them for their goodness when we are reasonably capable of doing so. If we have followed God's instruction, we will be led by His Holy Spirit to discern who is among the good and who is among the wicked. Wisdom and understanding will cause us to not only seek out goodness but to seek out good people with whom we can share our fellowship. If He has given us a spirit of joy and happiness, then that is what we have to share. If we have just suffered a tremendous personal loss that has temporarily removed our joy, then we really are not in a position to give away what we do not possess.

"Say not onto thy neighbour, Go, and come again, and tomorrow I will give; when thou hast it by thee" (Proverbs 3:28).

The word neighbor is translated from the Hebrew *reya*, which can include a brother, an associate, a friend, or a companion in addition to a neighbor.

When interest rates were in the double digits during the late seventies and early eighties, it became standard practice for businesses to hold on to money, due to be refunded, for as long as possible. The bigger the business, the longer they would keep your money. Solomon is telling us in verse 28 that this is not a righteous practice. This is more than procrastination; this is dishonest. When practiced on a personal basis this can be considered lying to whomever you owe, if you pretending to be unable to pay. It could even be viewed as stealing, on a temporary basis, which breaks the eighth commandment. It's easy to rationalize, "The government has held on to my refund for sixty days, so why can't I hang on to the money I owe my neighbor until payday?" Christians should always base their decisions on what the Bible says and not on what has become the accepted standard practice of society. The writings of Alcoholics Anonymous state, "Procrastination is really sloth spelled with five syllables." It is an unrealistic expectation for anyone to grow spiritually while living slothfully.

"Devise not evil against thy neighbor, seeing he dwelleth securely by thee" (Proverbs 3:29).

This verse was a very important command in Solomon's day. Being an agricultural society, the land owners of Israel depended on each other for their common well-being. Most people today do not have to worry about livestock or un-harvested crops being stolen, but we still need to refrain from doing our neighbors wrong. This includes gossip, which may be the most frequent breach of the intent of this verse in today's America. Proverbs 17:4 states, *"A wicked doer giveth heed to false lips; and a liar giveth ear to a naughty tongue."*

"Strive not with a man without cause, if he have done thee no harm" (Proverbs 3:30).

The Hebrew word used by Solomon for strive was *ruwb*, which can mean debate, complain, wrangle, or rebuke. The apostle Paul later instructed Christians to live peacefully with all men when possible (Romans 12:18). As long as Satan has any influence, we will encounter people who are difficult to get along with. Only through wisdom and understanding can the boundaries of any relationship be established as God would have them be.

It's obvious this verse is *not* saying Christians should ignore their personal or property rights. There are, however, real and imagined wrongs. Communications are easy to misinterpret, as are facial expressions and vocal tones. Truth and reality are not always easily recognized—it may take some time, effort, and especially prayer to arrive at the correct conclusions. If Christians feel it is necessary to pursue an aggressive course of action in response to oppression, it is their absolute responsibility to know for sure they have truly been oppressed. Satan loves spontaneous reactions toward misunderstood circumstances. Contempt prior to investigation is the breeding ground for ignorance of the truth. Proverbs 1:5 teaches us, *"A wise man will listen and increase his learning, and a discerning man will obtain guidance"* (HCSB).

"Envy thou not the oppressor, and choose none of his ways (Proverbs 3:31).

To oppress means to weigh down or to burden by means of excessive power or authority. No one wants to be oppressed, and God does not want His people to be bullied by tyrants. He will, however, sometimes use an oppressor to punish a person or even an entire nation who has defied his will. Oppression occurs at all levels of social interaction, from Congress to the schoolyard. It can even happen at church. There's a sign hanging in a military museum that quotes an army general as saying, "There are two types of people in this world, the oppressed and the oppressors." What that general did not know is that committed Christians who seek God's will, rather than leaning on their own understanding, are a third category of people. God can and will protect His people, who are not oppressive, from Satan's oppressors. Those with divine understanding know where to set their boundaries.

Solomon instructs us to not envy the oppressor. They do not need any encouragement—Satan is already all over that job. Oppression seems to be everywhere, yet Satan's favorite oppressor has not yet materialized. Scripture warns us of his coming, and of his extraordinary power that will subdue mankind. He is identified as the Antichrist, and will covertly enter as a man of peace, a "smooth talker," a political negotiator who will achieve what no US president has to date—a successful peace treaty between Israel and the Arab State.

This is what oppressors do; they first get themselves into a position of power before they openly carry out their self-serving plans. Some oppressors, such as the ancient Romans, operated with brute force, while others used the Trojan horse method. Regardless of the size, shape, age, or technique of the oppressor, Solomon says we are to choose none of his ways, even if the oppressor is a respected champion of his or her domain. Jesus told us, *"Blessed are the meek: for they shall inherit the earth"* (Matthew 5:5).

"For the froward is abomination to the Lord: but His secret is with the righteous" (Proverbs 3:32).

Solomon describes the oppressor as being "froward," as translated from the Hebrew word *luwz,* which describes a person who continues in the process of becoming an oppressor. A successful oppressor has to continually make sinful decisions if he is going to maintain his position of power. He has to remain corrupt and out of fellowship with God to keep his victims within their restraints. This requires him to continue being an abomination in the sight of our Lord. The Hebrew word *teebah* can be translated as detestable or disgusting, in addition to abominable, and it is often associated with idolatry. If a person sets himself above another by means of oppression, is he not committing idolatry by playing God?

Froward people who appear to have everything going their way, will always lack one tremendous asset. Part B of verse 32 tells us the froward will never benefit from the secret council of God. Psalms 25:14 has this to say: *"The secret council of the Lord is for those who fear Him, and He reveals His covenant to them"* (HCSB).

"The curse of the Lord is in the house of the wicked: but He blesseth the habitation of the just" (Proverbs 3:33).

The Bible can accurately be described as a book about the blessings and the curses bestowed upon man by God. The Bible's very first chapter records God blessing Adam and Eve so they could fill the earth and subdue it. At this point in time, everything God had made was not only good but very good (Genesis 1:31). Then sin entered the picture, and God cursed the ground, cursed the serpent, and multiplied Eve's (biological) sorrow. The last chapter of the Old Testament ends with the word curse. A lot of blessing and cursing goes on throughout the entire Bible. Solomon's proverbs can be summarized as a set of instructions that tell us how to receive the blessings and how to avoid the curses. Verse 33 tells us, in the simplest terms possible, who can expect to be blessed and who will be cursed.

"Surely He scorneth the scorners: but giveth grace unto the lowly" (Proverbs 3:34).

To scorn means to reject with contempt. The scorner is one who scoffs at meaningful concepts and duties. The New International Version of the Bible substitutes the word mock for scorn. Remember, a mocker is one who imitates in a disrespectful manner. This verse tells us God will treat the scorner in the same manner with which the scorner treats other people. Part B of this verse tells us about the opposite personality type of the scorner, which is the lowly or the humble, as described in the Holman Christian Standard Bible. Humility is often a misunderstood word. Our Lord is declared to be the most humble man that lived. *Unger's Bible Dictionary* states, "Christian humility is the grace which makes one think of himself no more highly than he ought to think." *Webster's* definition of humble is: "1) an absence of pride 2) reflecting a spirit of submission 3) an absence of vanity or arrogance 4) meek, modest or lowly, 5) an absence of wrath."

The apostle Paul had this to say in Romans 12:3: *"For I say, through the grace given unto me, to every man that is among you, not to think of himself more highly than he ought to think; but to think soberly, according as God hath dealt to every man the measure of faith."* Paul instructs us to have a sober mind, which, like humility, can also be a misunderstood concept. Paul is not just telling us to abstain from alcohol in this verse; he is describing a content mind, one which has been transformed through the saving grace of our Messiah. Jeremiah 9:23–24 provides an excellent description of a humble and sober mind. *"Thus saith the Lord, let not the wise man glory in his wisdom, neither let the mighty man glory in his might, let not the rich man glory in his riches: But let him that glorieth glory in this, that he understandeth and knoweth me, that I am the Lord which exercise lovingkindness, judgment, and righteousness, in the earth: for in these things I delight saith the Lord."*

On the topics of sobriety and humility, the thoughts of Bill Wilson, the founder of Alcoholics Anonymous and writer of the Twelve Steps, are most appropriate. Wilson writes, **"Humility is a keen awareness of our assets and liabilities."** Given this definition, Jesus was the world's most humble man because His assets were limitless, while His liabilities were absolutely zero. Yet our Lord chose to serve humankind and then willingly suffered the extreme cruelty of crucifixion.

The world's most humble man summed up His idea of humility very briefly, as recorded in the Gospels of Matthew and Luke. The first quote, in Matthew 18:4, was given to His disciples when they were arguing about which of them would be the greatest in the kingdom of heaven. Jesus summoned a small child to hold up as an example for them, and then, in reference to their desires to be the greatest in heaven, He replied, *"Whoever therefore shall humble himself as this little child, the same is greatest in the kingdom of heaven."* Later, in Matthew 23:11–12, in reference to the corrupt scribes and Pharisees, Jesus proclaimed, *"But he that is greatest among you shall be your servant. And whoever shall exalt himself shall be abased; and he that shall humble himself shall be exalted."* Luke 14:11 and Luke 18:14 both provide the same message, word for word, as Matthew 23:12 does. It seems all the writers of the New Testament Gospels, thought it was important for us to know what would happen if we lacked humility.

A lack of humility is a lack of self-awareness, which usually results in what Bill Wilson declared to be the deadliest of the seven deadly sins—pride! Solomon also placed pride first in the sixth chapter of Proverbs where he lists seven human characteristics the Lord finds to be abominations. Beginning with Proverbs 6:17, the seven abominations are (1) a proud look, (2) a lying tongue, (3) hands that shed innocent blood, (4) a heart that devises wicked plans. (5) feet that are swift in running to evil, (6) a false witness who speaks lies, and (7) one who sows discord among brethren.

"The wise shall inherit glory: but shame shall be the promotion of fools" (Proverbs 3:35).

Verse 35 tells us what the destinies are for both the wise and the fool. We were told in Proverbs 2:4 to seek wisdom as if it were silver—silver being the metaphor used to represent the eternal wealth of God's heaven. The Hebrew word for glory that Solomon used in verse 35 translates to splendor or honor, which also points us to God's heaven.

The fool who chooses to ignore wisdom's call will eventually be dragged down to the pit, as we were told in Proverbs 1:12. This is Satan's retirement plan for those who choose foolishness. Nobody sets out to become a fool; it's a process that usually begins at an early age with disrespect toward parents. Romans 1:22 states, "Professing themselves to be wise, they became fools." This verse tells us a fool does not realize he is a fool. Trying to tell a fool that he is a fool is like trying to convince a drunk he has had too much to drink or the rich man that he doesn't need more money. Proverbs 2:11 told us that discretion will preserve us. This means we should continually seek God's will if we want to remain in it.

Bill Wilson summed this up nicely in the eleventh step of his twelve-step program of Alcoholics Anonymous, where he wrote, "We sought through prayer and meditation to improve our conscious contact with God, as we understood Him." Wilson also wrote, "In spiritual matters there is no neutral." He believed we are in a perpetual state of either getting closer to or further from God. It's sort of like going from point A to point B on a map—regardless of which way we go, we are either getting closer to or further from point B. The only exception to this geometrical law is if we go in a circle, which would lead us back to where we started. The circles of sin are not the road to wisdom; they're the legacy of fools.

WISDOM SPEECH EIGHT

Proverbs 4:1-9

"Hear, ye children, the instruction of a father, and attend to know understanding. For I give you good doctrine, forsake ye not my law" (Prov. 4:1-2).

Chapter four of the Proverbs builds on information already provided in the previous three chapters. One obvious difference is the opening salutation, which is "Hear my children," rather than the customary opening, "my son". Some scholars believe the greeting, "my son," was used by Solomon because he had just one son, spoken of by scripture (I Kings 14:21). If Solomon in fact had just one son, despite his having one thousand wives and concubines, it raises the question, "Did God withhold children from Solomon?" First Kings 4:11 and 4:15 lists the names of two daughters Solomon had as well, which leads some to believe the opening call to attention, "Hear, my children," simply includes the daughters, Taphath and Basemath, in addition to Solomon's only named son, Rheoboam. It would not be logical to believe a man like Solomon, who had amassed such large collections of gold, horses, chariots, ships and even exotic animals, (I Kings 10:22) would be content to have had just three children. Perhaps Solomon's reason for marrying some of his many wives was a vain attempt to increase his chances of having more children.

Another possibility is, Solomon was writing this particular proverb to encourage all Israel's young people, to honor their parents by listening to, and obeying their own parental instruction. The Proverbs can also be interpreted as instruction to parents as well, emphasizing how important it is for them to train their children according to the guidelines of God.

After the loss of her first child Solomon's mother, Bathsheba, probably did everything in her power to impress upon her only son the importance of following God's law. Having observed the result of sin within David's family, Solomon and Bathsheba were both surely aware of the need for godly parenting. Being the wisest King of Israel, he might have understood it as a matter of national security.

Verse two which reads, "For I give you good doctrine, forsake ye not my law," is basically the same message as Proverbs 1:8, which stated, "My son, hear the instruction of thy father, and forsake not the law of thy mother". The word, doctrine, refers to an established belief system that promotes an organized system of life instruction.

Solomon addresses the children of chapter four as if they are older now, probably in their late teens or early twenties. Some verses of the fourth chapter remind the young students to remember what they had previously been taught, as Solomon will begin to quote what his father had taught him, in the next verse. This gives the young emerging adults of Israel a powerful example to follow when the wisest king of Israel is still humble enough to quote his own father. Perhaps the greatest example of humility is that of Jesus Christ Himself—who quoted his own human ancestors from the Old Testament, during His short ministry on planet earth.

It is wise for young adults to honor the moral and spiritual values which are handed down to them by their mothers and fathers. Proper parenting is a vital requirement for not only the survival of the family, it affects the community as well, which is why government also has an interest in how children are raised. There are some children, who will benefit from government regulated child rearing—but this is only because their own parents failed to be godly parents. Research would reveal most of these sub-standard parents had sub-standard parents themselves.

"For I was my father's son, tender and only beloved in the sight of my mother. He taught me also, and said unto me, let thine heart retain my words; keep my commandments and live" (Prov. 4:3-4).

The opening phrase, of verse three, indicates a change in the relationship between Solomon and his father, David. Verse three is written in the past tense, which means David is either dead, or incapacitated, and Solomon is now king. The Bible indicates Solomon was not David's choice for king, as indicated by 1 Chronicles 29:1, *"Furthermore, David the king said unto all the congregation, Solomon my son, whom alone God hath chosen, is yet young and tender, and the work is great: for the palace is not for man, but for the Lord God"*.

We're told in the previous chapter, the assembly David was addressing included all the leaders of Israel. This was probably David's final public appearance, as he announced Solomon was taking over as king, and would be the one to build God's Temple. The first chapter of I Kings tells us Adonijah, Solomon's older half brother, thought he should be king. He had earlier proclaimed himself to be king without David's consent or knowledge. This seems to indicate David's choice for his successor was not public knowledge. If Adonijah knew Solomon had been anointed to succeed David as king, he not only was in rebellion towards David, but also towards God. How could any prince of Israel show such disrespect to both God and his own father, who had led Israel into the zenith of her history?

It cannot be determined how many people knew Solomon was chosen to be the next King of Israel, but verse thirty, of 1 Kings chapter one, tells us David had previously promised Bathsheba her son would succeed him as the next king. We're also told Nathan the Prophet knew God had chosen Solomon to be the next king—it may have even been Nathan who had informed David of God's choice. If it had not been for Nathan and Bathsheba alerting David to Adonijah's rebellion, he might have succeeded in taking control of the kingdom. It is worthy to note, Solomon did not approach his father on his own behalf. We do not know the reason for Solomon's silence, but scripture tells us it was Nathan who spoke on Solomon's behalf. Whatever the reason, let's compare the personality of a young Solomon to that of a young David. The following verses record a fearless young David convincing a scared King Saul that he would defeat the Philistine giant, Goliath, who had paralyzed Israel's entire army with fear.

> And David said unto Saul, "Thy servant kept his father's
> sheep, and there came a lion, and a bear and took a lamb
> out of the flock: And I went out after him, and smote
> him, and delivered it out of his mouth: and when he

arose against me, I caught him by his beard, and smote him and slew him. Thy servant slew both the lion and the bear: and this uncircumcised philistine shall be as one of them, seeing he hath defied the armies of the living God (I Samuel 17:34-36).

David, even as a youth, feared no mortal enemy, whereas Solomon seems to have been rather reserved, possibly even timid at this point in his life. Despite their differences, God used both of these men to do His work. Solomon may have been the least likely son David would have chosen to succeed him as king. This is why an aged King David had to publically admit Solomon was not ready to assume the duties and responsibilities of being king. He was unable to go before Israel's leaders and proclaim, "I am happy to announce I am leaving my position in the hands of a younger, stronger and very capable leader." Instead he had to admit, God alone has chosen my son Solomon, who is young and unprepared to be your next king. You leaders of Israel will have to help him learn his job because I, King David, The Giant Slayer, failed to be the father this young man deserved to have. Would it be any wonder if Solomon had already begun to write an instruction manual for parenting known as the Proverbs?

Proverbs 4:3 goes on to describe a total different relationship between Solomon and his mother by saying he was the only one in her sight. This verse describes a dedicated mother who was probably willing to do about anything to get her son on the throne. She had a powerful ally in Nathan the Prophet who was equally determined to see to it that God's choice for the next king would indeed acquire the throne. These were the people God used to ensure Solomon was Israel's third king. It was probably only after the death of his mother, before Solomon began to wander from Wisdom's narrow path, by multiplying his collections of gold women and horses.

Verse four's phrase, **"Let thine heart retain my words,"** is the same advice found in proverbs 2:2, 2:10, 3:1, 3:3 and 3:5. If you are wondering why Israel's wisest king is so repetitive in his writing—it is because he had been shown through Israel's history that men tend to become spiritually complacent, and were then vulnerable to Satan's suggestions. Solomon knew that temptation tended to shorten men's memories. This means that when our brains fail to alert us of impending doom, we require a back-up warning mechanism. As children this was a function of our parents—as adults the repetitious teaching of God's Word will enable our hearts to deliver us from temptation when our brains fail us.

"Get wisdom, get understanding: forget it not; neither decline from the words of my mouth (Prov. 4:5).

Verse five restates the thesis of Proverbs with just four words. Beginning with chapter one, we were told, "wisdom calls aloud," and chapter two said, "incline your ear to wisdom," and chapter three declared, "The wise shall inherit glory," and now we are forcefully told in chapter four; **"Get wisdom! Get understanding!"** Remember these are David's words from his quote which began in the previous verse. The New King James translation adds exclamation points to these commands; indicating four very important words being spoken loudly, probably like a military command. David also had this to say about wisdom in Psalms 51:6, *Behold, thou (God) desirest truth in the inward parts: and in the hidden part thou shall make me to know wisdom."* David is telling us honesty is a must if we are going to seek God's wisdom. He wrote this psalm after being confronted by the Prophet, Nathan, of his own dishonesty, shortly after attempting to conceal his adultery with Bathsheba.

"Forsake her not, and she shall preserve thee: love her, and she shall keep thee" (Prov. 4:6).

Verse six begins by telling us to respect wisdom by not forsaking her. Since all righteous wisdom comes from God, we're being told here again, "Do not forget about God, or his instruction." This is the moral precaution we're told to put into practice. There's also an applicable physical interpretation as well. Let's consider the biological perspective of wisdom. We need a healthy brain, if we expect to accumulate any wisdom. The human brain is an amazing piece of God's creation. Men of science have only begun to understand its intricacies. Verse six can be interpreted as saying, "Take care of your brain; do not subject it to the pollutants of sin, do not subject it to unnecessary drugs or excessive alcohol, do not feed it with the visual or the audio data of sin. Protect your brain. If you have already had a concussion, make every effort to avoid having another brain injury, because the brain is not as resilient as are most other areas of the body." Take note of what the first High Priest of Israel was told by God to say to the other Priests who were under his authority.

> And the Lord spake unto Aaron saying, "Do not drink wine nor strong drink, thou nor thy sons with thee, when ye go into the Tabernacle of the congregation, lest ye die: It shall be a statute for ever throughout your generations: And that ye may put difference between holy and unholy, and between un-clean and clean"(Leviticus 10:8-10 OKJ).

God is very clearly telling Aaron alcohol will dull the brains ability to function. God wanted his priests to be able to see and to think clearly. He wants no less for his followers today. There can be no wisdom found in a drunken mind—no discernment, no discretion and certainly no fellowship with God's Holy Spirit. God is telling us to love wisdom and to love understanding, so we can sharpen our conscious contact with Him. This is what preserves us.

The protection provided by God for the preservation of His saints is the second topic addressed by verse six. God's protection and preservation, for His chosen people, is demonstrated countless times throughout the Old Testament. God has also managed to preserve His word, the Holy Bible, despite the many prolonged attempts by Satan's workers to destroy it. God is still preserving His saints through Wisdom's instruction found in His Holy Scriptures.

God's scripture is still warning His saints of future temptation and trickery to be executed by the devil. The Apostle Paul issued the following warning two-thousand years ago, about the devil's coming antichrist. We're told he will deceive all those who choose to follow the world's counterfeit wisdom, instead of God's truth.

> The coming of the lawless one is based on Satan's working, with all kinds of false miracles, signs and wonders, and with every unrighteous deception among those who are perishing. They perish because they did not accept the

love of the truth in order to be saved. For this reason God sends them a strong delusion, so that they will believe what is false, so that all will be condemned—those who did not believe the truth but enjoyed unrighteousness (II Thessalonians 2:9-12 HCSB).

Satan is not only a liar, he is the father of all lies, and his future ambassador, the antichrist, who is referred to here, in 2 Thessalonians as "the lawless one," will be a master of deception. When the antichrist appears, he will only be recognized by those who have a sober mind that is familiar with God's words. America has already embraced an educational system which encourages children to doubt the validity of God's Holy Scripture. This has resulted in a growing number of unbelievers among America's youth, who will not be able to recognize Satan's top recruiter, the antichrist, when he arrives.

If you are wondering, "How such a man will gain so much control," we are warned by Paul, in 2 Thessalonians, the people will be sent a "strong delusion, causing them to believe the lie." Solomon and David knew nothing about the coming anti-Christ, but they both did know the importance of inner honesty. They knew that without inner honesty and truthfulness, there could be no fellowship with God. No fellowship means there's no leadership to follow, which means we are on our own to battle an enemy who has had six thousand years of experience in diverting men and women from God's truth.

"Wisdom is the principal thing; therefore get wisdom: and with all thy getting get understanding" (Prov. 4:7).

The Holman Christian Standard Bible substitutes the word, supreme thing, to describe wisdom; making wisdom the highest priority. We have already learned from Proverbs 2:6 (HCSB), "The Lord gives wisdom; from His mouth come knowledge and understanding." The Hebrew word used by David, to describe wisdom, was ***reshith***, which means first in place time or rank. First in time takes us back to the very beginning, which is Genesis 1:1, when God created the heaven and the earth. God was not only the builder, He was the master architect of His creation. Prior to the creation of His heaven and earth, God's wisdom was already in existence. It was God's wisdom that laid the foundations of the earth and determined its measurements (Job 38:4-5) and (Prov. 3:19). Solomon has already told us how valuable wisdom is—now, through David's words, he is emphasizing absolutely nothing is more important.

"Exalt her, and she shall promote thee: she shall bring thee to honour when thou dost embrace her" (Prov. 4:8).

Remember, this is still a continuation of David's early instruction to Solomon which began in verse four. Most of the modern translations indicate this with Quotation marks, while the Old King James does not. When David said, "Exalt her," he used the Hebrew word, ***calal,*** which means to raise up. God always wants to raise His children up spiritually. Being His children, it is then our job to reciprocate, by raising Him up for those around us to see. We do this through worship, by praying, and studying His words. We also do this through our obedience to His perfect will, which will result in our being promoted, as we are told here in verse eight.

He might promote you to being a father or a mother, or better yet, eventually a grandfather or grandmother. His promotion could be in the form of a spiritual gift. First Corinthians, chapter twelve is an excellent source of information about spiritual gifts, with verse seven saying the Spirit of God is manifested in each one of us—which means every child of God has at least one spiritual gift. We exalt Him by being a faithful example of Godly wisdom to all those who observe our actions, hear our words and sense our thoughts and motivations. If we are inwardly in pursuit of selfish accomplishments, people around us can usually pick up on that. The Lord considers our motives along with our thoughts, words and actions, which are all taken into an account by our Lord, before we are honored as Proverbs 4:8 says we can be.

David's words, spoken to Solomon in verse eight, were also a prophecy, which was soon fulfilled, as confirmed in 2 Chronicles 1:8-12 (HCSB). God promoted Solomon with greater wisdom, wealth and understanding than any other king of Israel.

And Solomon said to God: "You have shown great and faithful love to my father David, and You have made me king in his place. Lord God, let Your promise, to my father David now come true. For You have made me king over a people as numerous as the dust of the earth. Now grant me wisdom and knowledge so that I may lead these people, for who can judge this great people of Yours?" God said to Solomon, "Since this was in your heart, and you have not requested riches, wealth, or glory, or for the life of those who hate you, and you have not even requested long life, but you have requested for yourself wisdom and knowledge that you may judge My people over whom I have made you king, wisdom and knowledge are given to you. I will also give you riches, wealth, and glory, unlike what was given to the kings who were before you, or will be given to those after you."

Both David, who instructed his children to embrace and exalt wisdom, and Solomon, who wrote David's words for the following generations to benefit from, are telling us what God had done for them. David and Solomon were both magnificently promoted. We are given a marvelous opportunity to be blessed, as they were; because we are given the very same set of Divine instructions—**Get Wisdom! Get Understanding!**

"She shall give to thine head an ornament of grace: a crown of glory shall she deliver to thee" (Prov. 4:9).

Verse nine reminds the reader of what was earlier stated in **proverbs 1:8-9**, which also promised an ornament of grace as a reward for obedience. David is saying in verse nine to a young Solomon that wisdom is the true source of life's rewards. The collective promise of the Proverbs is all children who are fortunate enough to receive godly instruction at an early age, and are obedient to their parent's instruction, and then as adults go on to obey the instruction of God's word will eventually receive a crown of glory. This verse can be interpreted as a prophecy describing what all true followers of Christ, who remain loyal to the end, will receive in heaven as we are told in Revelation 2:10 (HCSB). *"Don't be afraid of what you are about to suffer. Look, the devil is about to throw some of you into prison to test you, and you will have affliction for ten days. Be faithful until death, and I will give you the crown of life."*

David's words, from chapter four of Proverbs, and God's words, as given to John in the second chapter of Revelation, are just as true and just as applicable today as they were on the day they were spoken. We have been warned of a coming satanic storm, and we have been instructed how to be saved from that storm. We're told many will perish, so we are expected to help others to be prepared as well. It requires a sober mind filled with wisdom and understanding, for this mission from God to be accomplished. Then we can expect to hear Him say, "Enter in thou good and faithful servant."

WISDOM SPEECH NINE

Proverbs 4:10–19

"Hear, O my son, and receive my sayings; and the years of thy life shall be many. I have taught thee in the way of wisdom; I have led thee in right paths" (Proverbs 4:10–11).

Verse ten expands upon the same promise found in Proverbs 3:1–2, where Solomon told us, "My son, don't forget my teaching, but let your heart keep my commands; for they will bring you many days, a full life, and well being" (HCSB). Solomon advised his young student in chapter three to remember what he was taught so he could profit from the practice of obedience, as taught through godly parental instruction. Verse ten reminds the now-older student that his obedience will be rewarded with longevity. Verse 11 then follows by declaring he has not only been told what to do, but he has been shown what to do as well by having been led "in right paths."

Solomon is claiming to have set a proper example for his student to follow. We must assume this verse was written early in Solomon's life, prior to his fall from God's will. First Kings 11:4 tells us how Solomon's heart was turned from God in his later years by his foreign wives. No father can talk the talk without first walking the walk. He could no longer make a claim of righteousness to his only named son, Rehoboam, or to any other student of wisdom after his heart had been turned from God.

"When thou goest, thy steps shall not be straitened; and when thou runnest, thou shalt not stumble" (Proverbs 4:12).

Verse 12 continues the thought of verse twenty-three, from the third chapter which said, "Then you will go safely on your way; your foot will not stumble" (HCSB). God does not want us to falter. He always wants to strengthen us when we walk, or even run in His way. He makes things easier for us in ways we are often un-aware of. David wrote in Psalms 18:36, *"Thou hast enlarged my steps under me, that my feet did not slip."* There were probably numerous occasions in David's life where he experienced Divine help while fleeing from his enemies. When writing this psalm, David probably remembered some of those situations, and may have wondered, "How did I ever climb that cliff, or jump over that creek without stumbling?" Verse twelve not only assures us we will be helped, it tells us how we will be helped. God will help us the same way He helped David elude King Saul and his 3000 man army for approximately twelve years.

"Take fast hold of instruction; let her not go: keep her; for she is thy life" (Proverbs 4:13).

Verse 13 is the key verse for chapter four. The language used here in the King James Version is easy to understand—it plainly tells us that successful living depends upon our understanding and following wise instruction. This verse can be considered a universal truth or natural law; it can be applied in the physical or spiritual plane. It's true for the old or the young, for the wise or the simple, for the Christian or the pagan. It was true in the garden of Eden, and it will be true in the valley of Armageddon when Christ comes back to rule and reign. The recognition, understanding, and obedience to wise instruction will result in better health, peace of mind, and, in most cases, prosperity.

The New King James Version tells us to take a firm hold, rather than a fast hold, as seen here in the Old King James Version. The verbs firm and fast imply we should not delay in getting good instruction, and once we get it, we then must make every effort to keep it. This is the same message given earlier in Proverbs 4:5, where it shouts, **Get Wisdom! Get Understanding!**

These are the first exclamation points used in the New King James translation of Solomon's proverbs, indicating just how important these verses are for expressing the purpose and the power of Solomon's message. These two short sentences, consisting of only four words and two exclamation points, provide us the *mission statement* of Solomon's proverbs.

The Hebrew word *tsuwm* is what the King James Version translated as *fast*. Surprisingly, it means to cover over the mouth. Tsuwm was the word used in the Old Testament era for the Hebrew ritual of fasting. It takes a serious commitment and a lot of determination for an individual to go without food. Fasting is a means of learning how to discipline our biological urges. Hunger is an instinct with a necessary purpose—it helps to keep us alive by telling us when to eat. When used properly, our hunger instinct can guide us to consume the specific type of nutrition our body needs at a given time. When used improperly, it will cause us to consume unhealthy food, which eventually will cause a multitude of problems, beginning with obesity and then on to more serious conditions, such as diabetes or heart disease. Our instincts are God-given but can be manipulated by Satan to distract us from God's will for our lives. This is why we are instructed to take a fast hold of wisdom. We are being encouraged to hold on to wisdom with the same mental discipline as a person who is fasting or with the strength and determination of a rodeo cowboy taking hold of the saddle. This is how we prepare for any situation, good or bad, that God allows into our lives.

"Enter not into the path of the wicked, and go not in the way of evil men. Avoid it, pass not by it, turn from it, and pass away" (Proverbs 4:14–15).

Victorious Christian living depends upon the continual maintenance of our spiritual condition. God expects His children to take the high road in order to remain in His will. This is how we stay within His hedge of protection and away from the pit mentioned in chapter one. In addition to being the future home of Satan and his followers, the pit can represent a state of mind or spiritual status right here on planet earth. Solomon kept this passage simple and direct in an effort to alert Israel's young people to the reality of sin's various pits, whether it's as obvious as the pit of rebellion or as subtle as the pit of depression. Even wise people sometimes have difficulty recognizing when they are approaching the edge of the pit, especially when satanically distracted. David, in the first psalm, informs his readers how important it is to avoid those who hang out around the edge of the pit.

Blessed is the man that walketh not in the counsel of the ungodly, nor standeth in the way of sinners, nor sitteth in the seat of the scornful. But his delight is in the law of the Lord; and in His law doth he meditate day and night. And he shall be like a tree planted by the rivers of water, that bringeth forth his fruit in his season, his leaf also shall not wither; and whatsoever he doeth shall prosper. The ungodly are not so: but are like the chaff which the wind driveth away. (Psalm 1:1–4)

These beautifully written words can inspire even a rebellious soul to turn from evil. My own earthly father had some very direct words about hanging out with the "people of the pit." His crude language, which would offend some people, cannot be quoted directly, but let it be understood that his personalized version of Solomon's and David's warnings was very easy to remember by everyone who heard it. His words lack the beauty of the first psalm, but they were very effective. His mid-twentieth–century country vernacular compared the social interaction with the sons of sin to making physical contact with biological waste produced in the solid state of matter. Dad's words were fewer and more direct; let's just say his opinion was that whatever you played with, *it* would get on you! In the simple words of Hollywood's Forrest Gump, *"It happens."*

If you agree my earthly father's unprintable words were probably offensive, this is good because that means you should be able to understand how our heavenly Father feels about sin. It's ugly, it's diseased, and it stinks! In our physical world, it takes a lot of effort and disinfectant to clean up a dung heap. In the spiritual realm, the only solvent for sin is the blood of Christ. It will cover that ugly, stinking sin mess and separate it from your spirit, as far as the east is from the west. In the eyes of God, it will render your soul as white as snow and as smooth as silk. We, as Christians, have so much to be thankful for.

"For they sleep not, except they have done mischief; and their sleep is taken away, unless they cause some to fall. For they eat the bread of wickedness, and drink the wine of violence" (Proverbs 4:16–17).

Verse 16 reminds us of another reason to be grateful for what God does for us. We have all, at one time or another, had trouble getting to sleep when we can't quiet our minds. Solomon is telling us there is a type of sinner who enjoys sin so much that he or she cannot get a good night's sleep without committing enough sin to satisfy his or her fallen nature. We're told that a lack of sin can cause a habitual sinner physical withdrawal symptoms, similar to those of an addict needing a fix. Hitler was probably this type of sinner. The coming Antichrist will be as well. He will be so full of Lucifer's wickedness he will probably never sleep, which will enable him to promote evil twenty-four hours a day. What a contrast this is to the child of God who is assured by Solomon, "When you lie down, you will not be afraid; you will lie down and your sleep will be pleasant" (Proverbs 3:24 HCSB).

Verse 17 uses the metaphors "the bread of wickedness" and the "wine of violence." Bread is the translation for the Hebrew word *lechem*. This word appears over a hundred times in the Old Testament, and it always means the same thing—bread. This verse describes a type of sinner who is literally dependent on evil. God hates all sin, but wickedness refers to evil acts that are especially vile in nature. Like bread nourishing the physical body, wickedness nourishes the dark spirituality of this type of sinner. This type of sinner is demonically possessed. These sinners think they're in control—but they're not. Satan is their lord and master, and they may not even know it; they are Satan's slaves who enthusiastically promote his dark kingdom.

The "wine of violence" is a special treat for these corrupt people. Unlike the word bread, the word wine is translated from nine different Hebrew words in the Old Testament. The Hebrew word *yayin,* used in verse 17, refers to intoxication or banqueting. We are being told that those who are this wrapped up in Satan's will take extra delight in violence. They enjoy it so much they are infatuated or intoxicated by it. Solomon warned us of this dangerous type of sinner in chapter one. "If they say—come with us! Let's set an ambush and kill someone. Let's attack some innocent person just for fun! Let's swallow them alive, like Sheol, still healthy as they go down to the Pit" (Proverbs1:11–12 HCSB).

"But the path of the just is as the shining light, that shineth more and more unto the perfect day. The way of the wicked is as darkness: they know not at what they stumble" (Proverbs 4:18–19).

Light and darkness represent good and evil throughout the Bible. Jesus tells us plainly He is the light of the world in John chapter three. Next to Genesis 1:1, John 3:16 might be the most commonly known verse in the Bible. This single verse gives its readers a condensed yet very precise instruction on how to receive eternal life. John refers his readers to the grace provided to all humankind by the Son of God. The verses following John 3:16 go on to explain that the "light," who is none other than Jesus Christ, produces an awareness that forces men to choose between good and evil.

> For God so loved the world, that He gave His only begotten son, that whosoever believeth in Him should not perish but have everlasting life. For God sent not His Son into the world to condemn the world; but that the world through Him might be saved. He that believeth on Him is not condemned: but he that believeth not is condemned already, because he has not believed in the name of the only begotten Son of God. And this is the condemnation, that light is come into the world, and men loved darkness rather than light, because their deeds were evil. For every one that doeth evil hateth the light, neither cometh to the light, lest his deeds should be reproved. But he that doeth truth cometh to the light, that his deeds may be made manifest, that they are wrought in God. (John 3:16–21)

God has no problem with full disclosure of His plan for us because He knows the future. Satan only thinks he knows the future. Our heavenly Father, however, does seem to limit His explanation of spiritual matters to those who still exist in the physical world, as Jesus explains to Nicodemus in John 3:12. The darkness of sin in the physical world, referred to in verse 19, is what prevents the natural man from understanding the spiritual truths Jesus spoke of to Nicodemus. The more time we spend in the light, the greater our capacity for understanding spiritual concepts. With enough exposure, we begin to absorb that light, and it will saturate our inner persons—our souls and our spirits. This is what happens when we accept the Lord Jesus Christ as our God and personal Savior. Through this spiritual connection, we then become a part of that light, of which our Lord spoke to Nicodemus and as we are told in Matthew 5:14–16: *"Ye are the light of the world. A city that is set on a hill cannot be hid. Neither do men light a candle, and put it under a bushel, but on a candlestick; and it giveth light unto all that are in the house. Let your light so shine before men, that they may see your good works, and glorify your Father which is in heaven."*

In Revelation 1:20, John reveals a vision of seven lamp stands. He is told in his vision that the lamp stands represent the seven churches of Asia Minor. God then gave him messages for each of those seven churches. The first church was the Church of Ephesus, which was located on the west coast of what is now Turkey. It was the Roman capital of Asia Minor and was where John spent his last years before being exiled to the Isle of Patmos, where he received God's revelation. This church was well known to John. It had to have saddened him to deliver this rebuke from God. This warning is recorded in Revelation 2:1–7, and verse 5 reads, *"Remember then how far you have fallen; repent, and do the works you did at first. Otherwise, I will come to you and remove your lampstand from its place—unless you repent"* (HCSB).

The Church of Ephesus obviously had strayed from wisdom's path, and this was going to result in their light being put out. The absence of light allows for the presence of darkness, which is the way of the wicked, as Solomon states in Proverbs 4:19. He also says in part B of verse 19, *"They know not at what they stumble."* God will provide complete disclosure, whereas Satan wants to run a covert operation. It is Satan's hidden agenda that causes us to stumble when we have lost our lamp stand. Satan's happiest moments might very well be when a man blames God for his falling and then curses God for others to hear.

Such a man would perfectly fit the description of verse 19. People who curse God cannot do so and still be in the light. Having no light, they cannot see truth, so therefore they know not what makes them stumble. The choice is obvious. We can choose to walk in God's light, or we can remain in the ignorance of hell's darkness.

WISDOM SPEECH TEN

Proverbs 4:20–27

"My son, attend to my words; Incline thine ear unto my sayings. Let them not depart from thine eyes; keep them in the midst of thine heart. For they are life unto those that find them, and health to all their flesh" (Proverbs 4:20–22).

Verse 20 opens with Solomon's traditional call to attention. He is repeating the same advice earlier issued. "My son, if thou wilt receive my words, and hide my commands with thee; So that thou incline thine ear unto wisdom, and apply thine heart to understanding" (Proverbs 2:1–2). This was appropriate advice for the student of chapter two The difference in Proverbs 4 is that the young student is older now and is being told to not let wisdom's words depart from his eyes. Solomon is urging his student to review what he has been taught by rereading his lessons. A twenty-first–century Christian father could follow Solomon's example by telling his children, "When you leave my house and are out on your own, I urge you to continue reading the Bible so God's truth will always be in the center of your heart throughout your lifetime."

Solomon wanted wisdom's precepts in the center of the young man's heart, not just in his conscious mind. This is where it needs to be; it needs to be ingrained deeply into our innermost being, as suggested by the Old King James phrase, *"Keep them in the midst of thine heart."* This is where items of value belong so they can be guarded from those who wish to separate us from our spiritual treasures. You may recall Proverbs 2:4 compared wisdom to silver and hidden treasure. Wisdom and understanding of God's words are the gateway for all of His blessings, as He told Moses in the book of Deuteronomy.

> So keep the command—the statutes, and ordinances—
> that I am giving you to follow today. If you listen to and
> are careful to keep these ordinances, the Lord your God
> will keep His covenant loyalty with you, as He swore to
> your fathers. He will love you, bless you, and multiply
> you. He will bless your descendants, and the produce of
> your land—your grain, new wine, and oil—the young of
> your herds and the newborn of your flocks, in the land He
> swore to your fathers that He would give you. You will be
> blessed above all peoples; there will be no infertile male or a
> female among you or your livestock. The Lord will remove
> all sickness from you; He will not put on you all the terrible
> diseases of Egypt that you know about, but He will inflict
> them on all who hate you. (Deuteronomy 7:11–15 HCSB)

Life, by divine design, becomes busier and more complex as we progress through the stages of our human development. The young man Solomon is now addressing may have had a wife and children, who would be very dear to his heart. He may have owned a business and had friends with whom he also was involved. These are all favorable things we want our children to have, but God does not want possessions and accomplishments to displace His words of wisdom from our hearts. Solomon steadily yet slowly continues to expand on his instruction but not without extensive review. He now begins the warnings pertaining to the pits of sin that young adults are most likely to encounter. Busy lives can produce profits, but they also tend to distract us from God's words and God's people. Satan will make it easy for us to think we're too busy to take time for prayer and the reading of God's Word.

When young people have been married long enough to take their spouses for granted, a whole new set of temptations come into play. It's easy for one spouse to become emotionally or physically needy if responsibilities consume more of the other spouse's time and energy. This is when extramarital sex, drugs, or alcohol can become a real temptation.

These types of temptations can quickly escalate into satanic traps, which seem to offer an escape from whatever reality with which a person is unhappy. Sex without the benefit of marriage will be the dominant topic of the next three chapters. These final eight verses of chapter four are designed to get their readers into tip-top spiritual condition before Satan throws his favorite age- and situation-appropriate temptations into the paths of God's young men and women.

"Keep thy heart with all diligence; for out of it are the issues of life" (Proverbs 4:23).

The Hebrew word used in verse 23 for heart is *leb*. The definitions associated with this word are feelings, the will, and the intellect. It was also used to refer to the center of an object, which is where God wants His words to be—in the midst of every human's heart. This verse is urging its reader to maintain the spiritual integrity spoke of in the three previous verses. The word diligence refers to the standards that are expected or required. After four chapters of instruction, Solomon assumes his young student knows by now what is expected of him. The Hebrew word for diligence is *mishmar,* which means to guard or protect. It could also refer to a prison or a ward. When God's wisdom has been acquired and placed in the midst of our hearts, as verse 21 instructs us to do, we are then to keep it there and guard it as if it were a prisoner.

The "issues of life" referred to in verse 23 are normally thought of as debatable or unsettled points of controversy. An issue can also be thought of as a matter ready for a decision. If a matter has become an issue, it is then deemed to be of importance. If our hearts are filled with God's words and God's wisdom, then we would possess a very similar or in some cases, even identical concept of what God considers to be an issue. This type of knowledge, followed by appropriate action, is what makes a human Christ like. As a Christian grows in knowledge and commitment, her or his issues and priorities will be rearranged in the order of importance, according to what God deems they should be.

"Put away from thee a froward mouth, and perverse lips put far from thee" (Proverbs 4:24).

Solomon had not yet mentioned a deceitful—or, as the King James Version puts it, a "froward"—mouth, but he did speak of discretion in Proverbs 2:11. Discretion was defined as the ability to adapt our conduct and speech appropriately to match our given situations and circumstances. If we are talking about "issues of life," as in the previous verse, it is every Christian's responsibility to talk diligently—or probably not talk at all. The last thing a child of God should want to do is to be deceitful. The second phrase of verse 24 is telling us we not only want to avoid speaking deceit, but we should not want to listen to it either. Our words are a window into our souls from which others will judge us. The same also can be said for the words we are known to listen to. In an effort to increase the ability of our being effective ambassadors for Christ, we will want to close our ears, our minds, and especially our hearts to all perversities a carnal human may consider legitimate issues.

"Let thine eyes look right on, and let thine eyelids look straight before thee" (Proverbs 4:25).

Ayin is the Hebrew word for eyes, as used in Proverbs 4:25. It can have a literal or figurative meaning in the Hebrew language. Like our mouths, the eyes can provide insight to what our hearts feel. *Ayin* can refer to one's countenance or appearance. When God asked Cain, *"Why has your countenance fallen"* in Genesis 4:6, it is most probable that Cain's eyes were a major contributor for what God was referring to. It's doubtful he was looking to God with clarity and truthfulness in his eyes when addressed by Him. *Ayin* can also be interpreted as a fountain. The Hebrew word for fountain has various meanings that can include a flow of water, tears, blood, wisdom, or happiness. Most of these definitions for *Ayin* can make sense when applied to this proverb, but the literal meaning (countenance or appearance) is the one that agrees best with part B of this verse. If the meaning of this verse were applied in today's society to a young married man, it might go something like this: "Thou shalt not twist thy neck to eyeball the pretty girl wearing the tiny bikini." Such behavior not only affects how others view Christians and Christianity, but it also determines the type of data we are feeding our brains. Satan seemingly has an unlimited number of devices from which he can choose to distract us.

Their sole purpose is to distract us from the direction where God wants our attention to be.

"Ponder the path of thy feet, and let all thy ways be established" (Proverbs 4:26).

The Hebrew word for ponder is *palace*. Its meanings include to roll flat, to revolve, or to weigh mentally. Both King James Versions seem to favor the "weigh mentally" definition. Given the previous verse's instruction to look straight ahead, it would seem the "walker" in verse 26 would be freed from distraction, which would allow him or her to enjoy having conscious contact with God while walking. The walker's ways would then be aligned with the will of God. The New International Version seems to support the "roll flat" definition, as it reads, "Make level paths for your feet and take only ways that are firm." The level paths are still referring to God's ways—the NIV is just describing them from a different perspective. Part B of the New International Version also supports the "roll flat" definition by saying, "Take only ways that are firm." The flattened path would more likely be the dry or firm one, as the flattening process should eliminate any potholes or ditches. The firm or flattened path would also be the one that reduces the "walker's" chances of falling into any pits, of which we have been warned repeatedly.

"Turn not to the right hand, nor the left: remove thy foot from evil" (Proverbs 4:27).

Solomon concludes this important tenth wisdom speech with words very similar to Deuteronomy 28:14. *"Do not turn aside to the right or the left from all the things I am commanding you today, and do not go after other Gods to worship them"* (HCSB). One cannot help but wonder just how much of an impact on history it would have made if Solomon had remained obedient to his own instruction for the entirety of his life. We know from the book of Genesis that God knew man's heart was continually evil and that it would require His Son to defeat the sin disease caused by Satan. Had Solomon remained loyal to God's wisdom, and his writings had successfully inspired the following generations of Israel to remain loyal to

God's law, just imagine what a difference that could have made for all of humankind.

Had Jesus found an obedient Israel instead of a nation defeated by sin, he might have began to immediately be their king; which theoretically could have ushered in the thousand-year reign, as described by the Old Testament prophets. This would have eliminated all the suffering Israel and all other nations have had to endure since the crucifixion. The high cost of low living is immeasurable. It required a cost that only God could repay. It's ironic that this immense debt began to accumulate with one seemingly insignificant garden temptation.

Solomon realized temptation usually begins with what the eyes observe. We cannot shield our eyes from all evil unless we enter into complete seclusion. This not only would be impractical, but it would be un-Christian as well. Solomon later wrote, *"One who isolates himself pursues selfish desires; he rebels against all sound judgment"* (Proverbs 18:1 HCSB). Christians are the light of the world—as we already learned when discussing Proverbs 4:18. Hiding our light is not only selfish, but it is sinful as well. We are commissioned to spread God's Word, and we cannot do this unless Proverbs 4:27 is the path we follow. Keeping our eyes on God's Word needs to be an ongoing lifetime commitment for all who want to share in God's blessing. This is how we keep our feet on the solid path of wisdom and righteousness, while avoiding the pits of temptation.

WISDOM SPEECH ELEVEN

Proverbs 5:1–23

The main topic of Proverbs chapter five is sex. It's been said God must have a sense of humor because of His having invented sex, but chapter five does not support that conclusion. What it does teach is that an improper response to the human sex instinct can be a life-changing event. Solomon briefly discussed the "seductress" in chapter two when he warned the young man, "Her house sinks down to death" (Proverbs 2:18 HCSB), and "None return who go to her" (Proverbs 2:19 HCSB). These verses were adequate warnings to discourage the curiosity of an inexperienced preteen or teenager whose virginity was still intact, but an older, more experienced young man will require much more instruction.

When young people ponder if they should continue maintaining their sexual purity or whether it's time to experiment," they are still dealing with an unknown. One's first sexual experience is often accompanied with considerable anxiety. This is especially true for those who are not following biblical instruction. Young people who are having sex without the benefit of marriage are committing fornication and will experience an immediate spiritual vacuum after committing sexual sin. This is God's Holy Spirit telling them, "You have sinned, so I must withdraw My presence until you repent of your sin." Those who exercise restraint long enough to have a proper courtship and learn how to love each other first will experience the joy of complete love, as God intended it to be, instead of the guilt caused by immorality.

If a young person does give in to sexual temptation, it will then be easier for him or her to do a second and even a third time. Sex, much like that first drink of alcohol or that first cigarette, may not begin as a pleasant experience, but it gets easier and eventually enjoyable with practice. Once people are comfortable with a specific sin, especially a sin as addictive as sex, Satan has penetrated their spiritual hedge of protection. Young Christians who have maintained their virginity are the ones who will benefit the most from God's hedge of protection, thus rendering Satan unable to inflict his full arsenal of sexual temptations. Sexual temptation is biologically aligned with our God-given reproductive instincts, which are responsible for the strongest urges most young males will ever experience. Sexual urges must be properly moderated if they are going to serve their God-intended purposes. What else is there to cause young people to put up with all the inconveniences and formalities of a proper courtship? Why else would a young man make the effort to learn social etiquette or how to dance? How else would the human race continue to flourish?

Chapter five addresses an older, sexually experienced young man who is probably in his mid-twenties by now. This claim is based on later verses; which inform us the young man is married, yet has become sexually interested in a woman other than his wife. Psychological research has discovered sexual fantasies and dreams have a prominent presence in the human mind. It is not abnormal for a sexual thought or urge to pop up in our consciousness, but it is sin if we choose to continually dwell on such thoughts. Sustained impure thoughts will usually lead to suggestive words, which will reveal our lust to whomever we are communicating with. This is how it begins; if allowed to go unchecked, seductive words often lead to seductive actions. Sexual thoughts, seductive words, and intimate physical contact all serve a legitimate purpose, once a heterosexual couple has made a lifetime vow before God to spend the rest of their natural lives together as one flesh.

For some reason, which is not explained in scripture, God allowed men in ancient Israel to acquire multiple wives when these urges surfaced. God instructed Moses to have Israel's army kill all the males of a conquered nation, while allowing the females to live. This practice allowed for an abundance of available women.

> When you approach a city to fight against it, you must make an offer of peace. If it accepts your offer of peace, and opens its gates to you, all the people found in it will become forced laborers for you, and serve you. However,

if it does not make peace with you, but wages war against you, lay siege to it. When the Lord your God hands it over to you, you must strike down all its males with the sword. But you may take the women, children, animals, and whatever else is in the city—all its spoil—as plunder. You may enjoy the spoil of your enemies that the Lord your God has given you. (Deuteronomy 20:10–14 HCSB)

Other surrounding pagan nations also took female captives. Later, in the following chapter, God gave Israel additional instruction for the lawful treatment of female captives.

When you go out to war against your enemies and the Lord your God hands them over to you and you take some of them prisoner, and if you see a beautiful woman among the captives, desire her, and want to take her as your wife, you are to bring her into your house. She must shave her head, trim her nails, remove the clothes she was wearing when she was taken prisoner, live in your house, and mourn for her father and mother a full month. After that you may have sexual relations with her and be her husband and she will be your wife. Then if you are not satisfied with her, you are to let her go where she wants, but you must not sell her for money or treat her as merchandise, because you have humiliated her. (Deuteronomy 21:10–14 HCSB)

There are additional laws found in Deuteronomy 21 concerning the treatment of unmarried female slaves. The first mention of polygamy is found in Genesis four, when Lamech took for himself two wives. Polygamy seems to have been common throughout the Old Testament among men who had the ability to support multiple wives. Beginning in the New Testament, the apostle Paul taught that bishops should have only one wife (1 Timothy 3:2). If God had wanted men to have multiple wives, why did He create only one wife for Adam? It cannot be denied that God allowed men to have multiple wives, but God also requires his followers to obey the law of the land. Few countries today allow for multiple wives; those that do are openly hostile toward Christianity. Multiple wives are no longer an option for a Christian sexually unfulfilled young man.

Today's multimedia society surrounds us with sexually explicit material, making it virtually impossible for young adults not to be influenced by advertised sexuality. Those who have no real biblical knowledge will think the media's moral standards are perfectly acceptable. The message "It's okay to have sex as long as a condom is used" will erode any sexual restraint that young, emerging adults should exercise. How will God judge a nation whose government and media promote sex outside of marriage? Is it really any wonder that the majority of marriages in twenty-first–century America end in divorce?

Young Christians need to be taught and then encouraged to pray for strength to remain sexually pure, instead of being given a free condom. They should be praying not only for themselves but also for their future spouses, whom they may or may not have met yet. Prayer, followed by meditation and obedience, will provide assurance that God has already created the right spouses exclusively for them. Regular prayer will also help young Christians to know: when to work and when to rest, when to speak up and when to remain silent, when to indulge and when to abstain. Solomon devotes two entire chapters, Proverbs five and seven, plus the last twelve verses of chapter six, to the topic of sex, so he must have considered it one of the greatest—if not the single greatest threat—to his young student's success.

The pertinent question that Solomon failed to address is, "How are young adolescents and especially unmarried Christian men supposed to relieve themselves of the biological need for a release of their reproductive fluids without committing fornication?" Masturbation is an issue on which Proverbs—in fact, the entire Bible—seems to be silent, but it's one that parents need to address. Because of the Bible's silence, I am unable to answer with certainty the question, "Is masturbation a sin?" It has been my observation that the same Christian parents of the past generation, who complained about sex education being taught in the public schools, were just like Solomon, in that many of them failed to address this awkward question with their own sons—the very ones who were given to them by God and for whom they are responsible to teach and to train.

Masturbation is not the only topic the Bible fails to address, but it may be the only one that religions, theologians, and, yes, even authors want to avoid discussing. It is not un-heard of for high-profile biblical speakers to publically confess sins such as adultery, robbery, and even murder, but have you ever read or heard the confession of a habitual masturbator? It is much more common for a forgiven sinner to admit having committed an ego-driven sin that caused harmful and sometimes even irreversible effects on innocent bystanders than it is to hear the humble confession of a masturbator who has never committed adultery, never beaten a child or woman, or ever made a drunken public spectacle of himself while in pursuit of a harlot's approval.

The Bible does give us a general guideline to follow; we are told to shun the very appearance of evil. Some sincere and dedicated Christians have interpreted this biblical principle as forbidding the consumption of alcohol, while eating their way to obesity or possibly even a diabetic coma. It obviously cannot be a sin to eat because our bodies require nutrition. The Bible may not tell me that I can't drink a beer, but being a recovering alcoholic who has not had a drink in thirty years, I can be certain it would be a sin for me (or any other recovering alcoholic) to belly up to the bar and order a cold one. Being a delivered alcoholic, I lost my privilege to enjoy a cold beer a long time ago. Common sense must prevail!

These are the same principles that need to be applied to sexual activities. For example, it is not sinful for a sick person to stay in bed all day, but it is sin for a healthy person to refuse to get out of bed when it's time to go to work. It is my conviction that lengthy or daily masturbation is sinful. The sole purpose of masturbation is identical to that of a laxative or an enema—it's to be used sparingly and *very discreetly* for the release of excess biological materials manufactured by the human body. The divine architect of our human bodies did provide for the biological release of the male reproductive fluids without any mechanical assistance, but to wait for a natural expulsion of semen can rob a young man of many hours' sleep, plus have a dominating influence on his overall thought patterns. God gave us our urges and instincts for necessary biological purposes—they are not a curse.

The production of semen begins with adolescence and continues every day for the rest of a man's life. Females are different; they are born with all of their reproductive eggs, and when they are all used, that's it—no more eggs are produced by the female body. Beginning with adolescence, human eggs are released into the womb from the ovaries, usually one at a time about once a month. Young girls need to know what is happening in their adolescent bodies prior to that first reproductive egg being released to avoid any potential embarrassing situations. It is easy for parents to procrastinate on this sensitive topic, but human physiology does not wait for reluctant parents. Children are maturing quicker than they used to do. It is not unusual for a girl to experience her first menstrual cycle when just eleven years old.

Boys, just like girls, will experience a release of their reproductive cells but by a different means. When the male body has produced and reached its limit of storage capacity for semen, it will then release some of that semen by means of a "wet dream." This, in addition to some sperm cells being reabsorbed by the body are nature's way of accommodating the male body producing as many as two hundred million sperm cells per day. An adolescent male's first wet dream will probably not be nearly as traumatic as an adolescent female's first period, but this does not excuse a father from informing his son about what is going to happen to his body. Men are known for being more uncomfortable talking about these matters than are women. If this is the case, get your son an appropriate book and make sure he understands it. Have the "talk" after he reads the book, and if he can't answer questions about human sexuality, make him read it again. If necessary, read it to him until he understands he will be held responsible for where his seed is sown.

Ignorance about sex does not constitute sexual purity. One advantage provided by modern America's sexually open culture is there are books, written by Christian authors, who teach the proper spiritual, social, and biological perspectives of human sexuality. Given modern America's politically correct attitudes and laws concerning sex, especially homosexuality, it is more important than ever for young people to learn from a scripturally compliant source of information.

If you are a young person who is being exposed to this information for the first time and are still reluctant to discuss these matters with one or both of your parents, then I urge you to ask them. It is perfectly normal to feel uncomfortable discussing these matters, especially the first time. If you, for some reason, are unable to talk with a parent, seek a trusted older brother or sister in Christ with whom you can feel comfortable talking confidentially. Do not rely solely on random information you may have already heard from other inexperienced adolescents.

"My son, attend unto my wisdom, and bow thine ear to my understanding: that thou mayest regard discretion, and that thy lips may keep knowledge" (Proverbs 5:1–2).

Verse one begins by telling the young student how to regard discretion and knowledge. The Hebrew word *shamar* is translated to *regard* by the King James Version of the Bible. Its definitions also include: "to put a hedge about, take heed, look narrowly, or to preserve." The Holman Christian Standard Bible translates shamar with the English word maintain, which implies that discretion and knowledge has already been accessed, but his teacher now shows concern for the possibility of future indiscretions. He knows from experience there are temptations his young student has not yet encountered. The gifts of knowledge and discretion are very valuable. They are among the reasons listed in the beginning of Proverbs chapter one for why Solomon wrote his proverbs.

Proverbs chapter two opened by advising the young student to cry out for God's wisdom and then to listen for His response. If the teacher has done his job well, his student will know how valuable knowledge of God's will is and that he must continue seeking it throughout his entire life. When godly wisdom and knowledge come into the young student's soul, they will bring with them discretion and understanding. Chapter two defined discretion as a gift from God, that enables us to adapt our conduct and speech appropriately to our given situations and circumstances. This is one of the ways God's Holy Spirit enables His obedient children to avoid the snares of Satan, which will rob them of their blessings.

Chapter five does not alter the already tried and proven formula for Christian living. The teacher is simply urging his maturing student to remain steadfast as new temptations reveal themselves. We can assume the young man has already benefitted from his lessons, so thus far Solomon's advice has been profitable. Verse two tells him discretion will enable him to speak knowledgably. Without discretion, he will risk reducing his conscious contact with God, which will then restrict his access to the

Holy Spirit's wisdom. Wisdom is the source of intelligent speech. When indiscretion mutes the Holy Spirit, we begin losing our effectiveness of being positive representatives for the kingdom of God. God wants our lips to be an accurate source of information that spreads the "good news" of His loving mercy and unlimited power. Verse three will now tell us how Satan inspires some of his people to use their lips.

"For the lips of a strange woman drop as an honeycomb, and her mouth is smoother than oil: But her end is bitter as wormwood, sharp as a twoedged sword" (Proverbs 5:3–4).

Life on earth will present to each one of us our very own garden of Eden experience. The decision of whether or not to digest the forbidden fruit is determined by our spiritual condition. Satan is smart enough and certainly experienced enough to know what will challenge each individual with his or her greatest temptation. The young student addressed in chapter five is probably in the stage of his life when sexual temptation is at its peak. The inexperienced hormone-driven child of chapter two was certainly at risk of incurring the penalties of sexual sin, but the older man of chapter five has an even greater array of potential problems from which he can suffer. These can include divorce, bankruptcy, and children who may never recover from the emotional and spiritual turmoil of a broken home.

Verse four describes the end result of adultery as being "bitter as wormwood." This phrase portrays a crumbling piece of rotten wood that has lost its strength and now has no usefulness or purpose. A knowledgeable woodworker would cull out this disease-infected wood so its parasites would not invade any remaining still-healthy lumber. The immoral man or woman just like those parasites, jeopardize the integrity of the community they live and work in. No one who's happily married wants their spouse working or socializing with an immoral person who's seeking a sexual partner.

Wormwood is a large species of about 250 different plants that belong to the thistle family. Several types of wormwood are called sagebrush in the western United States. *Webster's* also defines wormwood as something bitter or grievous, which is also a good fit for its application in verse four. There is a reference to wormwood in Deuteronomy 29:18, used to describe the harmful influence of foreign idols in Israel. To understand the meaning of the Deuteronomy reference, it is best to begin reading at verse ten. God uses the "root of wormwood" as a comparison to the bitter curse Israel will surely incur if they worship false gods. It is a worthy parallel to the Proverbs prediction of death and destruction being the end result of sexual involvement with an immoral person.

Proverbs 5:4 concludes by describing the immoral woman as being "sharp as a two edged sword." The distinction of a two-edged sword is that it cuts as it is going in, and it also cuts as it is being pulled out. Later in his life, Solomon wrote, *"I find more bitter than death the woman who is a trap, her heart a net, and her hands chains. The one who pleases God will escape her, but the sinner will be captured by her"* (Ecclesiastes 7:26 HCSB). Solomon is concluding in Ecclesiastes (probably from firsthand experience) that there is little, if any, hope for a young man to continually escape the pursuits of a skilled seductress, especially if he is living outside of God's will. He also wrote, *"The mouth of the forbidden woman is a deep pit; a man cursed by the Lord will fall into it"* (Proverbs 22:14 HCSB). The immoral woman of chapter five is every bit as dangerous as were the outlaw gangsters of chapter one who were also attempting to lure away wisdom's young student.

"Her feet go down to death; her steps take hold on hell. Lest thou shouldest ponder the path of life, her ways are moveable, that thou canst not know them" (Proverbs 5:5–6).

These two verses warn the young man of the type of woman Satan will choose to use for the purpose of arousing his carnal urges. The immoral woman's sexual allure is no accident; she has learned how to maximize her attractiveness. Her lips may appear to be dripping with honey, but behind that seductive smile and captivating eyes lies a trap ready to slam shut on its prey. She is different from the other women he has known because his parents and teachers had shielded him from the dangers associated with these types of people. The immoral woman probably grew up in a different culture, possibly one that promoted a sin-filled environment, which fostered a different set of values and skills than those taught in Israel.

The followers of Satan think differently than do the followers of God. The immoral woman of chapter five is not a beginner. She is an established sinner whose livelihood depends on her leading others down the path she has chosen. Her eyes are wide open; her motives are self-serving and they do not honor God. Our young student does not know her ways because wisdom's instruction has taught him to shun her reasoning and lifestyle. He is now standing at a crossroads where he has to make a decision. Satan will try to convince the young man that he will be able to secretly eat of the forbidden fruit without harmful consequences. Verse five, however, is reminding him just how severe those consequences can be if he chooses to devour her poisoned fantasies. It requires just one exposure to contract a sexually transmitted disease, and it takes only one jealous husband or ex-lover to put a knife in his back. Even if he successfully conceals his sin from others, there is still a price to pay. Remember, the eyes of God are all-seeing. Hidden sin is still sin, and if left unresolved, it will dissolve all fellowship with God.

The word ponder, used in verse six, is translated from the Hebrew word *palace*, which means to weigh mentally. No Christian mothers or fathers want their children to ponder the ways of sin. They know that continual pondering will eventually produce a bad decision because conscious contact with God cannot be maintained while sin is being pondered. The expression "curiosity killed the cat" is a fit warning for those who continue to ponder the ways of an immoral man or woman. The best defense for a child of God is to avoid all unnecessary contact with these types of people. An organized wholesome environment with godly guidelines for proper speech and activities will inspire young people to ponder the promised blessings associated with Christian living. If you are going to ponder, it is best to ponder rightly.

> **"Hear me now therefore, O ye children, and depart not from the words of my mouth. Remove thy way far from her, and come not nigh the door of her house" (Proverbs 5:7–8).**

These two verses tell us how to avoid pondering the ways of sin. Wisdom is crying out, "Don't go there! Get far, far away. Better yet; don't even look at or consider sin." One of Solomon's purposes for writing the

Proverbs was to help young people avoid the devastating harm sin can cause. This is why chapter two begins with "Receive my words and hide my commands with thee" (Proverbs 2:1), and why chapter three begins with "My son, forget not my law; but let thine heart keep my commandments" (Proverbs 3:1), and why chapter four says, "My son, attend to my words; incline thy ear unto my sayings" (Proverbs 4:20). All of Solomon's collective efforts are to prepare the young man for when Satan greets him at the crossroads with sin's temptation. Satan's plan will be well thought out and timed with precision. If he is not successful, there is no guarantee he will not reappear with an even greater temptation. The best biblical example of how to deal with satanic attack is recorded in the fourth chapters of both Matthew and Luke.

These chapters record the temptation of Jesus by Satan. The attack was well timed, as Jesus was completing a forty-day fast and was physically weakened. The attack was well planned; Satan quoted scripture (taken out of context) in an effort to justify sin. Satan's first attempt was aimed at the body's physical needs, which was also how he tempted Eve in the garden of Eden. Satan suggested to Jesus, *"If thou be the Son of God, command that these stones be made bread"* (Matthew 4:3). If Jesus had followed Satan's advice, he would have successfully sabotaged the mission Jesus had been assigned by His Father. Had Jesus succumbed to this satanic suggestion, it would have increased Satan's chance of getting what he really wanted, which was to deceive Jesus into worshipping him. *"Then the devil took Him to the holy city, had Him stand on the pinnacle of the temple, and said to Him, 'If you are the Son of God, throw yourself down. For it is written: He will give His angels orders concerning you, and they will support you with their hands so that you will not strike your foot against a stone'"* (Matthew 4:5–6 HCSB).

Satan was reciting Psalm 91:11–12. Fortunately, Jesus knew the scriptures well enough to know the verses being cited by Satan were not cited in their entirety and were thus used out of context. *"For He shall give His angels charge over thee to keep thee in all thy ways"* (Psalm 91:11). Had Jesus submitted to Satan's will, He would not have been following His own way; He would have instead been following the devil's way, thus making Psalm 91:11 inapplicable for this situation. The temptation of Christ shows us why we need the scriptures written on the tablets of our hearts, as Proverbs 3:3 suggests we do. Knowing scripture is what keeps the believer in God's will. Continual obedience will secure God's continual blessing, which is what Satan does not and never will have. Since he is ineligible to receive what Jesus has to offer, he does not want anyone else to have it either. The reality of Satan's jealousy is the source of all our spiritual battles.

When Satan misquoted Psalm 91:11, Jesus responded by saying, *"Thou shall not tempt the Lord thy God"* (Matthew 4:7). Matthew 4:8–9 goes on to tell us that Satan took Jesus to a mountaintop to show Him the magnificence of the world's kingdoms and offered them to Him—if He would just bow down and worship him. This was what Satan really wanted—if Jesus had bowed down to the devil, He would have broken the first and second commandments, which state:

> I am the Lord thy God, which have brought thee out of the land of Egypt, out of the house of bondage. Thou shalt have no other gods before Me. Thou shall not make unto thee any graven image, or any likeness of any thing that is in heaven above, or that is in the earth beneath, or that is in the water under the earth. Thou shalt not bow down thyself to them, nor serve them: for I the Lord thy God am a Jealous God, visiting the iniquity of the fathers upon the children unto the third and fourth generation of them that hate Me; and shewing mercy unto thousands of them that love Me and keep My commandments. (Exodus 20:2–6)

If Jesus had worshipped Satan, He not only could have begun to rule the world, but He would have avoided the pain and suffering He was destined to endure on Calvary's cruel cross. If He had sinned by breaking these commandments, His sacrificial blood would have had no power to cover our sin from the eyes of God the Father and His Holy Spirit. Jesus chose to combat Satan's attack, not once but three times, by simply quoting scripture.

It is very important to note that Jesus, the man who could perform miracles, did nothing more than just quote scripture. Despite His having the power to do whatever He deemed was appropriate, He chose to simply quote scripture. Unlike Jesus, none of us has turned water into wine or walked on water, but we are all capable of simply quoting scripture. If Satan is actively creating problems in your life, try quoting scripture when you are being tempted at your own personal crossroads. If we have the holy scripture in our hearts, we can put on the *"armor of God,"* which will protect us from Satan's powers and principalities, as Ephesians 6:10–18 tells us it will.

> Finally, be strengthened by the Lord and by His vast strength. Put on the full armor of God so that you can stand against the tactics of the Devil. For our battle is not against flesh and blood, but against the rulers, against the authorities, against the world powers of this darkness, against the spiritual forces of evil in the heavens. This is why you must take up the full armor of God, so that you may be able to resist in the evil day, and having prepared everything, to take your stand. Stand therefore, with truth like a belt around your waist, righteousness like armor on your chest, and your feet sandaled with readiness for the gospel of peace. In every situation take the shield of faith and with it you will be able to extinguish all the flaming arrows of the evil one. Take the helmet of salvation, and the sword of the Spirit, which is God's word. Pray at all times in the Spirit with every prayer and request, and stay alert in this with all perseverance and intercession for all the saints. (HCSB)

"Remove thy way far from her, and come not nigh the door of her house: Lest thou give thine honour unto others, and thy years unto the cruel" (Proverbs 5:8–9).

Solomon is warning all who read his proverbs that, just like Samson, if they keep hanging around the barbershop, they are eventually going to get a haircut. Verse nine begins the list of reasons why the young man should avoid involvement with the immoral woman. The first reason is that it will cause him to give his honor to others. This means his reputation is going to suffer. The word honor, used in both of the King James Versions, is translated from the Hebrew word *hewd*. Its meanings include beauty, comeliness, excellence, glory, and majesty. The HCSB version provides a very good translation for verse nine: "Otherwise you will give up your vitality (hewd) to others and your years to someone cruel." Had this verse been written to a young woman, beauty would have been the best definition for *hewd*. Our hewd is a gift from God that contributes to our own uniqueness as a human being. Being such a personalized gift, it is one that is often reserved to be shared only with those who are dear to us.

When sinners realize they are sinners and that God, who hates sin, is the only one who can remove sin from their souls, **a conscious decision has to be made**. Confessing sinners can either accept God as Lord and Savior, or they can reject Him by continuing to act as if they are their own gods, living their own lives in their own ways. If sinners ignore God, for whatever reason, the Holy Spirit will remain a stranger to them and thus will have no immediate reason to cultivate their hewd. Anyone who decides to use their hewd for the glory of God does so by first confessing Jesus Christ as their Lord and Savior and then entering into an eternal covenant with Him. This is the most important covenant that a woman or man will ever enter. The second most important covenant is the marriage covenant.

The lifelong marriage covenant is often used in scripture to symbolize the eternal covenant committed Christians are commanded to establish with God. Throughout the New Testament, the church is referred to as the bride of Christ. A Christian man is expected to share his joy and his hewd with God and his wife—not with an adulteress and certainly not with Satan.

Satan has the ability to take on different forms. He appeared as a serpent to Eve, but this was his demonic spirit taking control of the serpent's body. It is logical to conclude this is how Satan can manage to take on different bodily forms—through spiritual demonic possession. There is every reason to believe that Satan is capable of inserting his presence and imposing his will unto the bodies of living creatures, including unbelieving human beings.

One of the benefits of being a Christian is Satan cannot dwell in a human body that's filled with God's Holy Spirit. *"Blessed are the pure in heart, for they shall see God"* (Matthew 5:8). The believer has the benefit of God's hedge of protection, which guards against satanic penetration of the soul. There are, however, some believers who get distracted and then wind up in a temporary fallen or backslidden state. Any delay on the believers' part to become reunited with God's fellowship will leave them vulnerable and thus make it possible for Satan to use them as an instrument of seduction.

This is precisely why women are instructed to dress modestly (1 Timothy 2:9). Even an old man can be distracted by a young woman showing too much flesh. Church is no place for the seductress to be allowed to display what she is so proud of. There is a very real problem in America's churches caused by sensual displays that distract attention from God's services. Churches that allow such distractions into their sanctuaries are compromising the gospel message. How can a sanctuary continue to be a sanctuary if impure motives are openly displayed? How can we expect to have effective worship when there's a sideshow of seduction going on?

What Satan seeks is to "rob, kill, and destroy." His ultimate delight is to deceive us into thinking he is God. Satan's number-one target is the church because that's where believers assemble for the purpose of serving and worshipping God. Why would Satan distract people in a bar or a casino? He has no problem with what the people in those places are engaging in. The church crowd, however, poses a problem for Satan. He will persistently seek ways to interrupt worship by using displays of exposed cleavage and short skirts to defile America's sanctuaries. Why would a man, who is supposed to be worshipping God, go to God's house wearing a sleeveless shirt to show off a set of well-developed biceps and shoulders that may, or may not, be highlighted with tattoos? **Anything or anyone that purposely distracts attention from God in His house is sin and should not be there**. What God wants is for His worshippers to assemble with humble and contrite spirits.

Satan hates nothing more than God being loved and worshipped by sincere men and women. Blinded by his own pride, Satan once dared to think he could deceive God's very own Son into worshipping him. Being the "great deceiver," his goal is for all remaining humanity on earth to worship him, which is exactly what will happen during the great tribulation period after God has raptured His people up from the earth.

Revelation 13 informs us those left behind on earth who refuse to worship the beast will be killed.

> He was permitted to give a spirit to the image of the beast, so that the image of the beast could both speak and cause whoever would not worship the image of the beast to be killed. And he requires everyone—small and great, rich and poor, free and slave—to be given a mark on his right hand or on his forehead, so that no one can buy or sell unless he has the mark: the beast's name or the number of his name. Here is wisdom: The one who has understanding must calculate the number of the beast, because it is the number of a man. His number is 666. (Revelation 13:15–18 HCSB)

Those killed for refusing to worship Satan's Antichrist are known as the tribulation saints. They will be left behind when God's church is called up to be with Him. These are the men and women who believed there was a God but, for a lack of faith, were unable to commit to a lifestyle of obedience. They will refuse to take Satan's mark because the rapture will have convinced them the Bible really is the true Word of God. Their new knowledge will cause them to make a real decision to accept Jesus Christ as their Lord and Savior, giving them the strength to withstand the overwhelming demonic forces during the last days. Being a tribulation Christian will not be easy. Those who are not imprisoned or executed will have to live secretly as fugitives from the Antichrist. They will be faithful to the end because the last chapter of Revelation declares Jesus, not Satan or his Antichrist, is the eternal King of kings in His creation. Until then, it is our covenant responsibility to avoid the world's immoral strangers who want to absorb all of our spirituality (or hewd), leaving none to be share with those who seek knowledge of the only true God. God wants us to be a sure testimony of His presence in our lives. Our mission is to help get people saved before the tribulation period begins.

Lest strangers be filled with thy wealth; and thy labors be in the house of a stranger" (Proverbs 5:10).

The HCSB version for Proverbs 5:10 reads, *"Strangers will drain your resources, and your earnings will end up in a foreigner's house."* A good parallel commentary for this verse is Proverbs 11:29—*"He that troubleth his own house shall inherit the wind: and the fool shall be servant to the wise of heart"* (KJV). There is no quicker way to divide a family or to "trouble a house" than with sexual indiscretion. The high cost of divorce is well known because it is now so common in modern America. Older people have been around long enough to have observed the negative effect of divorce being handed down from generation to generation. They know just how costly immorality can be. Sin, like a virus, waits and watches for weakness within its host, and then, at the most opportune moment, it will strike to grow and reproduce.

This verse's warning is not exclusive to just those who are married and committing adultery; it includes anyone who is deliberately participating in sin. God created the human race with the intention of humankind being a monogamous species. As stated before, He did allow for Israel's men to have multiple wives and even concubines, but this was not his original plan. When God began His creation, He created only one wife for Adam. Then sin entered the creation, and men began to kill their fellow men. Killing must have been common during the pre-flood era, as murder and the consumption of blood were the only two sins addressed by God in His next covenant, given to Noah, as described in Genesis 9:1–17.

The few facts that are provided for us from the pre-flood era leave us with the question, "Did God allow for men to have multiple wives simply because there were more women than there were men?" There is no record of God's telling men to take multiple wives in the Bible, but the practice did become common and was even recognized by Mosaic law in Deuteronomy 21:15. It is this author's belief that polygamy was not a part of God's original plan; it was the result of Satan's interference. God might have allowed polygamy because He did not create man or woman to be alone. His initial command to both Adam and Noah was to be fruitful and multiply. Old Testament polygamy would be an example of God's permissive will, not His perfect will. The first child born, Cain, killed the next child born, Abel, and murder seems to have continued throughout the pre-flood period. The sin of murder went on to eventually manifest itself as feuds between families and war among nations, resulting in fewer males than females throughout history, thus creating an imbalance between the male and female populations.

"And thou mourn at the last, when thy flesh and thy body are consumed" (Proverbs 5:11).

Take note of the delay before mourning occurs. The wages of sin are a process, not an event. The process begins with a distraction that lures our attention away from God. Once we have lost conscious contact with God, our minds are then vulnerable to satanic suggestion. Without God's hedge of protection, it is easy for a young man to view a beautiful young woman as a sexual object, rather than as a daughter of God who was created by his own heavenly Father. If a woman who has captured a young man's attention is actively seeking a sexual partner, the probability of her male admirer's remaining obedient to God's law is next to nil, unless God's words are in the midst of his heart, as Proverbs 4:21 says they should be.

Verse 11 is telling us consumption has to take place before an addicted sinner can realistically evaluate his situation. If sin's process is allowed to continue, complete consumption will be the end result. The young man of chapter five was earlier warned, "The way of the wicked is as darkness: they know not at what they stumble" (Proverbs 4:19).

When Satan's spiritual deception is used to exploit our God-given biological instincts, even a man with good intentions can be oblivious to the harm being done to him. Once he is consumed, the immoral woman will cease to be attracted to him. She will then move on to find her next victim, leaving him in a fallen state that will drive him to search for more sex. His sexual addiction could then drive him to seduce his own victims, some of whom may include innocent friends from his youth. He might even wind up seducing a young lady with whom he once went to church or perhaps the daughter of a Christian neighbor who had always been kind to him. This is how the cycle of sin stays alive.

The Hebrew word *kalah*, which is translated into *consumed*, means to be utterly destroyed or wasted. Verse 11 specifies the consumption of both the flesh and the body, which would refer to both an internal and external diseased state of the sinner's mind and body. Solomon is likely referring to a venereal disease, which is taking away the only thing this poor, delusional sinner has left—his body. Another definition for *kalah* is "wholly reaped." Sexual sin had reaped, or taken, everything of value from the fool of verse 11. He refused to listen, and now the Grim Reaper is about to force this man's spirit to "lay hold of hell," as we were told in verse five.

Before Satan lays claim to this misfortunate sinner's spirit, his tortured mind looks back to determine when, where, and how he went wrong.

"And say, How have I hated instruction, and my heart despiseth reproof" (Proverbs 5:12).

This verse takes us back to the past, when the young man of chapter five had began to stray from wisdom's path. Some may have never gotten onto her path because from the very beginning they hated instruction. This verse could be addressing the teenager of Proverbs 1, who was actively seduced by the outlaw gangsters. The third wisdom speech told us (Proverbs 1:20) wisdom continued to cry out but to no avail because the young student had disdained all of wisdom's counsel (Proverbs 1:25).

He may or may not remember being told, "Turn you at my reproof: behold, I will pour out my Spirit onto you; I will make known my words unto you" (Proverbs 1:23). These words were among Solomon's earliest sermons to the young man, perhaps fifteen or twenty years earlier, when life was much less complex. Proverbs 1:22 inquired, "How long, ye simple ones, will ye love simplicity?" Solomon was urging the young man to get the big picture—to wake up and realize it is God's world, and it operates on God's schedule with God's rules, and breaking these rules carries predictable consequences—consequences which they (the simple) do not want to think about, leaving them free to ponder the immediate gratification of sin.

Ignorance of God's words had not yielded good fortune. It resulted in God's no longer attempting to reach out to the young man. "Since you neglected all my counsel and did not accept my correction, I in turn, will laugh at your calamity. I will mock when terror strikes you" (Proverbs 1:25–26 HCSB). This is when the consumed older man of chapter five had crossed the point of no return. It happened long before he realized it. God, the source of wisdom and understanding, had ceased crying out to him with rebukes and corrections to guide him. Having no moral compass, the young man was free to follow his natural urges and instincts, which began the consumption of his thoughts and energy and would end with his falling like an ox at the slaughter (Proverbs 7:22).

"And have not obeyed the voice of my teachers, nor inclined mine ear to them who instructed me! I was almost in all evil in the midst of the congregation and assembly" (Proverbs 5:13–14).

This is why he went wrong; he rejected wisdom. Verse 14 tells us where he was when his demise began—he was in the midst of the assembly. The Hebrew word used here for assembly is *edah,* which refers to the entire general population of Israel, not just a specific group. Solomon is warning the readers of his proverbs, that evil is not restricted to being only in the places where you would expect to find it—it's everywhere. Social acceptance does not constitute righteousness, unless that society is living under God's law. A review of biblical history will confirm there were only a few brief periods when God's people, Israel, could have been considered as living within God's will. Are there any reasons to believe twenty-first–century America is doing any better?

Being "almost in all evil" means the outer personality of these evil people will show just enough restraint to where they can be accepted by the society in which they exist. If the inner motives of their wicked hearts were to be openly exposed, their employer and neighbors would not feel comfortable around them. God always sees everyone's thoughts and inner motives, yet He continues to love us. Some people are very good at hiding their inner selfishness, while others openly work society's social and legal systems for all they can get to satisfy their wants without the burden of work. It is easy to become discouraged in a world full of sin, but God's people are instructed to be of good cheer and to have faith in Him to provide for all their needs. When the going gets tough, we can rely on the words of the Bible's last chapter where we are told, *"There shall be no more curse: but the throne of God and of the lamb shall be in it: and his servants shall serve him"* (Revelation 22:3). This is why Christians are commanded to make a joyful noise, they have much to look forward to.

As a society continues to drift away from the will of God, it will eventually become a requirement for the leaders of that society to compromise any Christian values they personally have managed to retain. This process of phasing out God is known as *political correctness*. God's judgment upon a nation usually begins with the removal of godly leaders. This is what political correctness is currently doing in America. One of the core principles America's founding fathers wrote into our nation's legal documents is the separation of church and state. They were aware of the need for a separation of powers so government oppression could be avoided. Every powerful country in Europe at that time had a state-sponsored church that would determine how the people within its jurisdiction would worship God. The signers of our Declaration of Independence wanted men to be able to worship God as they saw fit, without any government interference.

What our country's founders had not anticipated was that a third power would emerge and go on to lead America's people into a flawed system of moral beliefs. The news media has anointed themselves as the authority of what is right and what is wrong in America. They are the ones many Americans choose to listen to on Sunday mornings, instead of attending church. Many Americans who used to attend church have become indifferent and choose not to leave the comfort of their homes. They no longer seek the fellowship of God-fearing believers, led by a godly pastor who has devoted his life to learn and understand the ways of God. Such a group of believers will recognize if one of their members is getting off wisdom's path and will encourage them to repent of their sin. A spirit-filled, Bible-believing church will provide the guidance that immature Christians need to avoid going astray in the midst of an assembly.

"Drink waters out of thine own cistern, and running waters out of thine own well" (Proverbs 5:15).

The "drinking of water" in Proverbs 5:15 is used to symbolize sex within the marital relationship. Sex and water are both necessary requirements for the survival of the human race. Cisterns and wells were prized possessions in all ancient communities but especially so with those located in a desert environment. Water from a cistern is extra water—water that has been stored up rather than allowed to run off. Running water is fresh water and would normally be thought of as the best-tasting. Metaphorically speaking, life is full of floods and droughts, so there will be periods when we will have nothing except that "old cistern water" to drink, instead of the fresh "running water" that tastes so much better.

A Christian's sex life can sometimes be compared to that old cistern water. If one spouse looses the initial enthusiasm he or she once had for the sexual relationship of the marriage, the other spouse is going to sense that. It only takes one person to turn off the running water, which forces the other spouse to be satisfied with the "leftover cistern water" of the relationship. A true God-centered marital bond is stronger than any loss of physical satisfaction. Compromise through open communication should be able to restore—or, in some cases, replace—the lost joy of the sexual relationship. Solomon is trying very tactfully to say that even if you are getting bored with your sex life, you are better off "drinking from your cistern" than to consider stealing the fresh water from a neighbor's well.

The Hebrew word *mayin* was the word Solomon used for waters, in verse 15. When used as a euphemism, *mayin* can refer to urine or semen. A euphemism is the substitution of an agreeable or less unpleasant term for one that would likely offend or be unacceptable to speak of in a given social situation. Solomon frequently used euphemisms because wise men know that a brother, when offended, can be distracted from truth. The next three verses also make use of euphemisms.

> **"Let thy fountains be dispersed abroad, and rivers of water in the streets. Let them be only thine own, and not strangers with thee. Let thy fountain be blessed: and rejoice with the wife of thy youth" (Proverbs 5:16–18).**

Fountains is translated from the Hebrew word *mayanah*, which is very similar to the Hebrew word, *mayin*, from verse 15 that Solomon used for water. *Mayanah*, when used figuratively, refers to a source of satisfaction. The fountain of verse 16 is referring to the young man's strength, part of which is his sexual drive. The expression "rivers of water" refer to the immense number of sperm cells that are discharged in a normal male ejaculation (fifteen to twenty million). Solomon was not aware of this medical fact, but God was.

Verse 16 is asking the young man, "Do you really want to plant your seed in another man's field? Do you want your very own unique DNA to be reconfigured with that of a stranger, or should it be given only to the loving wife of your youth?" These are questions that should at least slow down the young man's compulsion to misuse his sexual powers. Verse 18 plainly tells us the young man's fountain is a blessing to be shared with the loving wife of his youth, not an immoral woman. The fourth chapter of the Song of Solomon, also known as the Song of Songs, describes the wife as being a "garden fountain, or a well of flowing water." This description from the Song of Solomon blends harmoniously with the next verse of Proverbs chapter five.

"A loving doe, a graceful fawn—let her breasts always satisfy you; be lost in her love forever" (Proverbs 5:19 HCSB).

The original language of the King James Version of the Bible instructs its readers to be "ravished always with her Love." This is how God wants us to be consumed. He wants us to be consumed with the soul mate He has specifically designed for us to be with here on earth. He wants the best for us. He does not want our bodies consumed with a sexually transmitted disease or our minds filled with immoral lust. Verse 19 describes a blissful state that no one, not even Solomon, can realistically expect to have at all times. Once we have been intoxicated with true love and enraptured with both the internal and external beauty of our spouses, we are to grab on to this precious gift from God and use it as a guiding force in our lives—even if it is presently just a memory of times past. If Satan manages to remove the "running water" from our house, an obedient Christian will be able to praise God for his cistern.

"And why wilt thou, my son, be ravished with a strange woman, and embrace the bosom of a stranger" (Proverbs 5:20)?

Now that true love, as God intended it to be, has been explained to the young man, Solomon is asking, "Why would you want to defile your marriage covenant?" Did you know divorce is a type of murder? Genesis 2:24 states, *"Therefore shall a man leave his father and his mother, and shall cleave unto his wife: and they shall be one flesh."* This is God's statement on marriage. God is referring to a physical union that is designed to enhance the social and emotional bond between a man and his wife. This triple bond (physical, social, and emotional) will then be strengthened even further by the legal commitment of marriage. Marriage is a compound process that blends the souls of two people into one, thus producing the strongest possible bond—the spiritual bond. Any separation or tearing of this God-ordained union does not please God and will cause Him pain. The dissolution of the marital union causes a living death that pleases Satan immensely. Divorce tears apart the spiritual bond of matrimony, which results in the spiritual death of the flesh that had been joined together by God. Solomon frames the question of verse 20 as if to say, "Do you really want to give up all of this for just some temporary physical pleasure? Is it really worth it?"

"For the ways of man are before the eyes of the Lord, and He pondereth all his goings" (Proverbs 5:21).

The statement of verse 21 should not be a revelation to anyone. Even Israel's surrounding heathen neighbors believed their man-made idols possessed a living conscientiousness and thus had an opinion of what was going on in the lives of their worshipers. The eyes of the living God are everywhere. This concept was rarely challenged until scientists finally fabricated an alternative explanation for the world's existence. How can anyone keep track of everything that goes on in the entire world, as verse 21 suggests? Now that we have the ability to fast-forward three thousand years from the time Proverbs was written, it's easy to believe and understand that through the use of technology, this can be done. If man has the capability to do this with a computer, is it unreasonable to believe that our Creator can equal that task?

God's Holy Spirit is that part of God that is everywhere and sees everything. He does not need a computer to know all. His eyes and ears sense every biological action of every creature throughout eternity. He knows every thought created within our brains by the input of our central nervous systems, which gather information and send data to our brains for evaluation. Information sent in the form of small electrical surges can cause our brains to sense immense pleasure or an enormous amount of pain.

Could God have been feeling pain when the events of Genesis 4:10 took place? When God said to Cain *"The voice of thy brother's blood crieth unto me from the ground."* Is it any wonder that God hates sin if it causes Him pain? Can you even begin to imagine how much pain God has endured because of sin down through the history of humankind?

It is this author's opinion that God's Holy Spirit reaches throughout the entire creation, much like our own central nervous systems do within our bodies. The Bible does not provide an abundance of information about the Holy Spirit, but we do know from Revelation 4:4 there are seven spirits before the throne in heaven. We also know Jesus had to die on the cross before He would send God's Holy Spirit, referred to as *"the Comforter"* in the King James Gospel of John. The last of the four references to the Comforter is found in John 16:7, which reads, *"Nevertheless, I tell you the truth; it is expedient for you that I go away: for if I go not away, the Comforter will not come unto you; but if I depart, I will send Him onto you."*

Jesus was able to make this claim because He knew His sacrificial blood was going to make possible the indwelling of God's Holy Spirit within the spirit of men. Solomon managed to tap into this concept of God's Holy Spirit being a comforter over nine hundred years earlier when he wrote Ecclesiastes 4:1, *"Look at the tears of those who are oppressed; they have no one to comfort them. Power is with those who oppress them; they have no one to comfort them"* (HCSB). They had no comforter because they had no means for forgiveness from sin. When the sinless blood of Jesus was shed, it covered the sin of those who willingly accepted Him as Lord and Savior. Then—and only then—can God's Holy Spirit commune with our own spirit. Anything that hinders this process comes from Satan. We have already discussed the oppressor in Proverbs 3:31, which read, "Envy thou not the oppressor, and choose none of his ways."

This is because the oppressor does not have the promise of eternal peace, as does the child of God. Any hope the oppressor has for happiness and contentment has to be acquired immediately because he lives for the present moment, instead of for the promised eternal joy that Christians have to look forward to. Proverbs 23:17–18 demonstrate this truth well. *"Don't let your heart envy sinners; instead always fear the Lord. For then you will have a future, and your hope will never fade"* (HCSB).

"A wicked man's iniquities entrap him; he is entangled in the ropes of his own sin" (Proverbs 5:22 HCSB).

Webster's defines iniquity as wickedness or gross injustice. Solomon again is telling the young man that wickedness will trap him. The teacher began warning the young man about the snares of sin in the second wisdom speech of chapter one. "Surely in vain the net is spread in the sight of any bird" (Proverbs 1:17). Three verses later, chapter one declares, "Wisdom calls out in the street; She raises her voice in the public squares" (HCSB). Wisdom continued her instruction to the young student and later assured him in Proverbs 3:23, "Then you will go safely on your way; your foot will not stumble" (HCSB). Proverbs 4:12 states, "When you walk, your steps will not be hindered; when you run, you will not stumble" (HCSB). Proverbs 4:19 says, "But the way of the wicked is like the darkest gloom; they don't know what makes them stumble" (HCSB). This verse was the conclusion of the ninth wisdom sermon. Now, in this eleventh sermon, Solomon describes the cause of stumbling and being trapped as being caught in "the ropes of his own sin."

This verse creates the visualization of cords or small ropes being thrown over the young man's body as he wanders aimlessly, further and further from the path of righteousness. As his sinning continues, the strands of entanglement become thicker and heavier to bear. His walk down folly's path becomes slower, as the cords of sin begin to take hold of his life. He continues to struggle but eventually loses his balance and falls to his knees. He fights to get up but is unable to do so because of the accumulated weight of sin's entanglements; he then begins to crawl. With his torso now parallel to the ground, he is an easier target for Satan's cords of imprisonment to be tossed over his body.

Being blinded by his sin disease, he tells himself, "I am stronger now because I'm using my legs and my arms to continue on," but the accelerated rate of sin's attachments slowly drain him of all of his strength and determination. He soon collapses flat on the ground and lies there exhausted, grasping for breath, as the satanic strands from hell continue to wrap around him and begin to strangle his life's force from his now-motionless body. He knows he must get up to survive but can no longer conjure up the willpower to fight hell's quicksand. He is now physically

exhausted and mentally consumed. Satan's Grim Reaper will soon be summoned to take him by the arm and drag him down to the pit, where his fallen spirit will be imprisoned for all of eternity.

"He shall die without instruction; and in the greatness of his folly he shall go astray" (Proverbs 5:23).

No parent wants this to be the conclusion of a son or daughter's life. Verse 23 declares the incubator of this needless waste of life was a lack of instruction. Solomon had observed the loss of young lives within his own father's family. He had witnessed how the cords of sin consumed the strength of Israel's greatest king—his father, King David. He had to have been devastated when his half brother, Amnon, raped his half sister, Tamar. It had to have saddened him when Tamar's brother, Absalom, took revenge by killing Amnon and then had to flee from David's presence. Both David and Solomon witnessed their families falling apart because of sin. This is why Solomon wrote his proverbs—he did not want any more of Israel's young men to be consumed by sin due to a lack of instruction.

Could an understanding of this ancient book of Proverbs prevent America's young men and women from falling into sin's bottomless pit? This author believes it can—but only if mothers and fathers pick it up first. They then must read it, study it, pray about it, meditate on it, and then continue to pray for understanding of it. Once an understanding has been reached; a decision needs to be made: "Do I want to trust and obey, or do I want to ignore and play?" Solomon would probably say, "Choose wisely. Your children's happiness depends upon it."

WISDOM SPEECH TWELVE

Proverbs 6:1–6:19

Proverbs chapter six begins by directing our young man's attention away from threatening sexual situations and toward yet another group of social predators, those who oppress the vulnerable. The teacher begins his twelfth wisdom sermon with a specific problem; our young man has become surety for his friend. This means he has agreed to become legally obligated to make sure a debt, incurred by his friend, will be paid. A modern example would be cosigning for a loan, making a loan, or posting a bond. The Hebrew word for surety is *arab,* which means to pledge, to occupy, to mortgage, or to become security. Making a pledge is essentially the same as taking a vow, something that God takes very seriously. Making and then breaking a pledge or a vow is a forbidden practice. God wants His people to be viewed by others as truthful, reliable, and dependable. How else can God consider a Christian worthy to be a faithful ambassador for His kingdom?

"My son, if thou be surety for thy friend, if thou hast stricken thy hand with a stranger" (Proverbs 6:1).

Proverbs 17:18 states, "One without knowledge enters an agreement, and puts up security for his friend" (HCSB). Proverbs 22:26 reads, *"Don't be one of those who enters agreements, who puts up security for loans"* (HCSB). There is nothing positive to be found in scripture concerning pledges. Making a pledge or a loan often becomes the beginning of a downward spiral, ending with a broken friendship. If you do decide to help a friend by loaning money, make sure it is money you can do without. If the money is more important than the friendship, you had better keep your money. The second phrase of verse one goes on to describe a situation that indicates even less understanding.

Part A of verse one describes an agreement made with a friend; part B describes an even riskier arrangement—an agreement made with a stranger. The word *stranger* is translated from the Hebrew word *zuwr*, which refers to a foreigner. It can also refer to an adulterer or one to be turned aside, especially for lodging. If becoming surety for a friend indicates a lack of understanding, as Proverbs 17:18 tells us, then making a pledge with a stranger would have to be considered outright foolishness.

Solomon has repeatedly assured us that wisdom and understanding will deliver us from the "snares of life." The ability to recognize potentially harmful situations is just one of the ways God's wisdom can protect us. We are encouraged to be confident our feet will not stumble when we remain on wisdom's path (Proverbs 3:23). Now that Solomon's middle-aged student has accumulated enough wealth to help another financially, he is informed about the responsibility of managing his given resources in a responsible manner.

Accurate interpretation of this verse should be accompanied by the concept that we own nothing—it was all created by God. This fact should lead any potential lender to ask, "Does God want me to lend His money, of which He has given me stewardship, to this person? Will this loan serve as part of God's plan, or is it enabling the borrower to continue living in an irresponsible manner?"

Solomon issues us a further warning in Proverbs 11:15—*"If someone puts up security for a stranger, he will suffer for it, but the one who hates such agreements is protected"* (HCSB). The suffering referred to here can take on forms other than just being without the money or whatever else may have been loaned. Once a loan has been made, a new commitment has been made as well. The borrower may begin to feel stressed by his or her new responsibility for repayment. He or she may begin to associate the lender with this new source of stress, which will result in resentment. The friend who was willing to help may suddenly be viewed as an uncompassionate miser who is interested in nothing except repayment of the loan.

It is also possible the lender may have had motives for lending the money other than just wanting to be helpful. Perhaps the lender perceived the loan as a means of securing a friendship which he or she is now planning to put more demands upon. Perhaps making the loan will enable the lender to feel he or she is superior to the borrower and is now qualified to issue unsolicited advice.

When entering a covenant with a stranger, how will one know what to expect? Solomon has already told us: you do not understand the ways of the sinner (Proverbs 5:6). They usually come from a different background and have a different concept of right and wrong. The Proverbs continually tell us to occupy our thoughts with God's wisdom, not the wisdom of the world. This is how we obtain the mind of Christ (Romans 2:16). Having the mind of Christ means we not only should hate sin, but we also should be uncomfortable with the workers of sin. Christian compassion is a beautiful virtue, but it sometimes takes the full wages of sin for a sinner to hit a productive bottom. It is sometimes necessary for Christians to ignore their instincts to help and allow a friend they care for greatly to learn what he or she can learn only by hitting his or her own personal bottom. This form of wisdom is known as "tough love" in the Twelve Step community.

Solomon later wrote instruction pertaining to a very special type of pledge—a pledge that is made to God. This type of pledge is usually referred to as a vow and should be taken very serious.

"When you make a vow to God don't delay fulfilling it, because He does not delight in fools. Fulfill what you vow. Better that you do not vow than you vow and not fulfill it. Do not let your mouth bring guilt upon you, and do not say in the presence of the messenger that it was a mistake. Why should God be angry with your words and destroy the work of your hands? For many dreams bring futility, so do many words. Therefore, fear God" (Ecclesiastes 5:4–7 HCSB).

"Thou art snared with the words of thy mouth, thou art taken by the words of thy mouth" (Proverbs 6:2).

Verse two is telling the young student his position has been compromised. His own words have caused him to stray from God's path of wisdom. The teacher is telling him what has happened because the student has not yet realized the full extent of his predicament. When he became surety for his friend in verse one, his motives were most likely honorable, but he now realizes his friend is struggling to make repayment, which leaves him in a precarious position.

The young man was previously told, "Your steps will not be hindered" (Proverbs 4:12 HCSB). Having been snared, something has obviously gone wrong. Assuming our student has managed to avoid the life-threatening traps set by the immoral woman of chapter five, we have reason to believe his home and family are still intact. If his family's financial needs cannot be met because of his friend's inability to make repayment, he now fully understands the seriousness of the mistake he made. He should not have loaned money that he could not do without.

God does weigh a man's motives, and the motivation here seems to have been of an honorable nature. He wanted to help another human being. Unlike the lust-driven sinner of chapter five, who simply wanted to feel good sexually, the middle-aged man of chapter six is not told his entrapment will lead down to death (Proverbs 5:5). Yet Solomon is warning his student to not be snared or taken by this type of commitment. Should the teacher help his student by loaning him money to cover his bills, or should he allow the student to work his own way out of his entrapment?

This is a difficult question to answer. One would have to first learn and consider all the circumstances pertaining to the situation. Once this knowledge is acquired, prayer for knowledge of God's will, followed by meditation, is the next step. A quick decision could possibly deprive everyone involved of an opportunity to grow closer to God if this need is not allowed to be met in God's way and in God's time. Scripture encourages us to be charitable and even goes as far to say we can be blessed for our charitable deeds if our deeds are honorably motivated.

> Be careful not to practice your righteousness in front of people, to be seen by them. Otherwise, you will have no reward from your Father in heaven. So whenever you give to the poor, don't sound a trumpet before you, as the hypocrites do in the synagogues and on the streets, to be applauded by people. I assure you: They've got their reward! But when you give to the poor, don't let your left hand know what your right hand is doing, so that your

giving may be in secret. And your Father who sees in secret will reward you. (Matthew 6:1–4 HCSB)

Jesus is warning the multitudes against playing the "big shot" by saying, "Yeah, if something goes wrong, no problem; I can cover that debt." When cosigning for a loan, the one we're really helping is the one who's making the loan—the same one who wants to collect interest from our friend without taking any risk. The lender has determined there is indeed a risk, and now he or she wants the cosigner to be responsible for that risk. This may not always be the case, but it often is. Solomon wanted his students to be aware of the financial and sometimes social implications of such an arrangement. It is not uncommon for a borrower to eventually come to resent the one who has loaned the money, even if the lender has done so with good and honorable intention.

The word "taken," used in verse two, is translated from the Hebrew word *yakad*. In addition to meaning to catch or to snare—yakad can mean to be frozen or held. This is what unresolved sin does—it spiritually freezes God's children, which prevents them from following His will. God wants us to be productive people. He does not want us to be frozen with fear. The teacher is now going to tell his student how to avoid being frozen.

"Do this now, my son, and deliver thyself, when thou art come into the hand of thy friend; go, humble thyself, and make sure thy friend. Give not sleep to thine eyes, nor slumber to thine eyelids" (Proverbs 6:3–4).

We are told, in very firm language, "Get busy. Go to work. Get the situation straightened out; even if you are tired and want to go to sleep." These verses are in reference to the first phrase of verse one "If thou be surety for thy friend." The Hebrew word *rahab,* from which the word *sure* is derived, means to urge severely or to strengthen. The Old King James language seems to be saying, "The friendship, not the verbal agreement, is what God considers to be more important."

This is why we are told to humble ourselves and then plead with our friend, even if it's in the middle of the night. On this subject the apostle Paul wrote, *"Be angry, and do not sin. Don't let the sun go down on your anger, and don't give the devil an opportunity"* (Ephesians 4:26-27 HCSB). This verse is telling us there will be situations and circumstances that warrant anger, but unresolved anger does not promote God's will. Paul reaffirms Proverbs 6:4 by telling us to deal with our anger and to settle the matter as quickly as possible, preferably before the sun goes down.

"Deliver thyself as a roe from the hand of the hunter, and as a bird from the hand of the fowler" (Proverbs 6:5).

Solomon, as you may remember from First Kings chapter four, studied animals. He probably had a specific reason for using the roe as a symbol for freedom from sin's oppression. Other versions, including the Holman Christian Standard Bible, substitute the word gazelle, an animal known for its ability to run swiftly and suddenly switch its direction, while defying gravity with its graceful leaps into the air. The King James language uses the term roe, which is short for roebuck, one of the animals listed in Deuteronomy 14:5 as being clean or suitable for the children of Israel to eat. The roebuck is a small deer, usually thirty-five to seventy-five pounds in weight. The male roebucks have short, erect antlers, which may also provide reason for the translation of gazelle. Both the roebuck and the gazelle are very fast and graceful animals. The roebuck is thought to have been abundant in Israel during Solomon's day but today is rarely seen.

The gracefulness of these animals inspired Solomon and others to use them as examples for freedom. When we are in an awkward situation, God wants us to act gracefully as we free ourselves from our oppression. You may recall Proverbs 1:8–9. "My son, hear the instruction of thy father, and forsake not the law of thy mother: For they shall be an ornament of grace onto thy head." We, as Christians, are commanded to be the light of the world. To help us to accomplish this purpose, God's wisdom will lead us through our trials in a graceful manner.

The "hand of the hunter" is an interesting phrase. There are numerous mentions of snares and traps throughout Solomon's wisdom speeches. However, there are only two previous verses in scripture that use the word hunter. Esau is described as a skilled hunter in Genesis 25:27. We are told later, in Genesis 26:34, that Esau married two Hitite women who were a source of grief to his father and mother, Isaac and Rebekah. Esau's descendants were known as the Edomites, who became the continual enemies of the children of Israel. The other hunter, Nimrod, is described in Genesis chapter ten. He was the great-grandson of Noah and is described as a mighty hunter. Nimrod went on to become the first world leader, and the father of false worship, which began at the tower of Babel.

Genesis chapter ten states Nimrod went on to build several cities, including Babel, where God scattered men across the earth and confused their language. Nimrod's kingdom was never really destroyed; it was just scattered upon the face of the earth (Genesis 11:8). Most scholars believe Babel went on to become Babylon, which has historically represented Satan's kingdom here on earth. Nimrod was described as a hunter of the sons of man in the Jerusalem Targum. Genesis 9:25 tells us Nimrod's uncle Canaan was put under a curse by Noah, in connection with his father's (Ham's) shameful actions in the previous verses. Regardless of what actually happened between Noah, Ham, and Canaan (Genesis 9:20–25), the eventual result was a rebellion against God at Babel, which is what Nimrod's name means—"Let us rebel."

Solomon is instructing his students to free themselves from the oppression of sin, which is referred to in verse five as "the hand of the hunter." The hunter, whether it is the likes of Nimrod, Esau, or some celebrity conman, are all empowered by none other than Satan himself, who is the original hunter of men's souls. The Hebrew word used here for hand, in verse five, is *Yad*, which refers to an open hand. You should be wondering right now, "Why would the hunter allow his prey to escape by opening his hand?" The hunter does not willingly open his hand. His hand is pried open by the power of Jesus Christ, when we pray to Him seeking deliverance from whatever oppression we suffer. Remember we are to do this before we allow sleep to come to our eyes. He will release us from the bonds of sin, but it is then up to us to stay clear from the "snare of the fowler," which is obviously whatever sin leads us into bondage. Whether it be drugs, alcohol, pornography, or laziness, get far away from the edge of sin's pit. Walk where the footing is secure.

Solomon now goes on to use one of God's lower forms of created life as an example for us to learn from. The ant is among the family of creeping creatures God made during the sixth day of Genesis chapter one. Solomon is going to use this lowly little animal as a means for teaching his readers the importance of continual hard work. What the ant doesn't possess in terms of size and strength he more than makes up for with his enthusiastic energy and his independent motivation to get things done.

"Go to the ant, thou sluggard; consider her ways and be wise" (Proverbs 6:6).

There are now over fifteen thousand species of ants worldwide. Investigation has shown that the ants of the Middle East show a greater amount of intelligence than ants in other areas of the world. Proverbs 30:25 says, "The ants are a people not strong, yet they prepare their meat in the summer." *Unger's Bible Dictionary* states,

> There are however, certain facts in regards to the ants of the Holy Land which settle this controversy (regarding the wisdom and foresight of the ant) in favor of the rigid accuracy in the author of the Proverbs. They are: (1) The ants of these countries lay-up vast stores of grain in their nests. (2) To facilitate this process of providence they place their nests as near as possible to the places where grain is thrashed or stored. (3) They certainly eat this grain during the winter season. (4) They encourage certain insects which secrete sweet juices to consort with them, and collect and store their eggs with their own, that they may have them at hand for future use when they shall have hatched.

The sluggard or lazy person is told to observe and learn from the ant. This is the first use of the word sluggard in the Bible, its usage is confined to the Proverbs only. Sluggard is translated from the Hebrew word *atsel* which means to be slothful, indolent or slack. Proverbs 10:26 tells us the sluggard is not a popular person—*"As vinegar to the teeth, and as smoke to the eyes, so is the sluggard to them that send him."* We're also told the sluggard is not a prosperous person. *"The soul of the sluggard desireth, and has nothing: but the soul of the diligent shall be made fat"* (Proverbs 13:4). Unlike the ant, the sluggard is not diligent—*"The sluggard will not plow by reason of the cold; therefore shall he beg in harvest, and have nothing"* (Proverbs 20:4). The sluggard has a distorted perception of reality—*"The sluggard is wiser in his own conceit than seven men that can render a reason"* (Proverbs 26:16).

Laziness and conceit are the reasons why the sluggard will not consider the ways of the ant. Solomon knew the sluggard would not learn from the ant. He wanted his student to recognize the contrast in results between the efforts of the hardworking ant and the lack of effort shown by the slothful sluggard. The sluggard lives in his own little world, often ignorant of reality, making him the textbook example of Proverbs 4:19—"The way of the wicked is as darkness; they know not at what they stumble."

"Which having no guide, overseer, or ruler, provideth her meat in the summer, and gathereth her food in the harvest" (Proverbs 6:7–8).

The ant does not require a taskmaster. It operates by an instinct given to it by God and passed on through its DNA from generation to generation. God made us different from the animals; He gave us free will. Like the ant, we do have instincts. Some of them we follow better than we are aware, especially during our youth; but unlike animals, we as humans are given the ability to override our instincts with intellect. One of humanity's instincts is to sin. God created us as free moral agents, which means we have the ability to choose what we do and say when we're able to reason. Sin has taken away the ability of the sluggard to reason, which is why he refuses to change. Like a pig wallowing in the mud, the sluggard is comfortable with his ways and surroundings until his basic needs scream loud enough to disturb his slumber.

The Proverbs repeatedly encourage us to be motivated workers who are both mentally and physically engaged. Unlike the sluggard, the wise man strives to be a self-starter who is motivated to expand God's kingdom by being a happy and productive person. The contrast between the ant and the sluggard is well expressed in Proverbs 10:13. *"Wisdom is found on the lips of the discerning, but a rod is for the back of the one who lacks sense"* (HCSB). This concept is reinforced by Proverbs 26:3, which reads, *"A whip for the horse, a bridle for the donkey, and a rod for the backs of fools"* (HCSB).

True Christianity includes compassion, so we cannot help but feel sorry for the poor sluggard because he indeed will wind up being poor. Jesus told the scribes, *"For ye have the poor with you always, and whensoever ye will ye may do them good"* (Mark 14:7). You may be wondering why God created sluggards. The answer to that question is God did not create sluggards; sin did! The sluggard is just one of many problems caused by sin in God's otherwise perfect creation.

Parents are instructed, *"Train up a child in the way he should go; and when he is old, he will not depart from it"* (Proverbs 22:6). When parents fail to give their children proper training, the chances of producing a sluggard are greatly increased. Contrary to twenty-first–century American political correctness, proper training does sometimes necessitate physical punishment. When a parent fails to provide God's instruction for the *complete* training of a child, sin has been committed and will limit that child's ability to become who and what God designed that child to be. Love is the dominant theme of God's curriculum for childhood development, but it is not the sole tool of godly parenting.

Proverbs 19:18 provides more evidence that God expects parents to include physical incentives when other forms of correction do not seem to be working: *"Chasten thy son while there is hope, and let not thy soul spare for his crying."* The Hebrew word *yacar*, which is translated to *chasten*, means to chastise, literally with blows or figuratively with rebuke. Chastening was earlier discussed in Proverbs 3:11–12. When loving mothers and corrupt lawyers, operating within a godless social system, legally took the paddle out of the hands of America's fathers, many children, especially boys, were condemned by sin, *not by God*, to a life of mediocrity. When strong-willed boys grow up without equally strong discipline, they become resistant to the statutes of wisdom and are then attracted to the folly of foolishness.

Proverbs 13:24 puts it a little more directly: *"He that spareth his rod hateth his son: but he that loveth him chasteneth him betimes (promptly)."* Proverbs 22:15 focuses on the sinful nature with which every child is born: *"Foolishness is bound in the heart of a child; but the rod of correction shall drive it far from him."* This all-inclusive verse gives the problem, the solution, and the result. And finally, a verse for those who may still insist a child should never suffer physical correction: *"Withhold not correction from the child: for if thou beatest him with the rod, he shall not die. Thou shall beat him with the rod, and shalt deliver his soul from hell"* (Proverbs 23:13–14). What more can be said to convince parents that the "board of education" occasionally needs to be applied to the seat of learning, when less aggressive means of instruction do not yield acceptable results? My father explained to me at a tender age, "The padding on your behind was put there by the good Lord for more than one reason."

The inconvenient truth is that life is very competitive, especially in the business world. Today's wavering economy has created an insecure working environment for many stressed-out employees who are constantly worried about keeping their jobs. Overworked and sometimes exhausted, many parents either struggle or are unable to provide adequate instruction for their children. Some are forced to choose between their work and their children. Parents whose jobs require travel and especially those parents in the military will have long periods of separation from their families. The alienation from long absences makes it difficult for parents to "love on" their children and to keep current with their children's changing needs. A child who has to raise herself or himself is at great risk of being raised by a fool.

"How long wilt thou sleep, O sluggard? When wilt thou arise out of thy sleep? Yet a little sleep, a little slumber, a little folding of the hands to sleep: So shall thy poverty come as one that travelleth, and thy want as an armed man" (Proverbs 6:9–11).

One of the Hebrew words commonly translated into the English word sleep is *shawkab*, which means to lie down, either for rest or for sex. It can also mean to ravish or to lodge. This is the word used in the opening question of Proverbs 6:9. The second question of verse nine uses the Hebrew word *shenah*, which is translated to the same English word, sleep, but *shenah* has no meanings other than sleep. The Hebrew word *tenoomaw*, used in the first phrase of verse ten, which is also translated into sleep by the King James Version, means drowsiness. Ironically, in the middle of the word drowsiness, we can find the spelling for sin. A drowsy mind results in a drowsy spirit—one that is not alert and is an easy target for the hunter of men's souls, who as stated earlier is none other than Satan himself. The devil is always ready to take advantage of a drowsy spirit.

Samson is a good example of a man who had a drowsy spirit. Despite being the world's strongest man, Samson was lured into a state of drow*siness* as he slumbered (*shakabbed*) with Delilah (Judges 16). The Bible describes how persistent and calculating Delilah was in her pursuit to extract secret information from the mighty yet drowsy Samson. Delilah's actions are identical to those of the immoral woman we have already studied in the previous wisdom speeches of Proverbs. Her bed indeed led Samson to failure and eventually down to death—poverty was on him like a bandit. Many of those who once owned successful businesses and who were later lured into slumber by alcohol, cocaine, or sex will confirm that when they were found out, they usually lost everything to pay off their debt. In almost all cases, when the end came, it came quickly. Christians need always to be alert, and be ready because Satan is no sluggard!

"A naughty person, a wicked man, walketh with a froward mouth" (Proverbs 6:12).

Verse 12 continues the description of the sluggard. Solomon wanted his students of wisdom to readily recognize a sluggard. A sluggard in the middle stages of development will sponge off his or her parents for as long as possible. At some point, Mom and Dad will not or cannot continue to support their underachieving child. When the sluggard is shown "tough love" and is put out of the house, he or she will have to come up with a new means of survival. If he or she is unable to find another relative or friend to rely upon, then—and only then—will a committed sluggard consider work. Occasionally, a job can be the trigger that transforms a sluggard into a functioning human being. Work can restore a person's confidence, which will energize and motivate him or her to "free themselves like a gazelle" out of the pits of depression and uselessness.

Verse 12 describes the sluggard who goes on to be a worthless person who is incapable of profit. This is what the Hebrew word *beliyaal* means. The King James Version translates *beliyaal* into *naughty person*. Both the King James and New King James texts add to the description of "a worthless person" with the additional description, "a wicked man." The sluggard has gone from useless to dangerous. Sin is a progressive disease that will continue to manifest itself unless treated by the Great Physician. The Holy Spirit still makes house calls, and His medicine is knowledge of the soul-cleansing blood of Christ, shed on that old rugged Roman cross two thousand years ago. If sin is not confessed and forgiven, the sluggard, like any other type of sinner, will continue in his wickedness and become even more evil. This is why Solomon writes "a worthless person" and then further writes "a wicked man." Laziness leads to worthlessness, which causes low self-esteem and then depression. Depression will go on to rob the already-poor sluggard of any energy and ambition he may have left.

Satan loves to see a human being in the misery of advancing sin. It hurts a loving God to view a suffering sinner who refuses to repent and ask for help. Satan will welcome any state of misery and use it to get what he wants; which is the soul and eventually the spirit of the poor sluggard. Satan has dominion where sin abounds because the Holy Spirit will not go where wickedness is welcomed. Sin creates fertile ground for Satan's Grim Reaper, who will suggest, "Why don't you just end your suffering by ending your life?" Suicide is the ultimate victory for the devil. The other alternative is Satan might decide, "I can use this person. With a little training, he could promote my cause." The devil will then energize this almost-lifeless shell of a human being to recruit him into his worldwide organization of demonic workers, earlier described as "the gang."

The description, which follows in verses 13 and 14, of the wicked man strongly resembles what is commonly known as the "con man." He is the one who has been energized by Satan, so he thinks he doesn't have to work for a living, as Genesis 3:19 tells us all to do. He believes he can make an "easy living" by outsmarting the hardworking people who have the misfortune of crossing his path. This is why verse 12 begins the description by saying the wicked man who "walks with a perverse mouth." The King James Version reads a "froward mouth," while the New International Version of the Bible translates this as a "corrupt mouth." The con man, who is the hunter, as described in verse five, will sprinkle in a few pleasing words to gain his victim's confidence, but just about everything this type of man says will be a self-serving lie. This is natural for one who has made a deal with the devil, who now rules the sluggard's mind. Solomon provides his readers with a detailed description of this type of individual so we can be aware of his ways and alert to his motives. God wants to shelter His children from the influence of Satan's sluggards.

"He winketh with his eyes, he speaketh with his feet, he teacheth with his fingers; frowardness is in his heart, he diviseth mischief continually; he soweth discord" (Proverbs 6:13–14).

These verses describe the body language of a deceitful person. He enhances the seduction of his false words with the distraction of his quirky gestures. The first warning we're given is the winking of his eyes. *Winketh* comes from the Hebrew word *qarats*. Its primary meaning is to pinch. It can also refer to the biting of lips or the blinking of the eyes as a gesture of malice. Qarats can also refer to an illegal act or can mean to cause harm without justification.

The second warning is "He speaketh with his feet." The Hebrew word *malaw* means to speak, often poetically. It is obvious that feet do not speak, but they are capable of "tap dancing" around the truth. It could possibly refer to someone nervously bouncing or rolling up and down on the balls of their feet, or it could refer to someone pacing back and forth while he talks. Solomon warns his readers that distracting actions, whatever they may be, are characteristic of one who has a deceiving spirit with a hidden agenda. The King James Version states, "He teacheth with his fingers," while the Holman Christian Standard Bible describes the sluggard as "gesturing with his fingers." The original Hebrew says he *yarahs*, which means to point or to aim. There is also a warning provided for us in the New Testament that instructs Christians how to discern whether a person is filled with a deceiving spirit or with a truthful spirit.

> Dear friends, do not believe every spirit, but test the spirits to determine if they are from God, because many false prophets have gone out into the world. This is how you know the Spirit of God: Every spirit who confesses that Jesus Christ has come in the flesh is from God. But every spirit who does not confess Jesus is not from God. This is the spirit of the antichrist; you have heard that he is coming, and he is already in the world now. (1 John 4:1–3 HCSB)

These verses do not mean every unbeliever on earth is filled with the "spirit of the Antichrist," but it does alert us to the fact that every unbeliever is a potential medium for the spirit of the Antichrist. When we're walking wisdom's path, the Holy Spirit will make us aware of the places where sin abounds. These are the places where it is much more likely that the people we meet can be possessed with an evil or deceptive spirit. There are many good unbelieving people, but the possibility does exist they can come under the control of an evil spirit because God's hedge of protection is not around them. Satan is not above using a good person who is close to you as a means of attempting to deceiving you.

Verse 14 begins to describe the inner workings of the oppressor: *"Perversity is in his heart."* Remember, this man thinks he is smarter than his victims; he is full of pride. Godly intelligence comes from humility, not pride. Job 15:12–13 asks, *"Why has your heart mislead you, and why do your eyes flash as you turn your anger against God and allow such words to leave your mouth?"* (HCSB). In Job's day, the flashing or the winking of the eyes was associated with ungodliness. King David wrote, *"Let not them that are mine enemies wrongfully rejoice over me: neither let them wink with the eye that hate me without a cause"* (Psalm 35:19). The winking of the eye could have been a means of luring the innocent or the naive into a false sense of security. This would allow the winker a means of access for his selfish manipulations.

Some biblical scholars feel the "winking of the eye" could be associated with witchcraft or hypnotism. Whatever it was, Solomon wanted his students to identify it and use it as a means to recognize an evil man or woman as soon as possible. Perverse businessmen are borderline criminals whose goals are no different than the bandits of Proverbs chapter one— they're just not in as much of a hurry as the armed robbers needed to be. They like to run covert operations, making them harder to identify. Godly parenting includes training children to discern a false or evil spirit. This type of training can begin with children learning how to identify the young troublemakers in the neighborhood so their influence can be avoided.

"Therefore his calamity shall come suddenly; suddenly shall he be broken without remedy" (Proverbs 6:15).

This verse tells us that once the wicked man's judgment begins, it will not take long for it to be completely carried out. Sinners may be allowed to practice their foolishness for years, maybe even decades, but when their demise comes, it is usually swift and sure. Like the prodigal son (Luke 15), sometimes a man has to hit his personal bottom before he can escape sin's pit. The wicked man of verse 15 never makes it out of sin's pit. Like the young man who fornicates with the immoral woman, the con man will be taken hold of and led down to death by the evil of his ways.

> **"These six things doth the Lord hate: yea, seven are an abomination unto him: A proud look, a lying tongue, and hands that shed innocent blood, an heart that deviseth wicked imaginations, feet that be swift in running to mischief, A false witness that speaketh lies, and he that soweth discord among brethren" (Proverbs 6:16–19).**

A commonly asked question is, which one of these seven sins does not fall into the category of what the Lord hates and is thus just an abomination? An abomination, as defined by the Hebrew word *toebah*, refers to something disgusting. A heart that devises wicked plans is different from the other seven sins, in that it is the only one that is internalized. The other six can all be recognized externally by surrounding people; thus having a possible effect on them as well. Planning wickedness is not good, but it's not as evil as the actual act of doing harm to others by carrying out the planned deed. You may think a proud look is not really carrying out an action either, but pride is actually the worst of these sins. Pride, which amounts to a total lack of humility, is the sin God hates the most. Pride is the result of our making ourselves our own gods. This is idolatry and breaks the first and most important commandment. You can be certain God hates pride.

Did you know pride was the first recorded sin? Isaiah 14:12–14 describes Satan's falling from heaven because he wanted to exalt himself above God. Proverbs 21:4 plainly tells us, *"A high look, and a proud heart, and the plowing of the wicked is sin."* Satan is so full of pride—to this day, he is still trying to exalt himself above God by luring godly people away from God's wisdom and towards sin's folly. Satan thinks he's pretty smart, but does it really take that much intelligence to encourage someone to follow his or her own nature? Even animals are capable of following their instincts. God expects human beings to set those instincts aside, which is why He gave humankind intelligence and freedom of choice. When we choose God's wisdom for our guide, we not only gain access to eternal life, we can expect our lives to improve on earth as well.

It is worthy to note that three of the seven deadly sins mentioned in these verses deal with the tongue. A "lying tongue" breaks the ninth commandment. Proverbs 12:22 states, *"Lying lips are abomination to the Lord: but they that deal truly are His delight."* Proverbs 6:19 lists two specific types of liars who hurt not only themselves but others as well. The false witness, who reinvents reality, is attempting to protect someone who is guilty. The false witness also can harm the innocent. It was false witnesses who helped the chief priests and elders to convict Jesus of blasphemy so He could be sentenced to an agonizing death. The other type of liar is the troublemaker, the one who sows discord among his brethren. The troublemaker spreads his discord through gossip, which may or may not contain an element of truth. There are obviously some truths that are best left unsaid, which is why God wants His followers to exercise discretion. The motives of a man's speech can serve as insight into his soul for an alert listener.

The devil loves discord. When the Acts church in Jerusalem first began, shortly after the death and resurrection of our Lord, its members were described as being with "one accord." Acts 1:14; 2:1, 2:46; 4:24; and 5:12 all utilize this phrase. Being with one accord did not mean they were all squeezed into one little Honda. It meant they were all united with one mind and spirit through their obedience to the one Holy Spirit. Rather than reasoning among themselves about their problems, they all turned to God for their solutions—this was the source of their unity.

The opposite of being in one accord is obviously being in a state of discord, to which Proverbs 6:19 refers. The worthless person of Proverbs 6:12, who was previously described as a sluggard in Proverbs 6:6–10, becomes wicked when energized by Satan. He then goes on to talk with a perverse mouth, as verse 12 tells us. Verse 14 tells us the mission for which Satan has prepared him: "He sows discord." Proverbs 6:16–19 again describe this lazy, perverse, and wicked man by telling us what evil deeds each part of his body tries to accomplish. Verse 19 completes the description of the energized sluggard by telling us he is now also a false witness. The sluggard has finally gotten off his mom and dad's couch and is now sowing Satan's "seeds" of discord among his brethren.

The sluggard is spreading the germs of his sin's disease through his words because he is still too lazy for any physical action. Those among his brethren who are fortunate enough to have studied God's Word will recognize the sluggard's words for what they really are—false and thus useless. The parable Jesus spoke in Matthew 13 reveals what happens to those who become infected by the seeds of discord.

> The Kingdom of heaven is likened unto a man which sowed good seed in his field: But while men slept, his enemy came and sowed tares among the wheat, and went his way. But when the blade was sprung up, and brought forth fruit, then appeared the tares also. So the servants of the householder came and said unto him, "Sir, didst not thou sow good seed in thy field? From whence then hath it tares?" He said unto them, "An enemy hath done this." The servants said unto him, "Wilt thou then that we go and gather them up?" But he said, "Nay; lest while ye gather up the tares, ye root up also the wheat with them. Let both grow together until the harvest: and in the time of the harvest I will say to the reapers, "Gather ye together first the tares, and bind them in bundles to burn them: but gather the wheat into my barn." (Matthew 13:24–30)

The words we speak, like seeds, are sown into the ears of those around us. These words, when carefully considered and accepted by the listener, will then become a part of that person's memory, which means they have the potential to later influence the listener's own thoughts and words. Our hearts will harbor what our minds interpret. If these words are words of gossip or maliciousness, they will produce tares instead of wheat. Christians do not need to sow bad seed, as the devil's workers are already all over that job. Even a sincere Christian's witness can be destroyed if he or she unknowingly sows tares. We need to approach every verbal exchange as one to which God is listening—because as God, He sees all, hears all, and knows all.

WISDOM SPEECH THIRTEEN

Proverbs 6:20–35

"My son, keep thy father's commandment, and forsake not the law of thy mother: Bind them continually upon thine heart, and tie them about thy neck. When thou goest, it shall lead thee; when thou sleepest, it shall keep thee; and when thou awakest, it shall talk with thee" (Proverbs 6:20–22).

These comforting verses have assured Christians throughout the ages that they would never be alone if they successfully download God's words into their hearts. These same verses also serve as instruction to parents for why it is so important to provide all the training that God wants His children to have before they leave home. What better assurance could a young soldier, going off to war, have than to know if he makes the ultimate sacrifice for his country, he will be going home to be with the Lord? God's blessed assurance is second only to His eternal salvation. The best way to assure children that God's precepts and protection are there for them when they need them is to make sure they grow up with them.

The schoolyard bully, the teenaged sluggard, the immoral woman, and the smooth-talking confidence man are no match for God's wisdom. A committed Christian will want to avoid making any unnecessary alliances with these types of people, but he first must be able to identify who they are—which is the main topic of this sixth chapter of the Proverbs.

"For the commandment is a lamp; and the law is light; and reproofs of instruction are the way of life" (Proverbs 6:23).

Matthew 22:37 identifies what the commandment is: *"Thou shalt love the Lord thy God with all thy heart, with all thy soul, and with all thy mind,"* which is why Jesus told us, *"I am the way, the truth, and the life: no man cometh unto the father but by me"* (John 14:6). When we don't follow the light, we will experience a "reproof of instruction." This means the blessings of obedience, or if we choose, the curse of disobedience will be proven to us time and time again because it is God's universe, and His universal laws never cease to function. It's our choice which type of reproof we will experience. Now, Solomon will review again; what is probably the strongest temptation a successful young or middle-aged man will encounter.

"To keep thee from the evil woman, from the flattery of the tongue of a strange woman" (Proverbs 6:24).

The evil woman is the female version of the wicked man, as identified earlier in Proverbs 6:12. Like the wicked man, she probably began as a sluggard and decided hard, honest work was not to her liking. She too has a perverse mouth and "winking eyes," which are used to lure in her victims. The Hebrew word *chelqah,* which is translated by the King James Version as *flattery,* implies smoothness. A smooth or seductive tongue encourages fantasy rather than reality. It should come as no surprise the first piece of information given to us about the evil woman is the same body part of which verse 12 warns us concerning the wicked man—the tongue.

The flattering tongue of the seductress is just as dangerous as the perverse mouth of the wicked man. The lips of the immoral woman were the danger talked about in Proverbs chapter five. Proverbs 2:16 described the immoral woman in an identical fashion: "The stranger which flattereth with her words." Solomon knew how vulnerable the male mind is when confronted by sexual temptation. It concerned him enough to write another entire chapter (Proverbs 7) on the matter.

Lust not after her beauty in thine heart; neither let her take thee with her eyelids" (Proverbs 6:25).

God created a beautiful world for us to live in. The sights and sounds of nature have the ability to totally captivate our attention, but nothing can catch a man's attention like a beautiful woman, which is precisely what *laquach*, the Hebrew word for *allure*, means. It is difficult but not impossible for a man to admire a woman's beauty without lust entering his heart. She should be seen not only as the daughter of another man but also as a daughter of God, who created her beauty for a purpose. A woman's beauty can be admired in the same way other forms of nature are admired, such as a babbling brook, a blooming orchid, or a doe gracefully leaping through the forest. Unlike the con man, a beautiful woman does not have to shuffle her feet or point with her fingers to get a man's attention. All she needs to do is to be herself and let nature take its course.

True beauty comes from within the soul, not the eyes. Like wisdom, beauty can have more than one origin. The type of women these verses are describing to the young man, lack inner or godly beauty. They have an ugly soul that drives them to destroy the souls of the ones they manage to lure away from God, as they pursue their own selfish desires. Their beauty is only skin deep. The teacher wants his student to recognize the seductress for what she really is, so he now begins to describe her inner self hidden beneath her outer charms.

"For by means of a whorish woman a man is brought to a piece of bread: and the adulteress will hunt for the precious life" (Proverbs 6:26).

The King James term "whorish woman" is translated from the Hebrew word *zanah*, which usually refers to those specifically practicing adultery instead of just committing general fornication. Proverbs 29:3 reads, "A man who loves wisdom brings joy to his father, but one who consorts with prostitutes destroys his wealth" (HCSB). It's all about the money, not love or even pleasure. The prostitute is a businesswoman; unfortunately for her, her business is sin for hire, and like all other forms of sin, is doomed to fail. This makes her a desperate and thus a dangerous person with whom to associate in any way. This is why Solomon describes her as a hunter of precious life. She needs her client's wealth if she is to live as she is accustomed.

"Can a man take fire in his bosom and his clothes not be burned? Can one go upon hot coals, and his feet not be burned?

So (is) he that goeth in to his neighbor's wife; whosoever toucheth her shall not be innocent" (Proverbs 6:27–29).

The two questions asked by verses 27 and 28 compare the effects of sexual sin to those of fire. After something has been burned, it is permanently scarred and will have the lingering odor of smoke. The lingering odor and burned remains of a consuming fire are being compared to the inevitable effects of sexual sin. Anyone who is infected by an incurable sexual disease will understand these verses well but probably will not use himself or herself as a public example for a warning to sexually inactive teenagers. No one wants to publically share the shame and embarrassment this type of sin causes. Raging lust may be short-lived but will still manage to incapacitate good judgment. Any bad decision made because of lust is capable of causing long-lasting consequences. This is why it is compared to the odor of smoke, which will continue to stink long after the fire has been put out, just as a sexually transmitted virus will continue to survive in its victim's body.

"Men do not despise a thief, if he steal(s) to satisfy his soul when he is hungry" (Proverbs 6:30).

Stealing is obviously sin, but if the thief is starving, this verse is telling us that people will understand that need, and will be sympathetic toward an attempt to fulfill it. The original Hebrew word translated as hungry is *raeb*, which can mean to hunger or to suffer. Proverbs 21:2 tells us, *"Every way of a man is right in his own eyes; but the Lord pondereth the hearts."* It is perfectly normal for any living organism to do whatever is necessary to survive. If people are alert enough to discern the difference between one's stealing to fulfill a need and stealing to fulfill a want, you can be sure God also understands that difference.

"But if he be found, he shall restore sevenfold; he shall give all the substance of his house" (Proverbs 6:31).

Judgment and punishment still will be carried out, even if the thief has a legitimate need. Unlike God, most men are not in the forgiveness business. Repayment is almost always required. It is not known why

Solomon says the thief must repay seven times what he stole, since Old Testament law does not require this degree of repayment. Seven is God's number of completeness, so this phrase could be interpreted as saying the debt will have to be paid completely, which could include more than just financial restitution. It could also cause a loss of social standing in the community. The thief may be banished or "put out."

Verse 31 is telling us he may have to give up all the substance of his house. Unlike modern homeowners, his house was probably not his most valuable possession—a house in Solomon's time was often a crudely fashioned lean-to or a patched-up tent. Exodus 22:3 reads, *"A thief must make full restitution. If he is unable, he is to be sold because of his theft"* (HCSB). This could include his being forced into slavery—as well as his wife and his children—until the debt is satisfied.

"But whoso commits adultery with a woman lacketh understanding; he that doeth it destroyeth his own soul" (Proverbs 6:32).

This verse reinforces what we read earlier in verses 27–28. Once the fire is extinguished, the odor of smoke remains, and burned skin remains scarred. Social sins such as adultery and gossip are remembered; they cannot be undone. The Hebrew word for destroy is *shachath*, which means to ruin, to lose, or to utterly waste. The adulterer's reputation will suffer; he may even have to find a new community to dwell in, due to an enraged husband eager to settle the score. If the young man of Proverbs chapter six is married, as was the young man of Proverbs chapter five, he will also have broken his wife's heart. How can anyone who understands all these harmful and usually permanent effects go on to have an affair with a married person? Adultery, unlike thievery, is a crime for which complete restitution cannot be paid. The memory of unfaithfulness, like the effects of smoke and fire, cannot be erased.

"A wound and dishonor shall he get; and his reproach shall not be wiped away" (Proverbs 6:33).

Nega is the Hebrew word from which *wounds* is translated. It is also the word used sometimes for plague in the Old Testament. *Nega* can also be interpreted to mean a blow or a stripe. The HCSB states, *"He will get a beating."* Both are good interpretations and are logical to use in association with the dishonor and reproach that cannot be wiped away. Verse 33 describes a lifetime of shame and dishonor to which he, his wife, and his family will all be subjected. In addition to being treated like a leper, he will still have to contend with an enraged husband, assuming the woman he became involved with was married.

"For Jealousy is the rage of a man: therefore he will not spare in the day of vengeance. He will not regard any ransom; neither will he rest content, though thou givest many gifts" (Proverbs 6:34–35).

These final two verses of chapter six again warn the young man about the wages of sin. They also provide one of the clearest examples of how sin can manifest itself. Sin, like a disease, progresses through its stages, which become more and more demanding upon its victim's life. If allowed to continue, the final stage of the sin disease is death. The first stage of sin is always the same—the victim allows himself or herself to become distracted from God's will. There is a quick and very effective cure for the sin disease during the first stage—all it takes is for the victim to cry out for God's help and then follow His directions. God's words, which make up His holy scriptures, are His directions. The Old Testament book of Proverbs provides some of the clearest and easiest to understand directions found in the Bible's sixty-six books.

The jealous husband's fury is the direct result of a past set of sins in which he was not directly involved. His rage is the result of his wife's adultery. He, however, may or may not be partly responsible for the situations that encouraged his wife's indiscretion. Maybe he was not being a good husband. Husbands and wives are both under the oath of their marital vows to remain loyal and loving to their marital partners. The list of possible past sins leading up to adultery could probably go on forever. They could begin with two good people who God never intended to be married to one another in the first place. Regardless of its roots, the sin of adultery has manifested itself into an out-of-control man who now wants to exact his revenge. Solomon later wrote, *"For love is as strong as death; ardent love is as unrelenting as Sheol. Love's flames are firey flames—the fiercest of all"*

(Song of Solomon 8:6 HCSB). The flame of jealousy continues to burn until all of its fuel has been devoured.

Adultery is a sin that can quickly escalate to murder. More than one jealous husband has either killed the wrong man or killed for an adultery that never happened. Imagine the pain a child of a slain adulterer must feel when he looks into the angry eyes of his other parent who has slain his mother or father. Adultery is a sin that will affect all the members of the involved families. Its effect can even spread to the neighboring households of the community, and then be passed on to the following generation. Given the seriousness of the possible consequences of adultery and having felt its devastation within his own family, it is not surprising Solomon decided to devote the entire next chapter to the sin of adultery. The next chapter may have been inspired by Solomon's own adulterous curiosity.

WISDOM SPEECH FOURTEEN

Proverbs 7:1–27

Proverbs chapter seven is the last of Solomon's personalized instruction to his beloved student, as chapters eight and nine are addressed to a general audience, rather than an individual. Like chapter five, the main topic of this chapter is sex. The key to understanding why Solomon devoted two entire chapters to the same topic is to focus on the differences between these two chapters, rather than the similarities. The most obvious difference is that beginning with Proverbs 7:6, the teacher begins to present his lecture from a third-person point of view.

The main character of the story is a fictional young man who, for the purposes of a twenty-first–century application, could be thought of as a student in his first year of college. The teacher who is narrating the story has developed a concern for this particular student, due to his lack of progress. He does not seem to be happy, and his grades are on a decline. As the story unfolds, we learn he is distracted from his studies by a spirit of restlessness. Perhaps his being away from home for the first time brought on a sudden need for social intimacy. So rather than turning to wisdom for comfort, he instead goes to the wrong place, and meets the wrong person in an attempt to soothe his loneliness.

From a chronological perspective, the story of chapter seven would seem to fit in with the earlier chapters, when the student of Solomon's proverbs was first warned about the immoral woman and the "the stranger which flattereth with her words" (Proverbs 2:16). Sexual temptation was not mentioned again until chapter five—when Solomon's student was warned about the dangers of adultery, and was reminded he now had a wife to whom he had vowed to be faithful. The readers of chapter five can reasonably assume the teacher's warning was honored and the student's family remained intact.

We are never told why the young man in chapter five had become interested in other women. Perhaps the catalyst for his roving eye was that his wife was now too busy attending to their children's needs to continue providing all the attention to which he had become so accustomed in the early years of their marriage. To their credit, mothers seem to be more aware of their children's needs than do most fathers. It makes sense that God would create mothers and fathers with differing abilities for a job as important as parenting. Assuming the chapter five marriage had indeed been blessed with children, it is possible the purpose of the chapter seven story was to be an incentive for the chapter five student/father to help teach his own children about matters of sexual correctness.

Another difference in the chapter seven story is the marital status of the woman with whom the straying student becomes involved. Proverbs 7:10 tells us the woman was wearing the attire of a harlot when stalking him. We later learn, in verse 19, that she is a married woman who is masquerading as a prostitute so she could discreetly search for a lover who could satisfy the needs her husband was no longer attempting to fulfill. Unlike a typical harlot, she was not looking to benefit financially from her sexual activity. Her husband was away from home on an extended business trip. He seems to have been a successful man, as verse 16 describes the elaborate furnishings he had provided for the home she was preparing to defile.

This story could also be perceived as advice to the chapter five student to be aware of his own wife's needs. The absent husband would not be the only man who had become so involved with his business that he lost interest in his marital relationship. The apostle Paul addressed this very issue in 1 Corinthians 7:1–8.

> It is good for a man not to have relations with a woman. But because sexual immorality is so common, each man should have his own wife, and each woman should have her own husband. A husband should fulfill his marital responsibility to his wife, and likewise a wife to her husband. A wife does not have the right over her own

body, but her husband does. In the same way, a husband does not have the right over his own body, but his wife does. Do not deprive one another sexually—except when you agree for a time, to devote yourselves to prayer. Then come together again; otherwise Satan may tempt you because of your lack of self control. I say the following as a concession, not as a command. I wish that all people were just like me. But each has his own gift from God, one person in this way, and another in that way. I say to the unmarried and to widows: It is good for them if they remain as I am. But if they do not have self-control, they should marry, for it is better to marry than to burn with desire. (HCSB)

Paul's marital guidelines were given about one thousand years after Solomon wrote the Proverbs. During that time, much had changed in the Hebrew culture. Moses had made a provision for divorce, as written in the Deuteronomy 24, but Jesus, when questioned by the Pharisees, later declared, *"Moses, permitted you to divorce your wives because of the hardness of your hearts. But it was not like that from the beginning. And I tell you, whoever divorces his wife, except for sexual immorality, and marries another, commits adultery"* (Matthew 19:8–9 HCSB). The Samaritan woman Jesus talked to at the well in John chapter four had had five husbands, which seems to indicate divorce was easily obtained in Israel during the days of Jesus' ministry.

When the disciples arrived, they were shocked to see Jesus talking to a Samaritan woman. Women, especially Samaritan women, were considered a lower class of human existence, yet Jesus showed compassion and treated her with the same kindness He would have shown to any man. When Jesus later rose from the dead, it was Mary Magdalene to whom He first appeared and instructed to tell the brethren that He had ascended. Jesus chose a woman to be the first to know of the risen Lord. What an honor, and what an example.

Multiple chapters of the gospel accounts record Jesus telling the disciples He would have to die and then would rise. Despite being told beforehand that Jesus would rise from the dead; none of the apostles would believe what the women told them. A woman's word was not considered valid in a Hebrew court of law; all legal claims had to come from men. If followers of Jesus from the first century were going to fabricate the resurrection account, they would have never credited a woman with being the first to see the resurrected Christ.

The disciples seemed to be almost as reluctant as the Pharisees to change their Old Testament mode of thinking. They refused to believe that Jesus had risen, as Mary Magdalene reported. They were still unwilling to treat her as an equal, despite her love and devotion for Jesus. Mark 16:14 reads, *"Later, He appeared to the Eleven themselves as they were reclining at the table. He rebuked their unbelief and hardness of heart, because they did not believe those who had saw Him after He had been resurrected."* (HCSB). The first order of business for the risen Christ was to rebuke the disciples' hardness of hearts toward the women who had showed Him so much love—probably more love than the disciples themselves had shown! We have no way of knowing exactly how many earthly appearances Jesus made after His resurrection or precisely what all He said, but we can be sure everything Jesus said during those forty days, between His resurrection and His ascension, should be taken as being of the highest importance.

Male dominance over women was carried to an extreme during Old Testament times. The resurrected Christ made women's rights His first lesson to the eleven remaining disciples as a group. Prior to seeing her risen Lord, Mary Magdalene and the other Mary saw two angels, who told them, *"Go quickly and tell His disciples, He has been raised from the dead. In fact, He is going ahead of you to Galilee; you will see Him there"* (Matthew 28:7).

As they then left the tomb to carry out their mission, the resurrected Jesus Himself appeared and told them a second time to tell the disciples He was alive and had risen, and would appear to them at Galilee. It seems Jesus wanted to make sure He was going to have the opportunity to teach His disciples on the matter of fairer treatment for women. Jesus knew their hearts, and He knew that just like the Pharisees, the disciples were reluctant to give up their privileged social status, granted to them by the Old Testament covenants.

It can be legitimately claimed that honor and respect for women was our Lord's final command prior to proclaiming, *"It is finished!"* John 19:27

states, *"Then saith He to the disciple, 'Behold thy mother!' And from that hour that disciple took her unto his own home."* Jesus wanted His mother to be taken care of. It was important enough for Him to make it His dying request.

Jesus always stood up for those being oppressed. The harsh treatment of women had come about as the result of some very selective interpretation of Hebrew law by the Scribes and the Pharisees. He reminded the Pharisees of God's initial marital guidelines, written in Genesis 2:24, *"Therefore shall a man leave his father and his mother and shall cleave unto his wife: and they shall be one flesh."* Paul supported the concept of fairer treatment for women by going so far as to say that one wife is all a man of God should have. He instructed men to love their wives, as Christ loved the church (Ephesians 5:24).

Only when the importance of marriage has been established can one really understand the seriousness in God's eyes of the situation presented to us in Proverbs chapter seven. Even Jesus Himself was tempted by the devil. Therefore, it would not be unreasonable to suggest that every young Christian will have a temptation that can go on to be the defining moment of her or his life. Some temptations will cause a person to make a bad decision, which will cause a spiritual setback, but it's one from which he or she will eventually learn and thus grow. Other temptations, however, will foster a bad decision from which there can be no recovery. The scene from Proverbs chapter seven, as described by the teacher, seems to be a situation that results in one of those unrecoverable bad decisions. Sexual temptation is probably the devil's most frequently used means of sin seduction, for young and middle age adults. It is also the most effective, as it affects more than just the people involved; it tears apart entire families.

"For at the window of my house I looked through my casement, and beheld among the simple ones, I discerned among the youths, a young man void of understanding" (Proverbs 7:6–7).

The chapter seven story begins from the teacher's perspective as he looks through his casement. In modern terms, he was peeping through the blinds. The teacher was observing a group of teenagers without their knowing it, much like God can observe any of us. The simple ones would be a group of students who had just been dismissed from their final class of the week. They are described as the "simple" because they are still unaware of how complex the world's stage can be. The teacher knew the tendencies of young men; he had been teaching for many years. Most of the group he was observing were either students or former students of his. He was quite familiar with one young man in particular. He was a troubled young man who was failing to recognize and honor life's early instructions. He had continually tested the boundaries of authority through-out his childhood. It was no surprise to the teacher that this young man was walking with other students who had also displayed similar difficulty submitting to wisdom's statutes.

"Passing through the street near her corner; and he went the way to her house, in the twilight, in the evening, in the black and dark night" (Proverbs 7:8–9).

As the group walked on, the troubled yet proud young man began to drop back to the rear of the group. Then, as they were almost out of the teacher's sight, he separated himself from the group by turning onto a different path that did not lead where the young men were supposed to be going—home for the weekend, where their families were expecting them. As he slipped away into the darkness out of the teacher's sight, a feeling of fear and disappointment filled the teacher's heart—he knew the troubled young man had made a very bad decision.

The teacher had earlier overheard several bits of conversations from the young man that had indicated he was not content with the instruction of wisdom's way. He was bored with his virginity and eager to learn more about the opposite sex. He had heard older boys in the school talking about a certain area of the city where the harlots would gather at night. He now knew why his parents had always avoided that area and why his father would make occasional critical remarks concerning the people who would go to the "dark side of town." Then it dawned on him: "They told me not to go there because that's where the fun is. They still think I'm not old enough to take care of myself. What could it hurt if I just walked around the outer square? I really want to see what's going on over there."

As the teacher shut the blinds, he shook his head and began to think about all the bad things that could happen to that young man if he continued down that dark path. He feared the worst for the young man as he thought back to earlier years, when he had seen previous students take that forbidden journey down to the dark side of town. This was where some conflicted young students would go, attempting to answer the questions they felt too embarrassed to ask—questions that had been discretely answered by the very teachings they were balking at accepting. Sin had blinded them of the evil responsible for their curiosity. This young man had failed to embrace wisdom's instruction and to carve them into the tablet of his heart.

"And behold, there met him a woman with the attire of an harlot, and subtil of heart" (Proverbs 7:10).

This was the moment the young man had been waiting for. His male ego told him, "That's what I came here to see. I really want to meet her. I want to learn all about her." Little did he know that what he perceived to be his prey was actually his predator. He thought the woman who was approaching him was a prostitute, but that was only her outward appearance. Verse ten states she was dressed as a harlot, but this was only a disguise—she was actually a married woman who was seeking an adulterous affair. The King James Version describes her as being subtle of heart. This is a form of the same word used in Genesis 3:1, which says, "Now the serpent was more subtil than any beast of the field which the Lord God had made."

Solomon had every reason to describe this wayward wife of a successful businessman with the same word used by God to describe the serpent of Eden. It is a logical assumption that the woman of chapter seven was very beautiful; she was probably a trophy wife. Satan was also a beautiful creature. We are given a description of him in Ezekiel 28:12. *"You were the seal of perfection, full of wisdom and perfect in beauty"* (HCSB). Like the serpent, the adulterous woman of chapter seven was looking good, while she carried out Satan's work. They were both Satan's chosen vessels by which Eve and the eager young man would be deceived. In addition to their beauty, they were both graceful in their movements.

Anyone who has taken the time to observe the movement of a snake will know how captivating a serpent's movements can be. The rhythmic movement of a snake's body can be mesmerizing as it slowly and fluidly moves toward its prey. The different colors of a serpent's scales, much like the beat of music, will flow together and then separate in a graceful and coordinated manner with precise timing. Watching a snake can be a hypnotic experience, much like the sight of a beautiful young woman, as the curves of her torso rhythmically flow with the movement of her legs and arms. Any woman who is experienced in the art of seduction will know how to dress in order to accentuate the gracefulness of her movements, along with her other physical assets. This is why the adulteress of chapter seven is dressed as a harlot. Once she found the man who could fulfill her sexual fantasies, she wanted to have the right bait—she wanted to captivate her target's attention. She set out to prime him for his own sexual fantasy, even if it would cost him his life.

"She is loud and defiant; her feet do not stay at home.
Now in the street, now in the squares, she lurks at
every corner" (Proverbs 7:11–12 HCSB).

Proverbs 7:11–12 give us more insight into the character and personality of the adulterous wife. We're told she was loud and rebellious. This means she had energy to burn. This is typical for a person who lacks a worthy purpose in life. Like the young man, she was probably young herself. Being loud means she had a lot to say and was not going to show any discretion about when or where she would say it. She craved attention and was determined to carry out her self-centered desires without any regard for social, legal, or religious protocol. She had probably been rebellious most of her life, beginning with her refusal to obey the rules throughout her childhood. Her attractiveness had allowed her to get away with things she should not have done and said. Now she was going to continue her established pattern of reckless disobedience, even if it would endanger the welfare of those she managed to recruit for her personal desires.

With her husband being out of town, there was nothing left to inhibit her self-serving motives, so she disguised herself as a harlot and began the search for a good-looking, healthy young man who could provide for her the sexual stamina her hardworking older husband no longer possessed.

The phrase "lurking at every corner" means she had a specific vision of who she wanted for a lover. Her search was exhaustive. If she could not find exactly what she wanted she would find the closest thing to it. She not only lacked morality and discretion, but she was impatient as well. She was not going to wait for her husband to return; she wanted her urges satisfied quickly.

"So she caught him, and kissed him, and with an impudent face said to him, 'I have peace-offerings with me; this day have I paid my vows'" (Proverbs 7:13–14).

Chazaq is the Hebrew word that both King James Versions translate as *caught*. The primary meaning for chazaq is to fasten onto. The Holman Christian Standard Bible says, "She grabs him and kisses him." Unlike a prostitute, she did not begin to negotiate a price. She instead continued to appeal to his senses, which is exactly what the devil did in both the garden of Eden and during the temptation of Christ. She had already appealed to his sense of sight with her suggestive clothing and her sensual movements. Being of a loud personality, as we are told in verse 11, she may have began talking to him before she managed to embrace him. She did not have to talk much because her body language was already screaming at the young man.

When she grabbed him, it was a passionate embrace. She had to make sure he was physically strong by pressing tightly against his aroused body. Her sexual fantasy required more than a handsome face; she wanted her lover to have a lean yet muscular body—one that was capable of satisfying all of her sexual demands. Having successfully appealed to his sense of touch and being close enough for him to smell her carefully selected perfume, she was now ready to move in for the kill. Just like Satan, she would appeal to his pride by telling him how special he was and that he was the one she had searched for. She told him of all the preparations she made to enhance the pleasure of their soon-to-be physical union.

As she continued to explore his body with her eager hands, her verbal seduction began. She sensed he wanted her badly, but she also knew this inexperienced young man thought she was a prostitute who had been swept off her feet by just his appearance. He had no idea he was kissing another man's wife. This was her biggest challenge to overcome; she had to convince this young man of Israel to become the willing partner of her predetermined adultery. She knew this was not what the young man had set out to do when he ventured out from his home turf. She wanted him to think this was going to be more than a simple sexual adventure—this was going to be an ongoing affair built on excitement, passion, and endless sexual pleasure. She had to convince him what she was offering was worth the risk of sleeping with another man's wife. To accomplish this final objective, she described how much thought and effort had gone into her preparations to maximize their anticipated physical ecstasy.

This was when she stopped kissing him and brazenly stared into his eyes to say, "I have peace offerings with me; today I have paid my vows." She still wasn't ready to reveal her marital status. Instead, she tells him she has paid her vows. We're not told to what vows she is referring, but it can be reasonably assumed she is claiming to be a religious woman. We do not know what religion this woman was claiming to practice, but we can be sure it was not the sanctioned religion of Israel. This too could be appealing to the young man, as he was already in rebellion against the rules of what he was being taught. He was drawn to this beautiful woman's uninhibited enthusiasm to fulfill her sexual desires without any guilt or shame. He was now deeply intrigued with the thought of having sex, without angering God. He reasoned this was made possible by her having made "peace offerings" to consummate this proposed physical union, with her god's approval. He now understood her god to be much more accommodating than the God of Israel.

"Therefore came I forth to meet thee, diligently to seek thy face, and I have found thee. I have decked my bed with coverings of tapestry, with carved works, with fine linen of Egypt. I have perfumed my bed with myrrh, aloes, and cinnamon" (Proverbs 7:15–17).

The crafty adulteress is now putting the icing on the cake. She not only was ready to delight him sexually, she was going to do it with style and in a luxurious setting. This was beyond any dream he had ever had—a woman who not only was beautiful and willing but was wealthy as well. He was too overwhelmed with sexual desire to wonder who was paying for all the comforts this sex goddess was describing. He didn't care—he was ready to do anything she wanted. Sensing he was willing to succumb to her proposal, she now tells him exactly what she wants him to do.

> **"Come, let us take our fill of love until the morning;**
> **let us solace ourselves with loves" (Proverbs 7:18).**

How could he say no to such a well-thought-out proposal? All he could think of was falling into that perfumed bed with this seemingly wonderful woman who had totally captured his attention. His body's senses were heightened with excitement, as a thousand thoughts raced through his mind. He briefly wondered how he would explain where he had been all night to his parents. He was at an age where being around his parents had become awkward. Maybe this lady would provide him with the means of getting out from under his parents' rule. Before he could respond, his fantasy of independence soon ended.

> **"For the goodman is not at home, he is gone a long journey.**
> **He hath taken a bag of money with him, and will come**
> **home at the day appointed" (Proverbs 7:19–20).**

The word *goodman* is translated from the Hebrew word *lysh*. Most modern Bibles translate this word to mean husband. Hearing this word should have put the brakes on the young man's lust; it should have had the same effect as a cold bucket of water. Some misled men will draw the line at adultery. The following verses tell us this particular young man was not one of those men. It varies greatly from man to man and from situation to situation when a man is able resist the opportunity to have immoral sex. There have already been multiple warnings about adultery in Proverbs. The final verses of chapter six should be enough reason to discourage any intelligent man from getting involved with a married woman. The many different societies throughout the world's history have had their own interpretation of what is and is not morally acceptable, but the rage of a wronged husband has always been a force worth considering. As should the rage of a wronged God, who plainly stated in Exodus 20:14, *"Thou shalt not commit adultery."*

**"With her much fair speech she caused him to yield, with
the flattering of her lips she forced him" (Proverbs 7:21).**

When anyone, man or woman, allows an erotic situation to develop,
immoral sex has already been contemplated. Christians are not immune.
Any Christian who sticks around the wrong place with the wrong people
long enough to engage in foreplay has already sinned. This is precisely why
Jesus said, *"Whosoever looketh on a woman to lust after her hath committed
adultery with her already in his heart"* (Matthew 5:28). Proverbs chapter
seven is a story that illustrates what not to do. It all began with, as verse
seven told us, "a young man who was devoid of understanding."

**"He goeth after her straightway, as an ox goeth to the
slaughter, or as a fool to the correction of the stocks; Till a
dart strike through his liver; as a bird hasteth to the snare,
and knoweth not that it is for his life" (Proverbs 7:22–23).**

When instincts kick in, actions are automatic, often without thought
or any regard for resulting consequences. This is what's happening in verse
22. The expression "He's dumb as an ox" may have been derived from this
verse. Like the ox, the foolish young man does not know that the path he
is being led down will end with his demise. The other possible outcome
given by this verse is the "correction of the stocks." Correction is good,
as we were told in Proverbs chapter three, but the stocks were one of the
most humiliating forms of correction in existence. They were, however, a
practical solution for those who could not learn from conventional means
of correction, particularly those whose actions threatened the moral fabric
of a given society. If a known adulterer were to survive the stocks, there
would still be an enraged husband waiting to extract further revenge.

**"Harken unto me now therefore, O ye children, and attend
to the words of my mouth. Let not thine heart decline to her
ways, go not astray in her paths" (Proverbs 7:24–25).**

Verse 24 begins the conclusion of the chapter seven story. The teacher
is preparing to issue his final plea for his remaining students to avoid the
dangers of immorality. Over his career, he had learned how to recognize

which students were destined for success and which were headed in the wrong direction. He wished he had been more successful at convincing the struggling students to recognize the evil of their ways. Ironically, the students who needed help the most were the very ones who would slam their minds shut upon hearing anything they perceived as critical. This was why the teacher told his story from a third-person point of view. It would allow him to illustrate the dangers of immoral sex without offending his troubled students. By creating fictional characters, there was no need to directly address those he was concerned about and would thus minimize the risk of alienating their attention.

Verse 25 brings the teacher's instruction back to the first-person perspective. The message is not a new one, but the teacher is praying it can take on a deeper meaning and will now be taken more seriously by the young man. The young man in the story had wandered from wisdom's path but not with the intention of committing adultery. He knew right from wrong, but he had no idea how strong his sexual urges could be under the right circumstances. If you hang around a slippery place, it increases the likelihood of a fall. The story of Samson's famous haircut illustrates this well.

"For she hath cast down many wounded: yea, many strong men have been slain by her" (Proverbs 7:26).

When a man hears of or directly observes another man's life being destroyed by sin, his pride will try to tell him, "I'm glad I am wise enough and strong enough to avoid falling into that trap." Sex was the sin used as the example in Proverbs chapter seven, but other sins can yield the same result. Satan has studied human behavior since the days of Adam and Eve. He knows each person's vulnerability. If our pride tells us we can hang out in the wrong places with the wrong people, we should ask ourselves, "Why am I attracted to these kinds of people?" Sin can strike quickly—quick enough to take down anyone outside of God's hedge of protection. Verse 26 reminds us that no one, not even strong men, are immune from satanic attack when they choose to wander down a sinful path.

"Her house is the way to hell, going down to the chambers of death" (Proverbs 7:27).

Chapter seven 7 concludes by reminding us exactly where the devil's trail of deception will lead those who defy God's rules. This was actually the third time Solomon issued this same warning about this specific sin. Proverbs 2:18 and Proverbs 5:5 both tell us that those who become enslaved by sexual immorality will find themselves in the "Pit of Hell," eternally separated from wisdom's beauty and grace. This is where the spirits of those who fail to follow God's commands will descend, never again to be comforted by wisdom's love. What really sets the chapter seven warning apart from the previous chapters, is our being told that these were all strong men who were eternally damned by their lack of self-control. The chambers of death are a sobering thought. Only a fool can ignore the promised outcome of this verse.

The young man's demise was a process. As the seduction continued, sin's hold became tighter and tighter. It is difficult to determine exactly when and where he crossed the point of no return. Was it when he took the path to her house? Was it when she "caught" him and began to kiss him? Maybe the verbal seduction was where she had him hooked. A wise man will not be interested in how he can indulge himself without getting caught because a wise man will know it is not worth the risk of a one-way trip to the chambers of death. A wise man will shun the very appearance of evil—or better yet, a wise man will flee the very appearance of evil.

This is exactly what Joseph, the son of Jacob, did. He, like the young man of chapter seven was "caught" by a married woman who wanted to desecrate her marital vows. Joseph had been sold into slavery by his own brothers. He eventually wound up in the house of Potiphar, captain of the Egyptian guard, who recognized God's blessing was upon Joseph. Potiphar, being a wise man, put Joseph in charge of his house, which allowed Potiphar to focus on his job as captain of the guard for Pharaoh. Mrs. Potiphar, like the immoral wife of chapter seven, felt neglected by her husband, so she too caught herself a young man (Genesis 39:7–18).

Unlike the young man of chapter seven, Joseph fled the very appearance of sin. Despite his obedience to God, Joseph still paid the price of a guilty sinner. He was falsely accused of attempted rape and thrown into prison. Being familiar with unjust treatment, Joseph remained faithful to God and not only was delivered, but he was promoted to the highest position in Egypt, second only to Pharaoh himself. Wisdom, faith, and obedience will never go unnoticed or unrewarded by God.

WISDOM SPEECH FIFTEEN

Proverbs 8:1–36

"Doth not wisdom cry? And understanding put forth her voice? She standeth in the top of high places, by the way in the places of the paths. She crieth at the gates, at the entry of the city, at the coming in at the doors" Proverbs 8:1–3)

Chapter eight begins with, and then quickly answers two rhetorical questions. Their purpose is to redirect the young man's attention from any distractions he may have encountered. These questions were already answered way back in chapter one verses twenty and twenty-one, which reads, *"Wisdom crieth without; She uttereth her voice in the streets. She crieth in the chief place of concourse, in the openings of the gates: in the city She uttereth words."* Notice verse three says, "She cries out," this is because "She" had lots of competition, and still does, especially within the concrete cities built by man. She has had to compete with both, the wisdom and the foolishness of man, in addition to the temptations of Satan's workers (the gang). It's no wonder God's Holy Spirit lead men like Moses, and Paul to the desert where He could train them without distraction. Our Lord Himself often withdrew away from the crowds so He could be alone, and free from distraction to pray.

Verse two gives us another perspective of wisdom's approach. It says, "She takes her stand on the top of the high hill." God's wisdom is always on display, especially in nature. The secluded, hard-to-get-to spots, such as the mountaintops, the forests, or the deserts, are where God's architecture abounds. These are the places where total concentration on His masterpieces is made available to us. If a sample of God's work, such as a leaf or a flower, were put under a microscope, its beauty would still be visible, even under extreme magnification. That same microscope focused on man's work, let's say a stainless steel hypodermic needle, will reveal flaws.

God's creation is more beautiful and symmetrical upon closer inspection—even on a molecular level. Wherever man's concrete has been poured, there is no such beauty—the closer you look, the more flaws you will see. When in the midst of man's concrete cities; wisdom must "cry out" to be heard. When alone within God's natural setting, the Good Shepherd can cause us to lie down beside still water and talk to us softly, tenderly, and wisely. This is the ideal setting for our souls to be nourished or even restored as the twenty-third psalm tells us.

"Unto you, O men, I call; and my voice is to the sons of man" (Proverbs 8:4).

This verse confirms that God has an interest in the entire human race, not just the children of Israel. It cannot be determined with certainty if this is what Solomon wanted to say; most Old Testament Jews received a great deal of pleasure in knowing they alone were God's chosen people. This prideful attitude may have contributed to the predicted downfall of Israel. When Jesus was born about nine centuries later, the religious leaders of Israel had made themselves so important and full of pride that they fulfilled Old Testament prophecy by failing to recognize Jesus, as the Messiah when He arrived. The main instruction given to the disciples by the risen Christ was, *"Go ye therefore, and teach all nations, baptizing them in the name of the Father, and of the Son, and of the Holy Ghost"* (Matthew 28:19).

God made salvation available for all men, but the Jews still retained a special status, as He told the disciples, "Repentance and remission of sins should be preached in His name among all nations, beginning in Jerusalem," (Luke 24:47) or as Paul put it, *"To the Jew first, and also to the Gentile"* (Romans 2:10). God reached out to all humankind, as Solomon told us, long before Jesus told His disciples about this truth, which His Father sent Him to speak. God will tolerate only so much sin before He eliminates it, as He did when He sent the flood. Sadly, sin soon returned to haunt Noah's family, as recorded in Genesis chapter nine, beginning with verse 20. This began another cycle of sin that lasted 350 years, when God broke communion with man and again started over with just one family. This time, He did so without destroying all of earth's inhabitants. Instead, He entered into a covenant with Abraham and his future descendents, the children of Israel.

This was the beginning of the Jewish nation, who were given the privilege of living under God's Old Testament law, while surrounding nations remained in ignorance. Unfortunately for Israel, idols would be brought into their Holy Land. Solomon, despite his wisdom, was one of those who allowed this to happen. Solomon allowed his foreign wives to bring their idols into Jerusalem, and they were never totally eradicated until the Babylonian conquest and exile of the Jewish people. Israel was not healed at this point, but scripture does not record the worshipping of idols in Israel after that point in history. They did, however, add to God's law their own laws, making it much more burdensome to keep and thus devised a system of worship that was very profitable for the religious elite. This was what Christ came to change when He put all men under the covenant of grace. Like God's grace, His wisdom is also available for all men. It is harder for some to obtain than it is for others, but it is still available, which is what the next two verses are about.

"O ye simple, understand wisdom: and ye fools, be ye of an understanding heart" (Proverbs 8:5).

The simple and the foolish are given extra encouragement to focus on what wisdom has to offer. They are reassured it will be worth their time and effort. The Hebrew word *P(e)thaiy,* which is translated as *simple,* can also mean silly, foolish, or seducible. This is the same Hebrew word used in Proverbs 7:7 to describe the group of young men whom the teacher of chapter seven was secretly observing. It was one of these "simple" young men that was eventually seduced by the adulteress who was pretending to be a harlot. This leads readers to believe that the simple young men of Proverbs 8:5, whom the teacher was expressing concern for, were lacking experience and sophistication more so than intelligence. They were listening to their bodies more than their brains. They lacked foresight, which allows them to live in the moment. Verse five tells these people to wake up and become aware of the likely consequences of their tendencies. This is the message of the Proverbs in a nutshell. They tell us what the consequences will be for a wide variety of sin, so future generations do not have to go out and learn these lessons the hard way.

You may recall one of the original objectives listed by Solomon for studying the Proverbs, was to give subtility (shrewdness) to the simple" (Proverbs 1:4). Later in chapter one verse 22 seems to establish a relationship between the simple and the foolish. "How long you simple ones, will you love simplicity? For scorners delight in their scorning, and fools hate knowledge."

Simplicity is usually thought of as being practical and thus a good quality, but the simple referred to here are demonstrating similarities to the sluggard of chapter six. Like the sluggard, the simple often do not want to complicate their lives. Change is what human development is all about—this is especially true for the spiritual development of a newborn Christian. A newborn baby goes through a rapid series of physical, mental, and emotional changes. When we experience the second birth, which is a spiritual birth, the same birth Jesus talked about to Nicodemus in John 3, we are led by the Holy Spirit to give up our *spiritual simplicity* and become obedient to His will. God wants us to voluntarily get out of our comfort zones so that we can grow to become the people He wants us to be. Spiritual development will temporarily retard or even eliminate other areas of human development our flesh wants us to pursue. This is the very concept the Jewish rite of circumcision demonstrates. It is a cutting away of the flesh of the outer man so that the inner man can be free to pursue God's will.

The simple, especially the ones who have the tendencies of a sluggard, will love their simplicity, as Proverbs 1:22 tells us. When the simple refuse to follow wisdom's advice and refuse to work, they will justify their slothfulness by scorning wisdom's commands. This will then become what they delight in, as Proverbs 1:22 tells us. When the first two conditions of Proverbs 1:22 are met, the third condition will soon follow!

The fools of Proverbs 8:5 are described by the Hebrew word *k(e) ciyl*. This is the same word used by Solomon in Proverbs 1:22 and 1:32, where we are told that fools hate knowledge and will be destroyed by their complacency. This makes the fool a dangerous person to be around, more so than the simple—dangerous enough for Proverbs 26:4 to advise us to not even answer a fool in his folly. Verse five tells us the heart, not the brain, is the source of the fool's condition. An understanding heart is God's remedy for foolishness; without it, the fool will remain a fool and never benefit from the excellence of wisdom's words.

> **"HEAR; for I will speak of excellent things; and the opening of my lips shall be right things. For my mouth shall speak truth; and wickedness is an abomination to my lips. All the words of my mouth are in righteousness; there is nothing froward or perverse in them" (Proverbs 8:6–8).**

These three verses are additional encouragement for those still hesitating to follow wisdom's path. The sins of foolishness and laziness can have a powerful effect on the human mind. This is especially true for the simple; remember they are the ones who can be easily seduced. They could be young and inexperienced, but regardless of the source of their simplicity, these verses are meant to convince them not only of wisdom's creditability but her authority as well. The perverse man, the oppressor, the one who flatters with the wink of his eye, and the seductress all need to be believable if they are to be successful. Sadly, their success is usually, if not always, at the expense of the simple.

This is why the Proverbs repeatedly give us warnings, such as Proverbs 5:3–4. "Though the lips of the forbidden woman drip honey and her words are smoother than oil, in the end she's as bitter as wormwood and as sharp as a double edged sword" (HCSB). Throughout nature, the strong prey on the weak. The simple are rarely among the strong; they are usually those who are "swallowed" alive and dragged down to the pit, as described in Proverbs 1:12. The pits of sin are deceptive and can vary in each individual's perception, but what's common in every case is that **God does not want anyone to go there!**

This is why God wants us to know we can depend on what He tells us. He "speaks of excellent things." He does not need to lie to us or deceive us because He does not need anything we think we have—*it's already His!* He can take it anytime He wants it, because He created it.

If we refuse to be the people He wants us to be, He can create more people on a planet our telescopes haven't even seen yet. There's a lot God chose not to tell us. He chose not to tell us about the electron and the proton, but He created them and created everything and everyone we see out of them. His inspired words that were preserved for us still contain truths yet to be understood by human beings. Science and history have both confirmed the complete infallibility of the Bible when its facts are understood correctly without bias. Correct interpretation of reality requires recognition of truth. God tells us he is the way, the truth, and the light (John 14:6). Without his spiritual guidance, our perspective is skewed by our human condition.

If anything appears to be flawed in God's words, just keep digging, and you will find all His verses are really true. There is nothing in them that are blemished. His words speak only truth and righteousness. A quick glance through church history will reveal an organized, well-funded effort to keep the Bible out of the common people's hands. This oppression went on for centuries. There truly was a Dark Age, as Satan's workers were successful in keeping men in the dark with no access to the light of scripture. The next verse speaks of those who are blessed by the light of God's Word.

"They are all plain to him that understandeth, and right to them that find knowledge" (Proverbs 8:9).

"Him that understandeth" refers to those with whom God's Holy Spirit is in communion. Communion with God makes communication with God possible. One way the Holy Spirit establishes direct communication with man is to grant understanding of His holy scripture to those who sincerely seek it—those who seek it with all their hearts. These are those who value the knowledge of God's wisdom above any worldly treasure. The next verses tell us just how valuable God's wisdom is.

"Receive my instruction, and not silver; and knowledge rather than choice gold. For wisdom is better than rubies; and all the things that may be desired are not to be compared to it" (Proverbs 8:10–11).

In this eighth chapter, as we are nearing the end of Solomon's wisdom speeches, he is still comparing silver and gold to the knowledge that determines our relationship with God. What does this tell us about the heart and mind of Solomon, who went on to collect more gold than probably anyone else in history? First Kings chapter ten tells us Solomon received 666 talents of gold annually from surrounding nations. This is the equivalence of approximately thirty-eight thousand pounds of gold. He also acquired gold from foreign visitors, merchants, and voluntary gifts from other kings and governors. The queen of Sheba alone gave Solomon 120 talents of gold, in addition to valuable spices and precious stones (1 Kings 10:10). He sat on a throne overlaid with pure gold and drank from golden vessels. He even made three hundred shields of hammered gold. As extravagant and magnificent all this was, it pales in comparison to the descriptions of heaven given to us by Jesus in the Gospels and by the apostle John in the book of Revelation. We're told in Revelation 21 that heaven's streets are made of pure gold!

Given the extravagance described in 1 Kings 10, it is no coincidence the very next chapter of 1 Kings tells us that Solomon loved many foreign woman, some of whom were from nations with which God had instructed the children of Israel not to intermarry. Perhaps this was the period when Solomon explored his mind, with alcohol acting as his guide to what he believed to be wisdom, as described in Ecclesiastes 2:3. It is also interesting to note the number representing the amount of gold that Solomon received annually—666 talents. This is the same number designated by God as the number associated with the beast of Revelation 13. Almost everyone today associates evil with this number. No one knows its exact significance, given the limited information provided by God about the beast and his number—yet here is that very same number used to describe Solomon's extravagance, just prior to handing his kingdom over to the impending doom of idolatry.

This gives reason to believe Solomon wrote the eighth chapter of Proverbs prior to, or shortly after, his becoming king of Israel. It is probable Solomon and his mother, Bathsheba, both knew David's problems were caused by his straying from the wisdom of God. The blessed life David had enjoyed as a poor shepherd boy and a fearless warrior was replaced with the certain punishment mandated by the sins of adultery and murder. Solomon was smart enough to know David's sin had affected his entire family, so he kept reminding himself, through his writing, just how important God's commands were. Yet years later, after becoming king and eventually becoming bored with all his riches, he turned to amusement. This was described when he later wrote, *"And whatsoever my eyes desired I keep not from them. I withheld not my heart from any joy; for my heart rejoiced in all my labor: and this was my portion of all my labor" (Ecclesiastes 2:10).* So Solomon, not wanting to become an adulterer, exercised what he must have perceived to be a loophole in God's law, and he began to marry every woman he desired. This author believes God responded by making Solomon impotent. This meant the great king, who was also the greatest collector of wealth, was unable to collect children. This theory would explain why Solomon had only one named son, Rehoboam, who was necessary for David's line to continue sitting on the throne of Israel, as God had promised.

In a society where children were considered a sign of God's blessing, this had to be a major embarrassment. This could have been one reason why Solomon began marrying so many women. He seemingly would marry or purchase any woman he thought could possibly produce for him another son suitable for a king. His heart was turned first by riches, which then led to pleasure, which he later referred to as his reward. Ecclesiastes 2:3 states Solomon turned to wine, guided by wisdom, to gratify his flesh. Could drunkenness have contributed to Solomon's downfall? This we will never know, but Solomon obviously snapped out of it in time to write that all his grand experiments had led to an emptiness in his heart, as described by the very repeated phrase found in Ecclesiastes, **"Vanity, vanity, all is vanity."**

The word vanity appears in every chapter of Ecclesiastes, except for chapter ten. It is written a total of thirty-three times in twenty-eight different verses. The same Hebrew word for each entry of vanity is used each time. This Hebrew word, *habel,* means vanity or emptiness. It can also be used figuratively to mean something transitory or unsatisfactory. A Hebrew alternative form of this word, *hebel,* refers to the sons of Adam. This is most appropriate, as being a son of Adam is total vanity when you can be a son of God!

As the apostle Paul tells us in 1 Corinthians 15, the first man, Adam, was made from the dust and became a living being. The second man, however, was the Lord from heaven. He was the second man, or as 1 Corinthians 15:45 says, *"The last Adam became a life-giving spirit"*

(HCSB). Proverbs 8:10–11 tells us, the wisdom of this same "life-giving spirit" is more valuable than silver, gold, and rubies. Solomon knew this, temporarily ignored it, and then went on to express his remorse with words of regret and emptiness, by using the word *habel* thirty-two times in the book of Ecclesiastes. He felt consumed despite being surrounded by the magnificence of all his earthly riches. Verse 11 concludes the answers to the questions at the beginning of this chapter. Solomon now goes on to give us a first-person account of wisdom's wealth and benefits.

"I wisdom dwell with prudence, and find out knowledge of witty inventions" (Proverbs 8:12).

Verse 12 refers us to the relationship between wisdom and prudence. According to *Webster's*, the prudent life is one that includes foresight, shrewdness, and discretion. Wisdom is still crying out as she did in the beginning of this chapter. She seems to be saying, "I do not want to be around foolishness. I am the very opposite of foolishness. I want to be in the presence of those who seek me by trying to be righteous. The greater their efforts, the more I want to be with them. Those who try to fool me are really only fooling themselves. This is why I inspired my servant Solomon to write, *'The way of the wicked is as darkness; they know not at what they stumble'* (Proverbs 4:19). Because of your obedience and because you respected the commands and advice of your parents, your teachers, and other wise people, you have listened to while while on earth. I wisdom, will grant you knowledge and discretion that you otherwise would not have had. This is why I inspired my servant Solomon, to write, *'When wisdom entereth into thine heart, and knowledge is pleasant unto thy soul; Discretion shall preserve thee; understanding shall keep thee'* (Proverbs 2:10–11)."

"The fear of the Lord is to hate evil: pride, and arrogancy, and the evil way, and the froward mouth, do I hate" (Proverbs 8:13).

This verse brings us full circle, back to the key verse of the Proverbs: *"The fear of the Lord is the beginning of knowledge, but fools despise wisdom and instruction"* (Proverbs 1:7). If you are wondering how many times Solomon is going to tell us to fear the Lord, the answer is, "How many times have you failed to honor the Lord? How many times have you failed to respect Him in the manner He requires?" This verse teaches; those who truly fear the Lord, will hate the same things that God hates. Evil eventually causes problems that no sane person wants to have. It can cause injuries up to and including death; thus, it is wise to fear the effect of sin. We should fear any association with sin, which leads us to the conclusion: *we should fear anyone or anything that distracts us from the only power capable of freeing us from sin.* Association implies relationship; relationship requires respect. God wants a relationship, but He requires respect first.

A humble submission to a higher power requires a healthy fear that is realized with the knowledge that God truly is who and what He claims to be. He is all powerful, which is why we fear Him. He is all knowing, which is why we respect Him, and he is all present, which is why we should always obey Him. We do this by adopting His code of living, which includes shunning any appearance of evil.

Note the emphasis on pride and arrogance in verse 13. These are the attitudes that initiate the straying from God's will. These are the thoughts—the feelings—that take our faith and reliance away from God. Distancing ourselves from God's wisdom will soon cause us to have confidence in our own abilities. This is the beginning of a delusion that can and will continue until we put God back in charge. The attitude of pride shades us from the light of God's wisdom. This is why *pride proceeds the fall.* A fall from God's grace immediately affects our thinking, then our words, and eventually our actions. If God is your copilot, you should switch seats!

The sin process is much like a recovering alcoholic picking up that very first drink. The first drink leads to a second and the second one to a third, and before the poor drunkard knows it, he can't stop. Was it the last drink, the third drink, or the first drink that caused his demise? It may surprise you to know it wasn't any of these drinks that led to this poor man's demise. What caused this mess was his thinking he could have just that one drink. He strayed from the wisdom of the very program that led him to sobriety. Pride and arrogance had convinced him he could secretly take that first drink. Thankfully, help is still available, as this next verse tells us.

"Counsel is mine, and sound wisdom; I am understanding; I have strength" (Proverbs 8:14).

These bold statements are actually very humble claims; given that they are the words of God. Any mortal making these claims would do so out of pride and arrogance. Only God can say these things with humility! To a limited degree, these four attributes have other sources, but God is the original source because He is the Creator. You may recall from chapter one, God does not like it when we refuse His counsel. He wants to counsel us because He loves us, so He bestows upon His selected people the ability to also give wise counsel. These are the ones whom God has filled with His Holy Spirit. They can usually be recognized by their own reliance on God. When their counsel is sought—they will ask, "Did you pray about that?"

Real wise men know the source of their strength and understanding. They know their wisdom is proportional to their closeness with God. They have presented themselves as instruments of righteousness. As the apostle Paul tells us, *"Neither yield ye your members as instruments of unrighteousness unto sin; but yield yourselves unto God, as those that are alive from the dead, and your members as instruments of righteousness unto God"* (Romans 6:13).

Paul is telling us we were dead in our sins, but are now made alive through God's gift of righteousness. This is cause for celebration! Our salvation through grace is an even greater gift than the wisdom described in Solomon's Proverbs—yet he repeatedly emphasizes the value of wisdom with phrases such as; "Seek her as silver, Her proceeds are better than profits of silver, She is more precious than rubies, She is a tree of life, a crown of glory, She will deliver." Those who pray regularly will tell you communication with God is sound counsel and is the source of their own strength and understanding. Wise men will seek even wiser men to explain to them their understanding of God. *"He that walketh with wise men shall be wise, but a companion of fools shall be destroyed"* (Proverbs 13:20).

No one wants to be thought of as a fool; therefore, we will all encounter people who are trying to appear to be wise. The Bible is clear in its directive to seek wise counsel, but it also warns us of those willing to counsel who are not any good at it. They are either lacking in their ability to discern godly wisdom, or they might purposely give bad advice for some hidden motive. This type of person was discussed in Proverbs 6. He is the con man who winks with his eye. He is the one who speaks with a perverse mouth. Our success will often depend on our ability to sense any existing evil and deceit in those who want to lead us from God's wisdom. This ability is known as discernment. We discussed the benefits of discernment and her "sister," discretion, in chapter one. They are the gifts from God leading to wise counsel. Everyone can benefit from sound counsel, but this verse carries an even greater importance for those whose decisions affect many lives. These are the people the next two verses address.

"By me kings reign, and princes decree justice. By me princes rule, and nobles, even all the judges of the earth" (Proverbs 8:15–16).

These verses remind us that those who appear powerful really have no power, unless it's given to them. It is imperative that kings receive wise council because their decisions affect many lives. Their power has been given from above. This is why Jesus is quoted as saying to Pilate, "*Thou couldest have no power at all against me, except it were given thee from above*" (John 19:11). The apostle Paul also had some thoughts about worldly authority.

> Let every soul be subject unto the higher powers. For there is no power but of God; the powers that be are ordained of God. Whosoever therefore resisteth the power, resisteth the ordinance of God; and they that resist shall receive to themselves damnation. For rulers are not a terror to good works, but to the evil. Wilt thou then not be afraid of the power? Do that which is good, and thou shalt have praise of the same. For he is the minister of God to thee for good. But if thou do that which is evil, be afraid; for he beareth not the sword in vain; for he is the minister of God, a revenger to execute wrath upon him that doeth evil. Wherefore ye must needs be subject, not only for wrath, but also for conscience sake. For for this cause pay ye tribute also; for they are God's ministers, attending continually upon this very thing. Render therefore to all their dues: tribute to whom tribute is due; custom to whom custom; fear to whom fear; honour to whom honour. Owe no man any thing, but to love one another; for he that loveth another hath fulfilled the law. (Romans 13:1–8)

**"I love them that love me; and those that seek
me early shall find me" (Proverbs 8:17).**

It makes perfect sense for us to love and to want to be loved by one who can be as beneficial to us as wisdom can be. Wisdom, by definition, knows what is best for us—she knows our needs. To know our needs, she has to know us. If she knows us, then she will be able to know if we really love her. Divorce is proof that people fall in and out of love all the time. It can be difficult figure out. "Do I love this person for who he (or she) really is, or do I love this person for what he (or she) can do for me?" God knows our hidden motives, and He knows us better than we know ourselves. Jesus told Phillip, along with the other disciples, *"He that hath my commandments, and keepeth them, he it is that loveth me: and he that loveth me shall be loved of my Father, and I will love him, and will manifest Myself to him" (John 14:21).*

The word *commandments* is translated from the Greek word *entole*, which means an authoritative prescription. Thus, this verse is telling us, "If we love Jesus, we accept Him as our authority, and we will follow His prescription." A prescription is normally thought of as a written order for the provision of a healing agent, unavailable to the common man. It takes a person with authority to write a needed prescription—a person who has the legal and moral right to make a claim of possessing the required knowledge and power to provide the correct healing agent. Jesus is telling us in verse 21, "Not only will I love you, but my Father will love you as well. Welcome to my Father's family, which is known as His church family. My Father loves you so much He actually thinks of His church family as being the bride of His only Son. I am very pleased with this arrangement, so much so that I am going to manifest Myself to you."

The word *manifest* is taken from the Greek word *emphanizo*, which means to exhibit, to appear, to disclose, or to inform plainly. This is what the Holy Spirit does for us. He will exhibit a change in our lives that others will notice. He will disclose to us the meaning of His holy scriptures, which were—and still are—inspired by Him. When this happens, we will be plainly informed of from where we came, who we really are, and exactly where we are going. Eventually, He will appear to us—you can bet your soul on it!

So what did the Holy Spirit want us to know when Solomon wrote the Hebrew word *shachar*, which was translated as "early" by the King James scribes? *Shachar* is defined as being up early at any task, to search for painstakingly, or seeking with diligence. When we pray first thing in the morning, we are putting God first. This is where He needs to be if we are going to express our love for Him properly. If we fail to do this, it is a much bigger loss for us than it is for Him.

There is no reason why this particular proverb cannot also be interpreted to mean that we should seek Him in the early years of our life. God will not honor the commitment of a man who tells himself, "I am going to have all the fun I can while I can, and when I'm too old to pursue and enjoy sin any longer, then and only then will I become a Christian. I will gladly and willingly give God the leftovers of my life." This would be a pathetic attempt to outsmart God.

God, by definition, is not only a higher source of power and intelligence than we are, but He is all knowing. This means we can't outsmart Him or manipulate Him. He knows our hidden motives. If we truly love Him and are truly seeking Him diligently, then we will feel led to take action now. The word *proverb* could be interpreted to mean approving of action. A verb is a word that shows action, and *pro* means to be in favor of, so a proverb can be words that inspire us to take action. Verse 17 urges us to take said action early in life and early in the morning.

"Riches and honor are with me; yea durable riches and righteousness. My fruit is better than gold, yea, than fine gold; and my revenue than choice silver" (Proverbs 8:18–19).

Proverbs 11:18 tells us, *"To him that soweth righteousness shall be a sure reward."*—not only sure but enduring, so enduring that scripture tells us it will last forever. Physical blessings will pass away with their physical existences, but those treasures of a spiritual nature will never pass away— they are eternal.

Verse nineteen refers to fruit, which is translated from the Hebrew word, *p(e)riy*. In addition to fruit, it can refer to a reward or the shoot of a tree. Taken in a literal sense, any fruit worth more than gold would have to be some very fine fruit. From a figurative perspective, those who follow God's instruction are an offshoot of His branch of knowledge. God's revenue, mentioned in verse 19 is taken from the Hebrew word *t(e)buwah*. It can mean income, fruit, produce, gain, or increase. His *tbuwah "Maketh rich, and He addeth no sorrow with it"* (Proverbs 10:22). Working tirelessly for the kingdom of God will not leave us physically or emotionally "wrung out," like climbing the corporate ladder does. He will provide for our needs, including physical energy, and He will make our sleep "sweet," as we are told in Proverbs 3:24. It's of the utmost importance to remember God's blessing may not include financial riches. Beware of the "prosperity preachers." Our Lord, unlike Solomon, did not enjoy material wealth during His time on planet earth. Despite all of his riches, Solomon writes, *"Better is little with the fear of the Lord than great treasure and trouble therewith"* (Proverbs 15:16). Our work is not to accumulate worldly wealth—we are placed here by God, to expand God's kingdom.

> Lay not up for yourselves treasures upon earth, where moth and rust doth corrupt, and where thieves break through and steal: But lay up for yourselves treasures in heaven, where neither moth nor rust doth corrupt, and where thieves do not break through nor steal. For where your treasure is, there will your heart be also. The light of the body is the eye: if therefore thine eye be single, thy whole body shall be full of light. But if thine eye be evil, thy whole body shall be full of darkness. If therefore the light that is in thee be darkness, how great is that darkness! No man can serve two masters: for either he will hate the one, and love the other; or else he will hold to the one, and despise the other. You cannot serve God and mammon. (Matthew 6:19–24)

"I lead in the way of righteousness, in the midst of the paths of judgment; that I may cause those that love me to inherit substance; and I will fill their treasures" (Proverbs 8:20–21).

These verses first tell us where to find God's wisdom and then what God's wisdom does for those who truly love her. The way of righteousness and justice is a part of the natural habitat for God's wisdom. If a person, corporation, or government chooses another path that deviates from righteousness, they are breaking-off fellowship with God. This begins the breeding of pride and arrogance, which was discussed earlier with verse 13. God's wisdom, we're told in verse 21, will fill our treasure.

We're also told in Proverbs 8:21 that God's wisdom will cause us to inherit wealth. Wealth—or substance, as translated in the Old King James Version—is taken from the Hebrew word *yesh*. This is a different word than the one Solomon used in Proverbs 1:13, 3:9, and 6:31. That word was *hewn*, which means wealth, riches, or substance. The word *yesh* in verse 21 means to stand out or exist. Before an inheritance is received, someone first must die. Those who love God's wisdom must first denounce the world's wisdom before acquiring God's superior wisdom. Our old character, that old personality or what scripture refers to as "the flesh," must die before we're given a new heart. The new heart, given to us by God's Holy Spirit, is part of what we inherit. Our new heart causes a total rearrangement of ideas, values, and attitudes. There will be a change in personality, which will indeed cause us to "stand out." The Holman Christian Standard Bible translates this verse to read, *"giving wealth as an inheritance to those who love me, and filling their treasuries."*

This verse ends the wisdom speech portion of Proverbs chapter eight. Beginning with verse 22, Solomon gives us a history lesson, dating back before the creation of the earth. This ancient account also acts as corroboration for the authenticity of God's Holy Trinity, which is first referred to in Genesis 1:26. This verse records God saying, *"Let us make man in our image, after our likeness."* God was not alone, as indicated by the word "us". The Gospel of John also corroborates the existence of the Holy Trinity. *"In the beginning was the Word, and the Word was with God, and the Word was God. The same was in the beginning with God"* (John 1:1–2). Both the Old and New Testament writers were inspired to write of Jesus Christ, the second member of the Trinity, as was Solomon.

"The Lord possessed me in the beginning of His way, before His works of old" (Proverbs 8:22).

Proverbs 8:1 began with the question, "Does not wisdom cry out?" Verse 12 identifies wisdom as the voice of Proverbs 8 by boldly declaring, "I wisdom dwell with prudence." The voice of wisdom then goes on to tell us about God—what He loves, what He hates, and even what He can and will do. The voice of wisdom seems to know God very well. Verse 22 explains wisdom is a significant part of God because He possessed wisdom from the very beginning.

The Hebrew word used, where we read *possessed*, is *qanah*, which, in addition to possess, can mean to own or to procure, but its primary root means to erect or create. "His works of old" would refer to His creating the heaven and the earth, as we are told in Genesis 1:1, which reads, *"In the beginning God created the heaven and the earth."* The same Hebrew word, *reshiyth,*(for beginning) is used in both Genesis 1:1 and Proverbs 8:22. Reshiyth means the first in time, order, or rank. We can be sure "His works of old" refers to God's creation because Genesis 2:2 tells us, *"And on the seventh day God ended His work."* The work He had ended was the creation that had taken place the previous six days.

Any work or creation requires thought and planning before it is built. Before a house can be built, a blueprint must be drawn; before a book can be written, knowledge and understanding of that knowledge first must exist. Wisdom consists of both knowledge and understanding, which inspires intelligence. Unfortunately for man, all intelligence does not necessarily produce wisdom. Wisdom knows how to interpret and utilize intelligence correctly because wisdom has known God from the beginning, as verse 22 tells us. The length and beauty of this relationship is more than the human mind can fully comprehend. When pride enters a man's mind, he finds it difficult to accept what he cannot understand. This lack of faith in the knowledge God has provided for us has allowed Satan's influence to cause some men to question the first four vital words of Genesis—*"In the beginning God."*

The prince of darkness has successfully convinced some intelligent men, who have acquired false beliefs, that God's "works of old" are really just a random series of events that happened by sheer coincidence. These unfortunate intellectual types cause the words of Proverbs 4:19 to come alive: "The way of the wicked is as darkness; they do know not at what they stumble." If today's scientific knowledge and the Bible were both disregarded, which would be easier to believe—that some form of intelligence guided creation or that it all happened by sheer coincidence?

As Solomon expounds on wisdom throughout his proverbs, it becomes increasingly obvious his references to wisdom really refer to God Himself. Proverbs 8:23–31 should be sufficient proof to remove any doubt of this claim. God's very first order of business (*reshiyth*, or works of old) was to raise up an extension (*qanah*) or another manifestation of Himself. This was His way, as described in verse 22 by the Hebrew word *derek*, which can be translated as a way of life; a mode of action; a custom, journey, or manner. Like eternity, the concept of a triune God is difficult to understand, but it should not be difficult to accept—after all, is not man also of a triune nature? Does not man consist of a body, which is created in the image of God; a soul; and a spirit, which like God lives forever?

The Bible is saturated with language, from Genesis to Revelation, that reinforces the concept of a triune God. Genesis records God saying to Noah and his sons, *Whoso sheddeth man's blood, by man shall his blood be shed; for in the image of God made He man" (Gen*esis 9:6). This conversation is recorded after the ark was unloaded, and Noah had built an altar and burnt sacrifices of every clean bird and animal, which produced a soothing aroma for the Lord (Genesis 8:20–21). There is every reason to believe this was a face-to-face, eye-to-eye conversation with "The Angel of the Lord," which is believed (probably by all studious Christians) to have been the preincarnate Christ. Old Testament references to the preincarnate Christ will read as, "The angel of the Lord," "His angel," or "Mine angel." These references to a specific angel are to the Son of God in a heavenly body, made visible only to those to whom he wanted to reveal Himself. Those verses refering to angels other than the preincarnate Christ usually read "an angel," "the angel," or make reference to multiple angels. Moses, as you probably recall, was told by God that he could not see His face and live. This was God the Father speaking, who identified Himself as **"I AM THAT I AM"** (Exodus 3:14). It was God the Father who explained to Moses why His face could not be seen, in Exodus 33:20. Genesis 9:6 records God (in first person) talking to Noah face-to-face and saying "He" (God in the second person) made man in God's image. This can only be God the Son talking to Noah about God the Father.

The first mention of the designation, "Angel of the Lord," is in

Genesis 16, when He appeared to Hagar, the mother of Ishmael. Note the capitalization of the title, Angel of the Lord, in most modern translations of the Bible. This denotes deity, meaning that this angel is God. Notice in Genesis 16:10 The Angel of the Lord is quoted as saying, *"I will multiply thy seed exceedingly."* No other entity identified as an angel, other than The Angel of the Lord, can make this claim. All scriptural references to angels will quote the angel as saying what God will do, or they quote what God sent them to say. Angels will tell any man who bows down to them to "get up" because all angels know that only God should be worshipped or bowed down to. This angel had to be a manifestation of God; otherwise, He would not have claimed such authority.

In Psalm 110, King David made reference to multiple members of the Godhead when he wrote, *"The Lord said unto my Lord, 'Sit thou at My right hand until I make thine enemies thy footstool.'"*

There is also reference to the Trinity in Luke 3:22. *"And the Holy Ghost* [first member of the Trinity] *descended in bodily shape like a dove upon Him* [second member of the Trinity] *and a voice came from heaven* [third member of the Trinity] *which said, 'Thou art My beloved Son; in thee I am well pleased.'"* The Bible is full of references to the Trinity, which all corroborate what Solomon writes in his eighth chapter of his proverbs. The next four verses continue in the voice of God the Son.

"I was formed before ancient times, from the beginning, before the earth began. I was born when there were no watery depths and no springs filled with water. I was delivered before the mountains and the hills were established, before He made the land, the fields, or the first soil on earth" (Proverbs 8:23–26 HCSB).

Wisdom, who we now can identify as the voice of our Lord Jesus Christ, gives us a description of the time period corresponding with Genesis 1:2, which reads, *"The earth was without form, and void; and darkness was upon the face of the deep. And the Spirit of God moved upon the face of the waters."* The earth being without form describes exactly what Proverbs chapter eight is describing—no depths, no fountains, no mountains, no hills, no fields, and no dust—just water.

Proverbs 8:23 says there was no earth at this point in time, which agrees with Genesis 1:2 because it says there was water before there was ever an earth in the solid state. Then, in Genesis 1:3–5, the light of God begins to shine on a shapeless mass of water clinging together by the cohesive forces of its hydrogen bonds. Hydrogen bonds are the weak polar bonds between the positive and negative regions of the hydrogen atom. Hydrogen is two of the three atoms which make a water molecule. Hydrogen bonds are the forces that enable water to bubble up into droplets or small pools, rather than spreading out flat on any given level surface. They also determine what floats, and what sinks in a contained body of water.

If there was a "big bang," you can be sure it was God who created, and released the energy involved in any such monumental rearrangement of matter. By verse six of Genesis the waters began to divide. This was when water vapor began separating from the liquid water that contained other minority atoms in suspension besides the hydrogen and oxygen atoms of the water molecules. So there would now be a huge collection of God's created elements gathered within an even larger mass of water, which was beginning to turn into gases because of the energy given off by God's Holy Spirit hovering above the waters, as described in Genesis 1:2.

In Genesis 1:5 we are told there is already day and night, despite the two great lights (the sun and moon) of verse 16 not yet having come into play. Just because the sun is the center of our solar system does not mean God created it before the earth. Genesis 1:1 told us *"God created the heavens,"* which means the atmosphere and the earth, which was still without form. Matter in the solid state has a form, or defined shape; matter in the liquid or the gaseous state does not have a definite shape. They assume the shape of their containers.

The earth was God's real object of interest. We now know there are millions of other suns out there, but no other planets that we know of are comparable to the earth. There might have been some light available from other distant stars, other than the sun of our solar system, but this did not happen until Genesis 1:14. It must have been the light of God that was responsible for the division of light and darkness. Did you know there will not be a sun in heaven? We are told in Revelation 21:23 that no sun or moon is necessary in heaven. *"The city had no need of the sun, neither of the moon, to shine in it: for the glory of God did lighten it."* Our God is its light!

As the waters were collecting, causing the shapeless mass to begin taking on a three-dimensional form, it would eventually be thick enough to shield the inner molecules from the light of God's hovering Spirit. Thus, there was a division of what was and was not exposed to the light. Some of the heavier atoms floating in suspension, were now beginning to bond together as a semisolid mass in the center of this huge mass of water. As the mass thickened, there were now some particles getting no light at all. This dark area of the liquid earth was "the deep" that was first mentioned in Genesis 1:2. As these inner particles began to solidify and cool, they formed a spherical shape in the center of the mass, as described in the following verse.

"When He prepared the heavens, I was there: when He set a compass upon the face of the depth" (Proverbs 8:27).

The heavens were created in Genesis 1:1, but it was not until verse 14 that God said, *"Let there be lights in the firmament of the heaven to divide the day from the night; and let them be for signs, and for seasons, and for days, and years."* This would include other stars and their solar systems. The gravitational fields of these distant heavenly bodies could not have been the forces God allowed to do the work described in Genesis 1:1–10. Whether or not you believe the days of creation were single days or entire geological ages is not important. What is important is that we all know God was and always will be able to create an earth and its solar system in six days if He chooses to do so.

This author believes the scriptures indicate God's preferred method of operation is to allow the laws of nature, which were designed and created by Him, to take their natural course. The laws of motion, thermal dynamics, electromagnetism, and chemical bonding were all already in effect and waiting to be harnessed for use by future civilizations before God had yet created man.

Wisdom was there when God the Creator *"set a compass on the face of the depth,"* according to Proverbs 8:27. The word, compass is translated from the Hebrew word, *chuwg*: which means circle. A sphere viewed from a distance always appears as a circle. A sphere is the only three-dimensional shape with a constant appearance, regardless of which angle or direction it is viewed from. This circle was the inner core of the earth, which was beginning to form deep below the surface of the waters. It is significant to note this proverb suggests the earth was round at a time when most men thought it was flat. Approximately 2,600 years later, the holy office of the Inquisition would still imprison anyone (including Galileo) who dared to think the earth was not the center of the universe. Those same narrow-minded religious authorities continued to believe the earth was flat until Magellan circled the world in 1522.

"When He established the clouds above; when He strengthened the fountains of the deep" (Proverbs 8:28).

Genesis 1:7 seems to give a parallel account of Proverbs 8:28; it reads, *"God made the firmament, and divided the waters which were under the firmament from the waters which were above the firmament."* The evaporated waters (clouds) above the firmament were a compound consisting almost entirely of water vapor and probably some other gases expelled from the now-cooling planet. These other gases consisted of the molecules which, like the water vapor molecules, were also light enough to be drawn away from the gravitational force of the cooling planet.

The heavier waters below the firmament were now beginning to take on an outer spherical shape, which was forming around the inner spherical "circle of the deep," formed in the previous verse. The inner fountains of the deep were now a semisolid mass of particulates that contained very few, if any, water molecules. The displaced water molecules were now the waters of the surrounding outside sphere. The deep was a mass of the heaviest elements, which were the first to drop out of suspension from the face of the waters. As the heat was drawn away from the elements of the deep by the surrounding waters, they now began to take on a solid state that gave them a stronger unity and a new permanent shape and position within the outer waters. This process was the *"strengthening of the fountains of the deep."* They were no longer fountains of molten lava; they were a strengthened, solid mass, which was now exerting its own gravitational field on the outer waters.

"When He gave to the sea His decree, that the waters should not pass His commandment; when He appointed the foundations of the earth" (Proverbs 8:29).

Verse 29 describes the waters gathering together and separating from the dry land, thus marking the shorelines of the ocean. It is important to remember that whatever was established at this point in time was rearranged about two thousand years later by the flood. The foundations of the earth are what support the dry lands and the ocean bottoms. Modern science still knows very little about the deep ocean floors. This verse suggests the foundations lie under those deep ocean bottoms, that we know so little about. We do know there is still volcanic action taking place under the ocean floor. Volcanoes and earthquakes are still rearranging the face of this planet above and below the limit God assigned to the sea.

"Then I was by Him, as one brought up with Him; and I was daily His delight, rejoicing always before Him" (Proverbs 8:30).

John 1:1–3 establishes the existence of the preincarnate Christ, as well as God the Creator and the Holy Spirit of God, who were all present in the beginning, as written 1000 years earlier by Solomon. *"In the beginning was the Word, and the Word was with God, and the Word was God. He was with God in the beginning. All things were created through Him, and apart from Him not one thing was created that has been created"* (John 1:1–3 HCSB). Other translations of Proverbs 8:30 identify the one by God's side as a master or skilled craftsman. Both Solomon and John are in agreement that more than one member of the Godhead was present when the one in whom He delights was working by His side on a daily basis.

"Rejoicing in the habitable part of His earth; and my delights were with the sons of men" (Proverbs 8:31).

Note that God's world is now inhabited, which would seem to indicate a gap of time between the events of verses 30 and 31. It is the inhabited world that pleases Him most, so it would seem man is the crown jewel of His creation. The Holman Christian Standard Bible also emphasizes the significance of man, as compared to the rest of the creation, with its translation, *"I was rejoicing in His inhabited world, delighting in the human race."* Given the reference to "the inhabited world," it would seem this verse is referring to the earth after "the fall" in the garden of Eden, so the rejoicing and delight took place despite man's sin. This verse ends Solomon's historical review on a happy note, and now he reissues wisdom's formula for success and happiness.

"Now therefore, hearken unto me, O ye children; for blessed are they that keep my ways" (Proverbs 8:32).

This verse could be considered a single-sentence summary for the book of Proverbs. All throughout the Proverbs, Solomon has personified wisdom, calling out to her son or to her children, as verse 32 does. He also wrote of the blessings an obedient son will certainly acquire if he obtains the understanding of wisdom's way. The inspired words of Solomon continually encourage readers to become intimately acquainted with: who wisdom is, what gives her pleasure, and what she hates.

Beginning with Proverbs 8:22, after 223 verses of instruction, we are suddenly given the origin of wisdom and told she was actually in God's presence, working as a master craftsman by His side on a daily basis. When cross-referencing the Proverbs account of creation with the Genesis account, we found verses where God makes reference to Himself in a plural designation (Genesis 1:26 and 3:22). The obvious conclusion is that "Lady Wisdom," as written of by Solomon, was really no lady at all—it turns out she was and still is the Holy Spirit of God. Solomon has finally told us just how powerful the words of his proverbs really are—they are the inspired words of God!

Starting with Proverbs 8:32, the final five verses of chapter eight tell us, in a very short and direct manner, the certain penalty incurred by ignoring the wisdom of God. Proverbs 1:7 reads, *"The fear of the Lord is the beginning of knowledge, but fools despise wisdom and instruction."* This verse was identified as the key verse for the entire book of Proverbs. It could also be considered a short synopsis of the last five verses of chapter eight; which reads as follows:

> "And now, my sons, listen to me; those who keep my ways are happy. Listen to instruction and be wise; don't ignore it. Anyone who listens to me is happy, watching at my doors every day, waiting by the posts of my doorway. For

the one who finds Me finds life and obtains favor from the Lord, but the one who misses me harms himself; all who hate Me love death" (Proverbs 8:32–36 HCSB).

The message of this short sermon is consistent with all the previous wisdom speeches. The difference is that these words are understood to be the words of God, as revealed to Solomon and given to us from the first-person perspective, rather than just the words of a wise old king who wanted to be a good father. Solomon no longer is trying to persuade the reader by repeatedly comparing wisdom's worth to silver and gold. The message of these five verses is as certain as any mathematical equation:

Obedience + knowledge = wisdom, and wisdom + work = prosperity

and

Pride + disobedience = foolishness, and foolishness + laziness = death

"Hear instruction, and be wise, and refuse it not" (Proverbs 8:33).

This verse is not saying that hearing God's instruction will automatically make the listener wise. It's telling us to act wisely in accordance with the information that has been given to us. Proverbs 10:17 tells us, *"The one who follows instruction is on the path to life; but the one who rejects correction goes astray"* (HCSB). Proverbs 13:18 tells us more about "he who refuses correction"—*"Poverty and disgrace come to those who ignore discipline, but the one who accepts correction will be honored"* (HCSB).

"Blessed is the man that heareth me, watching daily at my gates, waiting at the posts of my doors" (Proverbs 8:34).

We're now instructed to listen and watch daily at the doorposts of God's gates. The entrance to God's kingdom is wherever the Holy Spirit is. Matthew 18:20 tells us where the gates of the kingdom can be found on earth: *"For where two or three are gathered together in My name, there am I in the midst of them."* This tells us we need to be where fellow believers are, so we can listen to and be with them daily. Every day we make conscious choices between strengthening the kingdom of God or validating Satan's dark domain. We make these choices by what we listen to on the radio, which websites we click on, what kind of books we read, and what kind of people we socialize with. We cannot expect to commune with God by going into the local tavern or casino. God knows our innermost thoughts and motives. When our intent is honorable, He makes Himself available to us for spiritual fellowship.

"For whoso findeth Me findeth life, and shall obtain favour of the Lord" (Proverbs 8:35).

What an uplifting verse this is! How much more could we possibly ask for or expect? Psalm 128 provides similar inspiration:

> Blessed is everyone that feareth the Lord; that walketh in his ways. For thou shalt eat the labor of thine hands: happy shalt thou be, and it shall be well with thee. Thy wife shall be as a fruitful vine by the sides of thy house: thy children like olive plants round about thy table. Behold, that thus shall the man be blessed that feareth the Lord. The lord shall bless thee out of Zion: and thou shall see the good of Jerusalem all the days of thy life. Yea, thou shalt see thy children's children, and peace upon Israel.

"But he that sinneth against me wrongeth his own soul; all they that hate me love death" (Proverbs 8:36).

Sin will always have consequences. Unrepentant sinners will carry the consequences of sin with them into eternity. It is a most unnatural act for a man to "wrong his own soul. To "love death" is probably about as unnatural as it gets. The conscious choice to hate God's spirit of wisdom makes about as much sense as an alcoholic continuing to drink, despite no longer enjoying it. Like drugs, alcohol, or rich foods, sin can be an addiction. Most addictions do their participants much harm, up to and including an early death. Some addictions can provide pleasure but always have some negative effects which eventually will outgrow any benefits they provide. The workaholic, for example, will benefit from his or her earnings but often at the expense of his or her long-term health and happiness.

Many people, both Christian and non-Christian alike, are quick to associate God with love or even proclaim that God is love. Seldom will you hear people voluntarily talk about God hating anything or anyone—but He does! Verse 13 told us God hates the perverse mouth. Verse 13 also instructs us to hate evil—that's because God hates evil more than any human is capable of hating it. Chapter six, of Proverbs, beginning with verse 16, listed six things the Lord hates. Despite God's infinite capacity for love, there are those who because of ignorance hate Him, as Proverbs 8:36 tells us. These are people who are spiritually dead. They are the ones who like a pig, will continue to wallow in the mire. It's been said you can judge a man by his enemies. If your enemies are the same as God's, you can consider yourself in good company.

WISDOM SPEECH SIXTEEN

Proverbs 9:1–18

This is the last chapter of Solomon's wisdom speeches. Chapter ten begins the second section, or what some call the couplets, or the second book of Proverbs. Most of the verses found in chapters 10–24 of the Proverbs will compare, contrast, or complete single nuggets of truth. Chapter eight revealed who and what wisdom really is. Chapter nine goes on to further describe the character of Wisdom and the extent of her efforts to teach and comfort her children, whom she loves, as we were told in chapter eight.

God's Spirit of Wisdom was delighted with man, regardless of Eve's disobedience and Adam's inability to discern her error in judgment. Adam's failing to be the leader of his house might have been Solomon's inspiration for writing Proverbs 7:22–23, which reads, *"He follows her impulsively like an ox goes to the slaughter, like a deer bounding towards a trap until an arrow pierces its liver, like a bird darting into a snare—he doesn't know it will cost him his life"* (HCSB). Sin's influence did not depart from Adam's house. Adam and Eve's failures in Eden were bad enough, but sin, as always, multiplied itself. It did not take sin long to manifest itself into murder. Yet we're told Wisdom's delight was still with the sons of man! Much like most parents, Wisdom forgives the shortcomings of Her children, and now informs us of Her plan for abundant provision.

"Wisdom hath builded her house, she hath hewn out her seven pillars" (Proverbs 9:1).

Solomon begins chapter nine using metaphors of architecture. The house Wisdom has built is not an earthly shelter; it is, however, still a type of shelter. Its roof and walls provide protection from the continual storms of sin, as described in Proverbs chapter one. *"When terror strikes you like a storm and your calamity comes like a whirlwind, when trouble and stress overcome you. Then they will call me but I won't answer"* (Proverbs 1:27–28 HCSB).

This warning was issued to those who earlier had ignored Wisdom's plea. Wisdom had begun crying out in the chief concourses and the town's open square (Proverbs 1:20–21) and continued to cry aloud throughout the following chapters of the Proverbs. Proverbs 1:27–28 were written in reference to those who had refused to enter Wisdom's house, despite her invitation. They chose instead to enter the house of the dead.

Solomon wrote praises of Wisdom by describing repeatedly her wonderful plan for prosperity and security. He also warned us repeatedly of Wisdom's nemeses, foolishness and folly, whose cords of entanglement separate their victims from the path of righteousness and eventually pull them down to the house of the dead. We should not want to go there because the house of the dead will lead us to the pit, written of in Proverbs 1:12.

Proverbs 1:9 tells us Wisdom's house has seven pillars that she has hewn out. The word hewn tells us these are pillars of stone, not wood. They are built to last forever. Wisdom's pillars are the support system for her institution of higher learning for eternal living. They represent God's guidelines for proper thinking and actions that lead us into the sanctuary of God's wisdom. These pillars are the virtues and practices Solomon has been writing about since the first chapter of his Proverbs. They explain a form of education that either replaces or builds upon our childhood experiences. When God determines a child has become accountable, a choice will soon be made by that child. It may not even be a conscious decision, but it is one that determines whether or not God's Spirit will dwell and communicate with that child's spirit.

John the Revelator wrote about the seven spirits of God, about one thousand years after Solomon wrote of these seven pillars of wisdom. Whether or not this is a coincidence is not known. Some believe these seven pillars represent the seven spirits of God. Throughout the Bible, seven is God's number of completeness. Beginning with the seven days of creation in Genesis and ending with the seven angels with the seven vials filled with the seven plagues spoken of in Revelation 21:9—seven is

God's number. This author believes Solomon chose to describe Wisdom's house having seven pillars because he was inspired to do so by God's Holy Spirit, who revealed to John the Revelator, centuries later, that there are seven spirits of God. Revelation 1:4; 3:1; 4:5; and 5:6 all make reference to the seven spirits of God.

These unnamed spirits are somewhat of a mystery; but it is reasonable to assume they collectively make up God's Holy Spirit. There just is not much information given in the Bible about the Holy Spirit. These seven spirits could be described as seven different functions or characteristics of God. For example, a man can be thought of or described as a father, a son, a husband, a neighbor, a teacher, a judge, or a friend. If a man can assume seven different roles or identities, why can't God?

In some instances, the Spirit of God is described as coming upon certain men, causing them to do something extraordinary. For example, the Old Testament book of Judges provides references for three separate occasions when the Spirit of the Lord came *upon* Samson. Each time this happened, Samson then went on to execute a superhuman feat of strength. This type of spiritual visitation could be described as a manifestation of God's spirit of might, which is one of the spirits listed by Isaiah (Isaiah 11:2). The New International Version describes this particular Spirit of God as the spirit of power. There are also many scriptural references (especially by David and Isaiah) about God's strength, which also could be thought of as part of His glory. The spirit of power, the spirit of might, His strength, and His glory—could they all be or be of the same Spirit of God?

Almost every Old Testament account about the "Spirit of the Lord" records the Spirit coming *upon* its recipients. One exception would be Bezaleel, the craftsman, who was *filled* with God's spirit of wisdom, as recorded in Exodus 35:30–31. *"And Moses said unto the children of Israel, See, the Lord hath called by name Bezaleel the son of Uri, the son of Hur, of the tribe of Judah; and He hath filled him with the Spirit of God, in wisdom in understanding, and in knowledge, and in all manner of workmanship."* This was the man who crafted the ark of the covenant. No one else is recorded in the scriptures as having been filled with the Spirit of God until a young virgin Hebrew girl, Mary, was visited by the angel Gabriel in the small city of Nazareth, approximately nineteen hundred years later.

Wisdom, knowledge, and understanding seem to be linked together quite frequently in the scriptures, and the book of Proverbs is no exception. Could these three virtues make up or be a part of one of the Spirits of God? Maybe discernment could be included with this trio of gifts from God. On the other hand, discernment would fit nicely with discretion, judgment, equity, and justice. Perhaps righteousness, prudence, uprightness, and diligence could be grouped together to comprise another Spirit of God. A fourth group could include humility, gracefulness, obedience, and truthfulness. Joy, peace, and contentment would seem to all fit together; but from another perspective, couldn't wisdom fit with any of these groups?

If you are confused right now, that is good because anyone who presumes to understand the spiritual dynamics of the living God is fooling them self. Despite being forgiven of our sin, few, if any, of us have been given as much insight to the inner works of God's Holy Spirit as the New Testament writers. Therefore, this author has zero authority and very limited ability to define anything that the Bible does not plainly explain. The Bible is filled with unsolved mysteries leaving us with many unanswered questions. It is not sinful to speculate whether the seven pillars are representative of the seven spirits, but we should never attempt to assign any limit to who God is and what He is capable of doing. When the true believers arrive at their eternal destination, and God's mysteries are revealed, then—and only then—will they know the answers to God's mysteries of the scriptures.

Earth-bound Christians are called to be both students and teachers of the Word of God. This is accomplished by following Solomon's instruction as described in the early verses of Proverbs chapter two—where we were told to receive God's words and to treasure His commands in our hearts. This is a lifelong process that begins with the fear of the Lord but grows into a sincere desire to please God because of our love for Him. When a believer has begun to understand just how good God is, he or she will want to deepen his or her understanding of God's love and His mercy and especially of His grace. We can all do this by inclining our ears to His wisdom and applying our understanding of His will into the actions of our lives (Proverbs 2:2). As we get closer to God and grow in knowledge of His will, we must never forget there is always more to be learned from God's Holy Spirit. Humility is what keeps us from becoming so heavenly minded that we are no earthly good. We always need to cry out for discernment, as Proverbs 2:3 advises us. Knowledge of God's wisdom, tempered with discernment and expressed with humility, is indeed more valuable than silver and gold. For this reason, it is wise for us to continually seek closeness with the true source of wisdom.

So rather than attempt to define what the seven spirits of God are or how they manifest themselves in God's creation, it seems our human limitations should cause us instead to just consider some of the possibilities.

1.   Do the seven spirits of God provide spiritual gifts?
2.   If so, why does Paul say in 1 Corinthians 12:4, "There are diversity of gifts; but the same spirit."
3.   Is the Holy Spirit just one of these spirits, or do these seven spirits collectively combine to be the Holy Spirit?
4.   Could the Holy Spirit act as an overseer of these seven spirits?

These questions are just a small sample of what we don't know about the mysteries of God. We have only thus far considered the good and desirable effects of God's Holy Spirit(s). When the Lord confused the tongues at the Tower of Babel, (Genesis 11) is it correct to consider this was done by a spirit of confusion? If it is, would this spirit of confusion be a part of God's Holy Spirit, or did God just let the unclean spirits do what they do best—confuse men? It would be interesting to know what manner of spirit it was that hardened Pharaoh's heart when Moses plead with him to let God's people go.

One of the men whom the Spirit of the Lord came upon in the Old Testament was King Saul. Despite this tremendous gift, Saul later was disobedient, and the Lord's Spirit left him as we are told in 1 Samuel 16:14, *"But the Spirit of the Lord departed from Saul, and a*n evil *spirit from the Lord troubled him."* Note the first Spirit was of the Lord, and the second spirit was from the Lord. We do not know if this was an unclean spirit or not. The King James Version describes the second spirit as an "evil spirit from the Lord." The Hebrew word *ra* has definitions that include evil, wicked, bad, distressed, and troubled, but there is not enough information given to determine with certainty if it was an unclean or demonic spirit that entered Saul.

Jesus had this to say about those types of spirits: *"When the unclean spirit is gone out of a man, he walketh through dry places, seeking rest, and findeth none. Then he saith, I will return into my house from whence I came out; and when he is come, he findeth it empty, swept, and garnished* (in order). *Then goeth he, and taketh with himself seven other spirits more wicked than himself, and they enter in and dwell there; and the last state of that man is worse than the first"* (Matthew 12:43–45). These three verses may not answer our pending questions, but they are well worth remembering. Demonic spirits are nothing to play around with; they are capable of causing great harm.

God chose to be vague about most aspects of the spiritual world, but He has told us what we need to know. There are both good and evil spirits out there that can and will affect our lives if they are allowed to do so. Knowledge of God's Word, followed by obedience, will enable us to discern the good from the bad in both the spiritual and physical worlds. It's then a simple matter of choice concerning who and what we want to serve: God and His goodness or Satan and his evil.

> **"She hath killed her beasts; she has mingled her wine; she hath also furnished her table. She hath sent forth her maidens; she crieth upon the highest places of the city" (Proverbs 9:2–3).**

Wisdom is preparing to throw a party in her house. Remember this house is not an earthly shelter. The house of wisdom consists of those who are supported by the seven pillars representing the Holy Spirit of God. Those who stray too far from Wisdom's platform risk becoming entangled in the cords of death. The good life has already been provided for—God has already made the necessary arrangements for us to enjoy eternity in His heaven. If we prudently study God's Word and grow in His wisdom, then we will be able to digest the meat of His Word. It is unfortunate that some Christians try to walk the walk and talk the talk without first studying to show themselves approved, as the King James Version of 2 Timothy 2:15 tells us to do. They continue to dine on the milk instead of the solid food our Lord has made available for us. Those who refuse to grow are at risk of falling off the platform because they refuse to work their way into the middle of it.

The wine spoken of in Proverbs 9:2 is taken from the Hebrew word, *yayin*. It refers to a grade of wine that is worthy of being consumed at a banquet. When we drink the wine from our Lord's cup, it helps us to digest the meat of His Word. If we consume our Lord's wine with the same enthusiasm a drunkard has for worldly wine, we will receive the blessing of spiritual intoxication. This is the type of intoxication that makes us oblivious to Satan's temptations. Like a drunkard, those who are drunk with the Spirit don't worry about life's inconvenient realities, but unlike the drunkard, it is our faith in God's provision, not a dulling of the senses, that will comfort us.

Solomon's wisdom speeches are now addressing older adults, not children or young adults. Those stages of life were already addressed in the earlier chapters. The hard work and discipline earlier prescribed by God's Holy Spirit will be rewarded, but first there will be one more attempt made to persuade those who have thus far ignored her pleas. These verses mirror the parable of the wedding feast recorded in Matthew 22:2–14, which reads,

> The kingdom of heaven is like unto a certain king, which made a marriage for his son, and sent forth his servants to call them that were bidden to the wedding; and they would not come. Again, he sent forth other servants, saying, tell them which are bidden, Behold, I have prepared my dinner: my oxen and my fatlings are killed, and all things are ready: come unto the marriage. But they made light of it, and went their ways, one to his farm, another to his merchandise. And the remnant took his servants, and entreated them spitefully, and slew them. But when the king heard thereof, he was wroth: and he sent forth his armies, and destroyed those murderers, and burned up their city. Then saith he to his servants, The wedding is ready, but they which were bidden were not worthy. Go ye therefore into the highways, and as many as ye shall find, bid to the marriage. So those servants went out into the highways, and gathered together all as many as they found, both bad and good: and the wedding was furnished with guests. And when the King came in to see the guests, he saw there a man which had not on

a wedding garment. And he saith unto him, Friend, how camest thou in hither not having a wedding garment? And he was speechless. Then said the king to the servants, Bind him hand and foot, and take him away, and cast him into outer darkness; there shall be weeping and gnashing of teeth.' For many are called, but few are chosen.

Both Wisdom in the book of Proverbs and the king in the book of Matthew wanted their house full, but they both have specific requirements for their guests. Therefore they both continue to insist on filling their vacancies only with those who recognize and are willing to follow the directives of a higher and wiser power. Listen to their pleas.

"Whoso is simple, let him turn in hither: as for him that wanteth understanding, she saith to him, 'Come, eat of my bread, and drink of the wine which I have mingled'" (Proverbs 9:4–5).

The simple are those who have not been blessed with much ability. Proverbs 1:4 lists one of the reasons for studying Proverbs—to give prudence to the simple. Eight chapters later, Wisdom is still calling out to those who have been unable to comprehend the beauty and wealth of what God has to offer. They are among those addressed in the second sentence of Proverbs 1:4, those who lack understanding. Besides the simple: the fool, the evil, the sluggard, and the proud also lack understanding of God's holy wisdom because the Holy Spirit does not commune with these kinds of people.

Understanding was mentioned in the previous chapters of Proverbs—its importance is established by being mentioned fifty-four times in the Proverbs and another twelve times using other forms of the word, such as *understand* or *understood*. God's Word is described as the "Words of Understanding" in Proverbs 1:2; where we are urged to apply our hearts to understanding and to lift up our voices for it. We are then told to seek it as we would a treasure so we can understand the fear of the Lord.

Understanding is so important, Wisdom sends her maidens to cry out this urgent message from the highest places of the city. God wants His house filled! His house is a wonderful place to be. In an effort to encourage the slow of learning, they are told, "It's not too late; there is going to be a feast in God's house," but all participants must first understand and respect God enough to fear Him prior to their admission.

For some reason in verse five, Wisdom urges those who lack understanding to come eat her bread. What became of the meat? The bread and the wine just so happen to be the identical components of the Lord's Supper. This is yet another example of God's Holy Spirit inspiring Solomon to prophetically write about a very important future institution. The bread used in the Lord's Supper symbolizes the broken body of Christ. It therefore symbolizes the sacrifice made on our behalf. When partaking of the Lord's Supper we acknowledge the necessity for His death so we can receive that which was in His body, the sinless blood given to Him by His heavenly Father. Every other living human being receives his or her blood from his or her earthly father, whose blood contains sin. Like it or not, sin is in every man, woman, and child's DNA.

Anyone who has read chapter nine of Proverbs prior to possessing knowledge of the New Testament will not understand that the bread and wine of this verse symbolizes the sacrifice of Christ. It is of the utmost importance for the readers of the Bible to understand that God wrote His Holy Bible for all humans of all ages. It does not really matter if we cannot understand what Solomon was thinking when he wrote verse five; what matters is that God knew what He wanted written. The writings of God are capable of multiple layers of truth that are applicable throughout the ages of human history and beyond.

Verse six tells us what our mission is after we have eaten His bread and drunk His wine. We are to forsake our former lives and boldly step out to serve Him.

"Forsake the foolish, and live; and go in the way of understanding" (Proverbs 9:6).

We are now capable of carrying out this command because we no longer step out alone when we have invited God's Holy Spirit into our souls. Such a decision, if sincerely made, will inspire our obedience to His will and thus initiate a union of His Holy Spirit's life-force with our own God-given spirits. All life comes from God, but deliberate and continual sin will cause His Holy Spirit to depart from the sinner's spirit. This has to be because if the Holy Spirit dwelt with sin, He would no longer be holy. Solomon's ancestors were instructed to make blood sacrifices as amends for their sin. These Old Testament sacrifices were only a symbolic solution. They were a sign of obedience, which allowed those who complied to remain eligible for the well-documented foretold covering of their sin by the blood sacrifice made by Jesus Christ on Calvary's hill. Once this sacrifice was made, the Holy Spirit could dwell with the spirits of man and still remain holy. The perfect sacrificial blood of Christ makes it possible for the Holy Spirit to come into and dwell with a man's spirit. The New Testament saints were described as being "filled" with the Spirit because of what Christ *willfully* did on the cross. Prior to this very well-documented key event in history, the Spirit only would come upon His human recipients. It took a very significant and prominently established event for man to restart the human calendar at year zero. That event was the Crucifixion of God's Son, Jesus of Nazareth.

"He that reproveth a scorner getteth to himself shame: and he that rebuketh a wicked man getteth himself a blot. Reprove not a scorner, lest he hate thee: rebuke a wise man, and he will love thee. Give instruction to a wise man, and he will be yet wiser; teach a just man, and he will increase in learning" (Proverbs 9:7–9).

Verses seven and eight reinforce verse six. The scorner is nothing more than a specific type of a fool. The scorner is always angry and seeks to upset everyone who has the misfortune of crossing his path. We were warned about the foolish in verse six so we need to avoid fools because it's only natural for them to spread their foolishness. God's wisdom will point out for us who and where the fools are if we have followed the adopted lifestyle described in the Proverbs. Proverbs 13:16 assures us a fool is easy to spot. Proverbs 23:9 tells us, *"Speak not in the ears of a fool; for he will despise the wisdom of thy words."* Wisdom and foolishness, like darkness and light, do not mix. If we participate with a fool in his folly, any accumulated wisdom we have been granted, will begin to diminish because the Holy Spirit will not associate with foolishness. We were told in chapter two, discretion will preserve us, and understanding will keep us from the evil of perversity.

As Christians we are obligated to be workers for God's kingdom. We also have a need for Christian fellowship, whether we want it or not. We cannot totally isolate ourselves from society, seeking refuge from the fool, the perverse man, and the oppressor, if we are going to do God's work. When Wisdom cries out to the simple, it is often done through the words and/or the actions of an obedient Christian. Beginning with the latter part of verse eight we are told the occasion may arise when it will be necessary for a wise man to be rebuked. If a Christian brother spends too much time in the wrong places and with the wrong people, his spiritual stature will be compromised. It would then be another brother's job, one who has remained on Wisdom's path, to rebuke this weakened brother in a loving way. The goal is to help the "straying" brother recognize his departure from Wisdom's path. We want to help him to help himself so he can be restored to fellowship, and God's kingdom is not diminished. The brother we lift up may well one day be the brother who reaches out to give us a hand up from the quicksand of sin. We read earlier, "God wants His house filled." Until it is filled, He wants His body of believers working to fill it. This will not be accomplished if we stand by passively and watch a brother depart in ignorance.

On this very subject, the apostle Paul wrote, *"Love must be without hypocrisy. Detest evil; cling to what is good. Show family affection to one another with brotherly love. Outdo one another in showing honor. Do not lack diligence; be fervent in spirit; serve the Lord"* (Romans 12:9–11 HSBC).

These three verses (Proverbs 9:7-9) tell us our environment can and does have an influence on our spirituality. Christians should want their appearance, their words, their actions, and their homes to all be a reflection of their inner values. If we are wise enough to know that the way of the Lord is the only way we should want to go, we will not want to waste our time or our energy on the fool or the scoffer. Everything we have is on loan from God. He expects us to use His resources wisely, rather than to waste them on fools.

It is not always obvious who is a fool and who is not. Some situations dictate that we first observe those around us, because the fool will soon identify himself through his folly. Those who stay busy, attempting to maximize their productivity, are the ones who want to learn and are usually open to suggestion. If the Holy Spirit wants you to be a witness to a stranger, God will let you know—if your spirit is in communion with Him. The Holy Spirit will provide an opportunity for those who are alert and remain worthy to carry His message. Like any successful businessman, God does not hire just anyone, and He knows exactly who deserves a raise and who should be laid off.

> **"The fear of the Lord is the beginning of wisdom;**
> **and the knowledge of the Holy is understanding. For**
> **by me thy days shall be multiplied, and the years of**
> **thy life shall be increased" (Proverbs 9:10–11).**

Verse ten begins Solomon's summary conclusion of his wisdom speeches. The wise old king is now going to remind his graduating students of the highlights of his instruction. It is probably no surprise that he begins this final and very important section with the designated theme of his proverbs—all wise things begin with a fear of the Lord. Where there is no fear, there can be no genuine humility, and where there is no humility, pride and foolishness will soon follow.

Have you ever had the experience of a wounded or starving dog approach you for help? It will most likely come up to you, crawling or slowly walking, with its head, tail, and ears hanging as low as they can go. When you reach out to comfort the dog, it sometimes will wet itself because it's so scared. It is a pathetic sight to see an animal shaking with fear, but at the same time, it can be a heartwarming experience if you know that animal is about to be rescued, fed, comforted, adopted, and loved.

This is how a sinner is to approach God. When our spirits are infested with the filth of sin, God can rescue us, comfort us, and wash away our sin, but He cannot adopt us because we are already His. Like the prodigal son or the lost dog, we are simply going back to where our life-forces originated. It was the Lord God who breathed the breath of life into Adam's nostrils so that he could become a living soul, as Genesis chapter two tells us. He is the life force for all life.

The Hebrew word for soul used in Genesis 2:7 was *naphesh*, which refers to a breathing creature. This was when man received physical life in his body, which was created from the dust of the ground. It should come as no surprise that God, the source of life, is the one who determines when a physical body ceases to breathe. Verse 11 reminds us of this second truth, which we have read at least four times in the wisdom speeches. There are additional indirect suggestions about God's having numbered our days on the earth. Proverbs 3:2 leaves no doubt. *"For length of days and long life and peace shall they add to thee."* Proverbs chapter four, verse ten reads, *"Hear, O my son, and receive my sayings, and the years of thy life shall be many."* Proverbs 3:16 and Proverbs 4:22 also directly state God determines our length of life.

"If thou be wise, thou shalt be wise for thyself; but if thou scornest, thou alone shalt bear it" (Proverbs 9:12).

This verse is difficult to interpret. The Holman Christian Standard Bible translates Proverbs 3:7 as saying, *"Don't consider yourself to be wise; fear the Lord and turn away from evil."* It seems the Proverbs are telling us we can only be wise if we don't believe ourselves to be so. An accurate interpretation for both these verses will first require a distinction between godly and worldly wisdom. The reader seeking the intent of verse 12 will have to first understand that the message of Proverbs 9:12 can be applied differently to these two very different types of wisdom.

Godly wisdom includes humility, which by definition, means wisdom ceases to exist unless we give credit where credit is due. The only one worthy of such credit is our Creator, who is the sole source of all godly wisdom. A literal interpretation of verse 12 would require the reader to assume that the subject of verse 12 does not possess godly wisdom because this verse declares he is wise for himself. This would indicate the subject of verse 12 seeks to glorify himself, not God. Being devoid of humility, it is only a matter of time before Satan reduces this self-proclaimed wise guy to a scorner, who will seek to elevate his status by reducing the status of those around him. Verse 12 then gives its final warning to the self-sufficient wise guy by telling us he will indeed be left to his own devices, because God's Holy Spirit is no longer with him; thus, he will bear his sin without the saving redemption of a loving God.

The message of verse 12 can also be applicable to those fortunate enough to have been blessed with God's gift of wisdom. Solomon has explained repeatedly to his students that wisdom is more valuable than any of the earth's precious metals. Therefore, a wise man will benefit more from his wisdom than anyone else. This means he is wise for himself because he is the one benefiting the most from his given wisdom.

A wise man will realize his wisdom is a gift. Wisdom is not earned. True godly wisdom is granted to those who recognize God for being all that His holy scriptures proclaim Him to be. A wise man must labor in his studies to know our Lord Jehovah on an intimate level. A man who has acquired enough knowledge to know our Lord this well will realize his wisdom is surely God-given and thus can be taken from him at any time.

"A foolish woman is clamorous: she is simple, and knoweth nothing" (Proverbs 9:13).

Solomon has already warned his students of the immoral woman—she was the prostitute of chapter five. He then devoted all of chapter seven towards warning his young students about the seductress. The seductress of chapter seven, was a married woman who had observed her god's law by paying vows, as we were told in Proverbs 7:14. Yet she was willing to risk everything her wealthy husband had provided for her to pursue her carefully chosen young lover. Now Solomon is going to describe another type of sexual temptation that his young students will eventually encounter: the foolish woman.

This is the final warning issued in Solomon's wisdom speeches and a case could be made that he saved his most important warning for last. He is preparing to warn his young men about a third category of women who would make themselves easily available for sexual pleasure. Remember that the presumed targeted audience for Solomon's wisdom speeches were the young men who were being trained for the future leadership of Israel. These were the carefully chosen young men who probably would go on to enjoy a celebrity status, similar to that of today's athletes.

Verse 13 begins with a description of the type of young woman who is likely to pursue these types of men within that society's tolerable boundaries. She would not be like the prostitute of chapter five, for whom sex was a business. Her type was easily identified by the elder sages of Israel, who would strenuously deny her any access to the privileged social circles of Israel's future leaders—who were still being trained and educated and thus were to some degree, protected. The adulteress of chapter seven, who simply wanting to feed her lust for a specific young man, also would have been excluded by Israel's elder instructors. She was already married, so it would not make sense for her to have an affair with a high-profile individual. She could easily wind up under a pile of stones for her brazen behavior, according to Old Testament law. Solomon's final warning was reserved for foolish women who came from affluent families.

The Hebrew word used in verse 13 for foolish, *kciyiuwth,* is used only once in the scriptures, despite the Bible's many references to fools and foolishness. It means "silly or stupid." The obvious interpretation would be she was an unintelligent gold-digger. What she lacked in brains was probably compensated for by her beauty and her youth. She is described as *kciyiuwth* because she was trying to build a relationship on a foundation that lacked the necessary building materials. She was not smart enough to consider her competition. The rich and powerful of ancient Israel could buy slave girls for the sole purpose of male ego gratification. This could be why verse 13 ends with *"she is simple and knows nothing."* She is also described as clamorous; which is translated from the word *hamah,* which means to make a loud noise or commotion. She first had to get noticed before she could attempt to carry out her self-serving agenda.

"For she sitteth at the door of her house, on a seat in the high places of the city, to call passengers who go right on their ways. Whoso is simple, let him turn in hither; and as for him that wanteth understanding, she saith to him" (Proverbs 9:14–16).

How does a foolish woman manage to live in a house located in one of the highest places in the city? Note that verse 14 tells us this is where she was located. This verse is referring to a particular type of woman, and they have been around the "high places" in every civilization from the beginning of time because the men in those high places wanted them there!

Verses 14 and 15 can also be interpreted in a figurative sense. Solomon could be using the woman to symbolically represent sin and foolishness of all types, not just sexual sin. He himself would go on to have firsthand experiences with the clamorous women who sat in "high places." The queen of Sheba could be considered such a woman. She and Solomon lavished extraordinary gifts upon one another, as recorded in 1 Kings 10. First Kings 10:13 tells us, "Now King Solomon gave the Queen of Sheba all that she desired, whatever she asked." Who's to say that the queen did not want to have a child with the richest, wisest, and most powerful man known to her?

It may be coincidence, but after her recorded departure to her own land, as recorded in verse 13, the rest of 1 Kings 10 is devoted to the lavish extravagance of Solomon's lifestyle. Some of these extravagances were in direct conflict with Mosaic law. Did the visit from the queen of Sheba whet Solomon's appetite for the sin of extravagance?

It would seem so; as the very next chapter begins with, "But King Solomon loved many foreign women" (1 Kings 11:1). These were probably women who sat in high places before being brought to Israel for the purpose of pleasing important men, including the king. These were women with whom Mosaic law prohibited the children of Israel from intermarrying. These were the same women for whom Solomon built "high places," as we are told in 1 Kings 11:7–8.

Ironically, Solomon had previously written of the sure curse associated with the seductress and the immoral woman, and now we can add the foolish woman, spoken of here in chapter nine. Like his father, David, Solomon succumbed to sexual temptation, and like David—God spared Solomon's life—but this does not mean the warnings of Proverbs were not fulfilled. Solomon's sin was the catalyst for the decline of the whole nation of Israel, from what most theologians believe was the most magnificent kingdom the earth has ever known. It would be during the reign of Solomon's only named son, Rehoboam, when Israel would be divided by the northern ten tribes of Israel rebelling against his rule. This event soon led to a political crisis, causing northern Israelites to wage war against southern Israelites. Solomon's inability to control his carnal urges shortened the lives of countless young Israelites who had no choice but to go to war.

"Stolen waters are sweet, and bread eaten in secret is pleasant. But he knoweth not that the dead are there; and that her guests are in the depths of hell" (Proverbs 9:17–18).

You should recall Solomon's reference to stolen water in Proverbs chapter five. Here in chapter nine, water is again used as a metaphor to represent forbidden activities that wise Christians should shun. It doesn't really matter what the water and bread of chapter nine represents because we are told they are stolen. Regardless of the type of sin being promoted here by the clamorous woman, the result is the same as in all the previous examples given to us by God's Holy Spirit in Solomon's wisdom speeches. The "stolen water" represents the temptations of past, present, and future generations.

These temptations have lured the vulnerable away from our Lord's leadership, causing generations of deceived people to go astray. Like the "stolen water," the clamorous woman is representative of Satan's many false agents. Satan has been deceiving humankind for many centuries now. He is very good at what he does. Solomon's very last piece of information given to his now-adult pupils can be summarized by the old saying, "Birds of a feather flock together," and wherever Satan's dirty birds are congregating, you should not want to be there!

If Solomon was available to comment on this final thought and apply it to our current society, what advice do you think he would render? Where are the guests from the depths of hell hanging out in our present culture? Whoever you are, wherever you are, and whatever your circumstances, take the time and make the effort to seek God's will. If you are surrounded by the guests of hell, I suggest you run, not walk, from Satan's playgrounds, playmates, and playthings. Insulate your soul with God's wisdom and understanding found in His Word. It all begins by crying out to Him with the repentant sinner's prayer.

If you do not know the Lord Jesus Christ as your personal Savior, I am pleading with you to invite His Holy Spirit into your life right now, before it's too late. Get as far away as possible from the edge of Satan's pit. All you have to do is recognize you are a sinner and that Jesus has already paid that sin debt with His blood sacrifice. After these two admissions, it simply takes a sincere decision to make Him Lord and Master of your life. With this done, you can be certain He will never leave you or forsake you. You can bet your soul on that. Go ahead—lay all your chips on the table. Proclaim to everyone listening that you're all in.

May God's blessing be with each and every one of you in all that you do—Amen.

Printed in the United States
By Bookmasters